Imagining the Celtic Past in Modern Fantasy

Perspectives on Fantasy

Series Editors
Brian Attebery (Idaho State University, USA)
Dimitra Fimi (University of Glasgow, UK)
Matthew Sangster (University of Glasgow, UK)

The first academic series with an exclusive critical focus on Fantasy, *Perspectives on Fantasy* publishes cutting-edge research on literature and culture that brings sophisticated discussion to a broad community of debate, including scholars, students and non-specialists.

Inspired by Fantasy's deep cultural roots, powerful aesthetic potential, and reach across a broad range of media – from literature, film and television to art, animation and gaming – *Perspectives on Fantasy* provides a forum for theorizing and historicizing Fantasy via rigorous and original critical and theoretical approaches. Works in the series will cover major creators, significant works, key modes and forms, histories and traditions, the genre's particular affordances, and the ways in which Fantasy's resources have been drawn on, expanded and reconfigured by authors, readers, viewers, directors, designers, players and artists. With a deliberately broad scope, the series aims to publish dynamic studies that embrace Fantasy as a global, diverse and inclusive phenomenon while also addressing oversights and exclusions. Along with canonical Anglophone authors and texts, the series will provide a space to address Fantasy creators and works rooted in African, Asian, South American, Middle Eastern and indigenous cultures, as well as translations and transnational mediations.

The series will be alive to Fantasy's flourishing fan cultures, studying how audiences engage critically and affectively and considering the ease with which participants in Fantasy communities move from being readers and watchers to players, writers and artists.

Editorial board members
Catherine Butler (Cardiff University, UK)
Pawel Frelik, (University of Warsaw, Poland)
Rachel Haywood (Iowa State University, USA)
Robert Maslen (University of Glasgow, UK)
Ebony Elizabeth Thomas (University of Michigan, USA)
Anna Vaninskaya (University of Edinburgh, UK)
Rhys Williams (University of Glasgow, UK)
Helen Young (Deakin University, Australia)

Titles in this Series
Queering Faith in Fantasy Literature: Fantastic Incarnations and the Deconstruction of Theology, Taylor Driggers

Forthcoming Titles
Mapping Middle Earth: Environmental and Political Narratives in J.R.R. Tolkien's Cartographies, Anahit Behrooz

Imagining the Celtic Past in Modern Fantasy

Edited by
Dimitra Fimi and Alistair J.P. Sims

BLOOMSBURY ACADEMIC
LONDON • NEW YORK • OXFORD • NEW DELHI • SYDNEY

BLOOMSBURY ACADEMIC
Bloomsbury Publishing Plc
50 Bedford Square, London, WC1B 3DP, UK
1385 Broadway, New York, NY 10018, USA
29 Earlsfort Terrace, Dublin 2, Ireland

BLOOMSBURY, BLOOMSBURY ACADEMIC and the Diana logo are
trademarks of Bloomsbury Publishing Plc

First published in Great Britain 2023
Paperback edition published 2024

Copyright © Dimitra Fimi, Alistair J.P. Sims and contributors, 2023

Dimitra Fimi, Alistair J.P. Sims and contributors have asserted their rights under the Copyright, Designs and Patents Act, 1988, to be identified as Authors of this work.

For legal purposes the Acknowledgements on p. xii constitute an
extension of this copyright page.

Series design by Rebecca Heselton
Tree by Horastu/ iStock

All rights reserved. No part of this publication may be reproduced or transmitted in any form or by any means, electronic or mechanical, including photocopying, recording, or any information storage or retrieval system, without prior permission in writing from the publishers.

Bloomsbury Publishing Plc does not have any control over, or responsibility for, any third-party websites referred to or in this book. All internet addresses given in this book were correct at the time of going to press. The author and publisher regret any inconvenience caused if addresses have changed or sites have ceased to exist, but can accept no responsibility for any such changes.

A catalogue record for this book is available from the British Library.

Library of Congress Cataloging-in-Publication Data
Names: Fimi, Dimitra, editor. | Sims, Alastair J. P., editor.
Title: Imagining the Celtic past in modern fantasy / edited by Dimitra Fimi and
Alastair J.P. Sims.
Description: London ; New York : Bloomsbury Academic, 2023. | Series: Perspectives on fantasy |
Includes bibliographical references and index.
Identifiers: LCCN 2022041472 (print) | LCCN 2022041473 (ebook) | ISBN 9781350349995
(hardback) | ISBN 9781350350038 (paperback) | ISBN 9781350350007 (pdf) |
ISBN 9781350350014 (epub)
Subjects: LCSH: Fantasy fiction–Celtic influences. | Fantasy fiction–20th century–History and
criticism. | Fantasy fiction–21st century–History and criticism. |
LCGFT: Literary criticism.
Classification: LCC PN3435 .I47 2023 (print) | LCC PN3435 (ebook) |
DDC 809.3/8766–dc23/eng/20220926
LC record available at https://lccn.loc.gov/2022041472
LC ebook record available at https://lccn.loc.gov/2022041473

ISBN:	HB:	978-1-3503-4999-5
	PB:	978-1-3503-5003-8
	ePDF:	978-1-3503-5000-7
	eBook:	978-1-3503-5001-4

Series: Perspectives on Fantasy

Typeset by Integra Software Services Pvt. Ltd.

To find out more about our authors and books visit www.bloomsbury.com
and sign up for our newsletters.

Contents

List of illustrations	vii
List of contributors	viii
Series editors' preface	x
Acknowledgements	xii
Note on spelling	xiii
Introduction *Dimitra Fimi*	1

Part One   Celticity as fantastic intrusion

1. Mad, bad and dangerous to know: The Celtic fairy realm in Susanna Clarke's *Jonathan Strange & Mr Norrell* *K.A. Laity* — 11
2. The evolution of Alan Garner's Celticity in *Boneland* *Gwendolen Grant* — 29
3. Woman as goddess in the Irish fantasies of Jodi McIsaac *Kris Swank* — 53

Part Two   Celtic fantasy worlds and heroes

4. The heroic biographies of Cú Chulainn and Connavar in the *Rigante* series *Alistair J.P. Sims* — 73
5. Classical ethnography and the world(s) of the Rigante *Anthony Smart* — 91
6. Celts in Spaaaaace! *Cheryl Morgan* — 117

Part Three   Celtic fantasy beyond the anglophone

7. From *Vertigen* to *Frontier*: The fate of the Sidhe in Léa Silhol's fiction *Viviane Bergue* — 137
8. 'Chaidh e nas doimhne agus nas doimhne ann an seann theacsaichean': Gaelic history and legend in *An Sgoil Dhubh* by Iain F. MacLeòid *Duncan Sneddon* — 155

Part Four Fantastic perceptions of Celticity

9   The Celtic Tarot in speculative fiction *Juliette Wood*   175
10 Celtic appropriation in twenty-first-century fantasy fan
    perceptions *Angela R. Cox*   195

Index   209

Illustrations

Figure

3.1 Saint Brigid of Ireland's Cross (Knott 2006)   64

Table

1 The Heroic Biography Pattern as outlined by von Hahn, with Nutt's additions in italics, as combined by Ní Mhaoileoin   81

Contributors

Viviane Bergue is an independent scholar and the volunteer editor of *Fantasy Art and Studies*, the journal of les Têtes Imaginaires. Her research interests focus on Modern Fantasy fiction, especially in relationship with myth and fairy tale, Urban Fantasy and quest narratives. She is the author of *La Fantasy, mythopoétique de la quête* (2015), a revised edition of her PhD thesis.

Angela R. Cox is an independent scholar who most recently worked at Ball State University. Her research interests include genre, game studies, fan studies and the fantastic. She has published chapters on the *King's Quest* fantasy game series by Sierra On-Line in *Feminism in Play* (2018) and most recently in the forthcoming *Fifty Key Video Games*.

Dimitra Fimi is Senior Lecturer in Fantasy and Children's Literature and Co-Director of the Centre for Fantasy and the Fantastic at the University of Glasgow, UK. She has published award-winning monographs on J.R.R. Tolkien and Celtic-inspired children's fantasy, and co-edited Tolkien's manuscripts on invented languages.

Gwendolen Grant is an independent researcher. Her research interests focus on mythology, speculative fiction and the occult. Her recent publications include an article on 'Sound and Ritualistic Language in Charles Williams' *War in Heaven*', published in *Aries: Journal for the Study of Western Esotericism* (2021).

K.A. Laity is Associate Professor of English at The College of Saint Rose where she teaches medieval literature, medievalism, film and digital media, and crime fiction. In addition to Clarke's work, her current research includes the medieval Scots tale *Rauf Coilyear*, women writers of noir fiction and the magical traditions of surrealist artists.

Cheryl Morgan is an independent scholar who works in the fields of speculative fiction and ancient history. Her most recent publications on speculative fiction have been in *Worlds Apart: Worldbuilding in Fantasy and Science Fiction* (2021), *Ties That Bind: Love in Fantasy and Science Fiction* (2020) and *Fafnir: The Nordic Journal of Science Fiction and Fantasy Research* Vol. 7:1 (2020).

Alistair J.P. Sims is an independent scholar, bookseller and publisher at Books on the Hill, Clevedon. His research focus is on mythology in modern fantasy literature. His most recent publication is 'Teutonic VS Celtist: Does the Battle Still Wage in Modern Fantasy?' in *Fantasy Art and Studies* (2019).

Anthony Smart is Lecturer in Ancient and Medieval History at York St John University, specializing on the intellectual and political histories of the ancient world and the early Middle Ages. Recent publications include articles in *The Classical Journal* and *Classical World* (2020), entries in *The Greenwood Encyclopedia of the Daily Life of Women: How They Lived from Ancient Times to the Present* (2020) and the *Tacitus Encyclopaedia* (2022). He is currently completing a book on grief and sorrow in the Roman republic, and editing a volume on the political culture of Rome in the early principate.

Duncan Sneddon is a Lecturer in Celtic at the University of Edinburgh. He gained a PhD in early medieval Scottish History (Edinburgh, 2018) and has taught at the University of Aberdeen and Sabhal Mòr Ostaig. His main research interests are in early medieval hagiography, Gaelic folklore and modern Gaelic literature.

Kris Swank is a librarian and faculty member at Pima Community College, Tucson, Arizona, and at Signum University, an online educational institution. Her research interests include the works of J.R.R. Tolkien, fantasy literature and medievalism in literature, film and television. She is currently pursuing a PhD at the University of Glasgow in English Literature. Kris has contributed to *Tolkien Studies*, *Mythlore*, the *Journal of Tolkien Research* and several edited collections, most recently *Critical Insights: The Lord of the Rings* (2022) and *The Arthurian World* (2022).

Juliette Wood is Associate Lecturer at Cardiff University who works in the fields of folklore and Celtic literature. She has written extensively on the Holy Grail (*Eternal Chalice. The Enduring Legend of the Holy Grail*, 2008) and has provided expert consultation for television and radio. Her recent publications include *Fantastic Creatures in Mythology and Folklore* (2018) as well as contributions to *The Ashgate Encyclopedia of Literary and Cinematic Monsters* (2014) and *A Companion to J.R.R. Tolkien* (2022).

Perspectives on Fantasy

Series editors' preface

It has traditionally been difficult to reach a consensus definition of Fantasy. Critics generally agree that fantasies deal with the impossible, but beyond this, they have directed their attention variously to arcane subsets of literature or vast swathes of cultural production. That Fantasy powerfully evokes different meanings at different times for different people is one of its virtues as a vector for exploring culture. Depending on one's approach, Fantasy can be said to arise in our earliest myths and legends, to build on 'taproot' texts that abstract and crystalise human hopes and fears, or to represent a relatively contemporary means of negotiating with pasts, presents and futures through retrenchment, reconfiguration or visionary reforging.

Fantasy's flexibility has brought it to particular prominence at the dawn of the third millennium. Successful film and TV series have adapted classic and modern works and created deep and dazzling new worlds on screen. Innovations in aesthetics, artifice, media, narrative, improvisation and play have reenergised Fantasy with modern modes, tropes and techniques, and the rise of the internet has allowed for unprecedented forms of community collaboration. These developments have created myriad new fantasies and amended, resynthesised and extended a powerful tradition in which the impossible is evoked to contrast with, probe the limits of and call into question our mundane realities.

However, despite this burgeoning richness, academia has been slow to develop a set of tools for addressing Fantasy as a major cultural form. Fantasy lags considerably behind Science Fiction, crime fiction and the Gothic in terms of critical attention. The *Perspectives on Fantasy* series addresses this lack by providing a space in which the best new scholarly and theoretical work can be drawn together to catalyse an increased understanding of a mode that is both artistically distinctive and deeply meaningful for a vast range of creators and audiences.

We chose the title *Perspectives* to reflect the fact that Fantasy is not a problem to which there is a single solution, but rather a range of territories that look different to different eyes, territories which we all explore better when we have a wide variety of lenses to look through. Our series is keen to extend the theorisation of Fantasy, with a special focus on expanding and diversifying existing critical approaches. Important work has been done tracing the roots and emergence of modern genre Fantasy, but there is much more to be accomplished in this area, and a pressing need for work that explores different cultures, politics, poetics, forms, tropes and methodologies. Though innovative monographs on major writers are very welcome, the series recognises that Fantasy promiscuously crosses media. We therefore also encourage scholarship focusing on film, television, boardgames, role-playing games, video games, comics, art and animation. Within given groupings of fantastic works, we would like to see contributors examining themes and structural elements such as world-building, the operations of magic systems, the construction of evil, the (re)negotiation of histories and creators' engagements with ethical, social, economic and ecological issues. We are eager for the series to be alive to Fantasy's flourishing fan cultures, exploring how audiences engage critically and affectively with fantastic creations and considering the ease with which participants in Fantasy communities move from being readers and watchers to players, writers and artists. Last, but not least, we are keen to provide a space for cogent critique. In considering how we imagine other worlds and peoples, the series will seek to be vigilant in exposing the limitations of fantasies, as well as the potencies of the equivalences they draw. Fantasy lets us rethink the world; in contemplating such rethinkings, we are keen to acknowledge oversights, exclusions and suppressions, as well as the flickering utopian potential of Fantasy's playful sidelong glances.

Brian Attebery, Dimitra Fimi and Matthew Sangster

Acknowledgements

This volume has been so long in the making that we can hardly believe we got here in the end! Our amazing team of contributors went through so much disruption, not least the Covid-19 pandemic, and we are so grateful for their patience and resilience, besides their wonderful insights and diverse range of essays.

For constant support in double-checking Irish linguistic and textual matters, we would like to thank Geraldine Parsons of the University of Glasgow.

Alistair J.P. Sims would like to thank Professor Raimund Karl, who supervised his PhD on fictional narratives in archaeology at the University of Bangor.

Kris Swank is grateful to Jodi McIsaac for answering her questions.

Juliette Wood wishes to thank her instructors, Rev. Bernard McMahon and Dr Angela Carson, at the College of New Rochelle (USA) who introduced her to the poetry of T.S. Eliot and the world of medieval literature.

Angela R. Cox would like to acknowledge Joshua Byron Smith at the University of Arkansas, who initially helped her identify Celticism in her data corpus.

The editors are grateful to family and friends whose support was invaluable from the inception to the completion of this project. Special thanks from Dimitra Fimi to Andrew Davies, and from Alistair J.P. Sims to his parents, to Chloe Smirk, and to the staff at Murrays of Clevedon.

Note on spelling

For the spelling of Irish names and titles of medieval Irish and Welsh texts, this volume follows John T. Koch's *Celtic Culture: A Historical Encyclopedia* (Santa Barbara; Oxford: ABC-CLIO, 2006).

Introduction

Dimitra Fimi

Powerful female goddesses who fight in battle and shape-shift. An alliance of rebellious 'barbarian' tribes battling against a mighty empire. Supernatural figures with possible pagan origins transforming into modern Saints. Lost languages and cultures of the British past evoking a sense of melancholy and romanticism. All of these images fit with one or more popular perceptions of the Celtic past. For some people, the Celts are the Iron Age indigenous inhabitants of Britain and Ireland, crushed under-foot by the might of the Romans, leaving behind only archaeological remains and the observations of their conquerors. For others, the term 'Celtic' points to the medieval texts and cultures of Ireland and Wales, full of wonder and the supernatural, but also clearly dominated by the Church, and showing links between the pagan past and the Christian and folkloric present. For yet others, what is more tangibly Celtic are the Celtic languages still spoken in Britain, Ireland and beyond: Welsh, Irish, Scots Gaelic, Breton and the remnants of Manx and Cornish. When we talk about the ways in which contemporary fantasy engages with the Celtic past, therefore, we are already in a saturated terrain, in which different, and often competing, perceptions of the 'Celts' or things 'Celtic' are combined, mixed and re-mixed, modified, adapted and reshaped to suit a modern mode and genre, and an (intended or unintended) ideological stance.

The term 'Celtic' itself has different meanings depending on scholarly or popular contexts. Different academic disciplines have variant uses for it. In linguistics and philology 'Celtic' refers to a family of languages, a branch of the Indo-European family tree (often called 'proto-Celtic') which, later, divided into two sub-groups: the Brythonic languages (that in time gave us Welsh, Breton and Cornish) and the Goidelic languages (that developed into Irish, Scottish and Manx). In ancient history, the earlier attestation of the term 'Celtic' comes from Greek *Keltoi*, a term used loosely to refer to northern 'barbarian' tribes.

In archaeology the term 'Celtic' was for many years habitually used to refer to the material remains of central European Iron Age peoples with particular art styles (primarily the Hallstatt and La Tène cultures – the latter featuring characteristic intricate spiral and interlace designs), some of whom eventually ended up in Britain and Ireland and formed the indigenous population prior to the Roman and Anglo-Saxon invasions. In folklore studies, Celtic is still often used to refer collectively to the folk beliefs and narratives of modern Ireland, Wales, Scotland, Cornwall, Isle of Man and Brittany.

These disciplines were combined in the eighteenth and nineteenth centuries to form the popular idea that the people the Greeks and Romans called the Keltoi or Gauls, the people of the Hallstatt and La Tène cultures, the people who spoke 'proto-Celtic' and later modern Celtic languages, and the contemporary people producing folklore in the 'Celtic fringes' of Britain and Ireland were (and are) one and the same, with an unbroken history and shared identity. Thus the 'conventional' history of the Celts was born: a linear story, in which some of the Iron Age Celts left their homeland in central Europe and migrated to Britain and Ireland, bringing their language with them. In time, and against attempts at cultural appropriation or extermination by other invaders, these people developed into the modern nations of Ireland, Scotland and Wales, their language separating into branches and giving us modern Irish, Scots Gaelic and Welsh. They also, the story continues, maintained their own cultural heritage (their stories, pre-Christian myths and traditions) well into the Middle Ages, something that can explain the supernatural, semi-divine, pagan-flavoured figures and heroes of texts such as the Irish *Táin Bó Cúailnge* and the Welsh *Mabinogion*. They maintained their individuality and reclaimed their ancient heritage and identity with the rise of Romantic Nationalism into the nineteenth century, successfully linking their contemporary folklore with echoes of their 'lost' mythologies and cultures (see, for example, the Irish Literary Revival), and influencing artistic movements (e.g. Art Nouveau) with the 'trademark' of 'Celtic' art: interlacing design.[1]

But from the 1980s and on, the concept of a homogeneous 'Celtic' people in Britain begun to be challenged and deconstructed. There is no evidence that the peoples the Greek and Romans called Keltoi or Gauls ever called themselves that, or even thought of themselves as anything other than separate tribes with their own agendas and conflicts. The intricate spirals and interlace designs that

---

[1] For more detailed overviews of the 'conventional' history of the Celts, see James (1999) and Fimi (2017: 8–9).

were supposed to be exclusive to 'Celtic' archaeology are also often found in remains of Germanic cultures. The peoples of Ireland and Wales in the Middle Ages had no knowledge of the affinities between their respective languages and did not think of each other as sharing a common cultural identity. Moreover, the huge distance in time between whatever pagan, pre-Christian beliefs their ancestors could have held, and the medieval texts of the supernatural they preserved and cherished is so big (several centuries) that the claim of unbroken continuity between ancient myths and stories written in a Christian milieu is very difficult to defend. To cap it all, the eighteenth- and nineteenth-century Romantic nationalism movement often engaged in the 'invention of tradition', and was particularly good at constructing these large, overarching, rather seductive narratives of unbroken national and cultural heritage going back centuries – but modern scholarship is much more suspicious (and rightly so in most cases) of the politics, shortcuts and wishful thinking of these processes.[2] A fair amount of taking apart the 'conventional' narrative of the history of the Celts has been done – but this hasn't necessarily fed into the popular consciousness, and even less so in popular culture.

And an important portion of popular culture is what this volume is concerned with: fantasy literature, a literary mode and genre very much rooted in the historical and mythological past for many of its tropes, motifs and structures. Whether one adopts the 'long' history of fantasy, in which the fantastic goes back to the beginning of time, encompassing the magic and supernatural elements of folk narratives, ancient epics and medieval romances; or the 'short' history of fantasy, in which fantasy is a modern phenomenon, a reaction to the rise of the realist novel and the dominance of scientific thinking, contemporary fantasy has mined the mythological past of different cultures and traditions, re-shaping it to fit new contexts.[3] The Celtic past, historical and mythological, has been particularly popular for modern fantasy writers. Some have re-imagined the Iron Age 'Celts' and their cultures as worldbuilding ingredients. Others have creatively re-used medieval texts in Celtic languages featuring strong supernatural elements, such as the Irish *Lebar Gabála Érenn* ('The Book of Invasions') or the Welsh *Mabinogion*. And many have connected ancient or medieval perceptions

---

[2] For studies that dismantle the 'conventional' history of the Celts, see Chapman (1992); Sims-Williams (1986, 1998 2012); James (1999) and Collis (2003). For a summary, see Fimi (2017: 9–12).
[3] Proponents of the 'long' history of fantasy include Neil Barron (1990) and Brian Stableford (2005), while the 'short' history of fantasy is supported by scholars such as Clute and Grant (1997), Richard Mathews (2002) and C.W. Sullivan (2004). For a longer discussion, see Fimi (2012).

of the Celtic past with modern folklore, and with often stereotypical portrayals of the modern 'Celtic' nations and their peoples.

Two terms that take account and respond to the discrepancy outlined above, between the scholarly versus the popular understanding of things 'Celtic', are particularly useful for readers of the essays in this volume: 'Celticity' and 'Celticism'. Celticity is defined as 'the quality of being Celtic' (Löffler 2006: 387), while Celticism is the study of the 'reputation of [the Celts] and of the meanings and connotations ascribed to the term "Celtic"' (Leerssen 1996: 3). As Tolkien once remarked: '"Celtic" of any sort is … a magic bag, into which anything may be put, and out of which almost anything may come' (Tolkien 1983: 185–6). In many ways, each of the fantasies explored in this collection is itself a 'magic bag' into which each author/creator constructs their own understanding of Celticity and responds with their own interpretation of Celticism. Some of the questions that underlie the arguments of the essays in this volume include: What does 'Celtic' mean to contemporary fantasy authors and why is it such a popular source of inspiration? What do their engagement with things 'Celtic' allow them to do in their creative practice and how is this linked to ideological underpinnings? How does their understanding of 'Celticity' relate to their perception of modern national/cultural identities? Which of the 'Celtic' medieval texts or more modern folkloric narratives are they creatively reshaping for their fantasies and why?

Previous scholarship on Celtic-inspired fantasy hitherto has mostly focused on source-studies of children's fantasy inspired by the Welsh tradition, such as C. W. Sullivan's *Welsh Celtic Myth in Modern Fantasy* (1989), and Donna R. White's *A Century of Welsh Myth in Children's Literature* (1998). My own *Celtic Myth in Contemporary Children's Fantasy: Idealization, Identity, Ideology* (2017) widened the discussion by engaging with the Celticism versus Celtoscepticism debate, and by focusing on texts reshaping both the Irish and Welsh tradition from the 1960s to the 2010s. However, contemporary fantasy addressed to adult readers is full of examples of complex, original and nuanced entanglements with the Celtic past, which have not attracted the attention they warrant. This edited volume aims to open a conversation about fantasy's multifaceted and enduring fascination with the Celtic past, and its various perceptions, focusing on texts from the last few decades that are written for and targeted at adult readers.

It should be noted that this collection is not aspiring to be a systematic, comprehensive or exhaustive exploration of Celticity in contemporary adult fantasy. Although major authors are included, such as Susanna Clarke, David Gemmell and Alan Garner (see essays by Laity, Sims, Smart and Grant), there are other recognizable figures missing – Robert Holdstock is an obvious example.

But the collection also makes the case that lesser-known authors should be considered as part of the Celtic-inspired fantasy phenomenon: earlier authors whose work invites a re-appraisal, such as Patricia Kennealy-Morrison (see essay by Morgan), rising stars whose fantasies are examined here for the first time from a scholarly perspective, such as Jodi McIsaac (see essay by Swank), and fantasists whose work is well-known within their own national and cultural boundaries, but which deserve more recognition from the anglophone academy, such as Léa Silhol and Iain F. MacLeòid (see essays by Bergue and Sneddon). Coupled with those author- and text-centric essays, we include two wider approaches to the Celtic fantastic, which examine tropes and perceptions of the Celtic past across different texts, writers and fandoms (essays by Wood and Cox).

The collection is divided into four parts, grouping essays into sub-genres of fantasy, language and wider themes. The first part, 'Celticity as Fantastic Intrusion', includes three essays on texts that can be defined as low fantasy (as in Clute and Grant's definition), or intrusion fantasy (in Mendlesohn's classification).[4] In Susanna Clarke's *Jonathan Strange & Mr Norrell*, Alan Garner's *Boneland* and Jodie McIsaac's *The Thin Veil* and the *Revolutionary* series, the Celtic past erupts into (and disrupts) a realistic setting, either a modern one, or an (alternatively) historical one. The respective essays by Laity, Grant and Swank examine the ways in which the Celtic past interacts with and affects each text's 'mundane' present. The second part, 'Celtic Fantasy Worlds and Heroes', examines texts that use different facets of the Celtic past to construct secondary worlds, in which elements of the Celtic past serve as raw material (to be re-shaped and adapted freely) to conduct worldbuilding and create compelling heroes and stories. Morgan's essay focuses on Patricia Kennealy-Morrison *Keltiad* novels, while Sims and Smart discuss David Gemmell's *Rigante* series, analysing how the novels engage with the Irish medieval tradition, and with the perception of the 'Celts' in classical ethnography respectively. The third part, 'Celtic Fantasy Beyond the Anglophone', offers two essays on texts written in languages other than English. Bergue explores French author Léa Silhol's sustained engagement with the Celtic past in her *Vertigen* and *Frontier* series, while Sneddon discusses Iain F. MacLeòid's *An Sgoil Dhubh* ('The Black School') within the canon of both fantasy and modern literature in Scots Gaelic. We end with the fourth part, 'Fantastic Perceptions of Celticity', in which the fantastic is situated within cultural practices perceived as 'Celtic', despite scholarly refutations. Wood examines how the popular idea of the Tarot as Celtic has informed speculative

---

[4] For these sub-categories of fantasy, see Clute and Grant (1997) and Medlesohn (2008).

fiction across the twentieth and twenty-first centuries, while Cox analyses perceptions of Celticity within fan communities of readers.

Though each essay approaches its material in different ways, some fascinating strands of common perceptions of the 'Celts' and the Celtic past arise from all texts, concepts and communities explored in this volume. Firstly, the majority of fantasists that are discussed in this volume of essays follow the older model of the linear history of the 'Celts'. That is to say, there is an active linking of Iron Age cultures of Britain and Ireland with post-Christian medieval texts through to more contemporary folklore, thus creating a pan-Celticism that erases geographical and regional differences, and collapses or disregards very real gaps in chronology. As the essays by Sims and Smart show, David Gemmell's *Rigante* series combines a version of the Keltoi observed by classical commentators, with medieval Irish mythological heroes such as Cú Chulainn. In their respective essays, Grant, Morgan, Bergue and Sneddon discuss how Alan Garner, Kennealy-Morrison, Léa Silhol and Iain F. MacLeòid merge disparate material from medieval Irish, Welsh and wider Arthurian sources, as well as more contemporary Irish and Scottish folklore, supporting a similar pan-Celtic vision. The essays by Wood and Cox confirm this general tendency, by demonstrating how elements from medieval texts and traditions in Celtic languages have been brought together, often haphazardly and indiscriminately, to create our modern understanding of the Tarot on the one hand (which has then fed into countless fantastic texts in turn), and, on the other, to shape the fandom responses and readings of modern fantasy.

Coupled with this pan-Celtic approach, in many of the fantasies explored in this volume, mythological and legendary figures from medieval Irish and Welsh material are unproblematically designated as 'gods' or 'goddesses'. The term 'Celtic mythology' is fraught with problems. 'Mythology' implies a (more or less) coherent body of folk narratives (myths, legends, folktales) which belong to pre-Christian cultures and account for the creation of the world and the nature of the gods, offer aetiologies for natural and cultural phenomena, and construct a particular worldview. Nineteenth- and early twentieth-century mythographers, such as John Rhys, Charles Squire and T. W. Rolleston, followed the model of classical mythology, and attempted to construct a Greek- and Roman-style pantheon out of otherworldly and supernatural beings in Irish and Welsh medieval texts, despite these latter being written down in a Christian milieu. By so doing, they conflated characters and motifs across different centuries, languages and cultural contexts. Nevertheless, the end result was to establish a popular concept of a pre-Christian, 'pagan' pan-Celtic religion that projected backwards, linked with archaeological remains from centuries earlier, and was accepted by many scholars as having already existed in the period of Iron Age 'Celtic' tribes (see, for example, the work of Proinsias Mac Cana, or Miranda J. Aldhouse-Green). As many of the essays in this volume show, this popular perception of 'Celtic' religion, mythology and gods/goddesses, endures in contemporary fantasy. In Gemmell's world of the Rigante, Irish mythological figures such as the Dagda and the Morrígan are unproblematically designated as deities (see Sims and Smart). In Léa Silhol's and Kennealy-Morrison's fantasies, the 'Celtic gods' are sitting alongside such deities from other mythologies, such as Greek and Egyptian (see essays by Morgan and Bergue), and this rather eclectic mix of Egyptian lore and 'Celtic myth' is also evident in the development of the Tarot (see Wood). What is more, the idea that some of these Celtic divinities survived and evolved into contemporary folkloric beliefs in fairies, or into specific figures of Christian saints (e.g., Brigit/Bríg and Saint Brigit), is also taken up by the fantasies of Jodi MacIsaac (see Swank).

A third and final strand of Celticity apparent in many essays in this volume is related to popular ideas about the 'Celtic character', which – once more – stem from the nineteenth century and are still very much with us today. Victorian ethnic preconceptions constructed a romanticized image of the 'Celts' as artistic, visionary, emotional and in touch with nature, in opposition to the excessive rationality, focus on progress and industrial achievements of the English. But this romanticized image could also be flipped and politically exploited to present the peoples of contemporary Celtic-speaking nations (especially the Irish) as primitive, backward, uncivilized and disorderly (see Sims-Williams 1986). Most of the fantasies explored in this volume tend to play with the more positive portrayal of 'Celtic' characters as somewhat superior to an Englishness that is obsessed with too much civilization and has lost its touch with the magical and numinous aspects of the world. Laity's essay shows the relevance of this view in Susanna Clarke's *Jonathan Strange & Mr Norrell*, in which Celticity is the organic, natural underbelly of the strict, quasi-scientific English magic of Mr Norrell. The same view is also sustained in Alan Garner's *Boneland*, in which – as Grant demonstrates – Celticity offers a magical, privileged link with the primeval past (and with the protagonist's psyche), as opposed to the materialistic present.

There is a lot of work still to be done on understanding the complexities and ideological nuances of 'Celtic'-inspired fantasy in contemporary culture, not just in literature, but also across media such as film, TV, games and gaming, and art. It is hoped that this volume will go some way towards opening an initial discussion that will bear further fruit in future research.

References

Aldhouse-Green, Miranda J. (2011), *The Gods of the Celts*, Stroud: The History Press.
Barron, Neil, ed. (1990), *Fantasy Literature: A Reader's Guide*, New York: Garland.
Chapman, Malcolm (1992), *The Celts: The Construction of a Myth*, London: Macmillan.
Clute, John, and Grant, John, eds (1997), *The Encyclopedia of Fantasy*, London: Orbit.
Collis, John (2003), *The Celts: Origins, Myths and Inventions*, Stroud: Tempus.
Fimi, Dimitra (2012), 'Tolkien and the Fantasy Tradition', in Claire Whitehead (ed.), *The Fantastic (Critical Insights)*, 40–60, Ipswich, MA: Salem Press.
Fimi, Dimitra (2017), *Celtic Myth in Contemporary Children's Fantasy: Idealization, Identity, Ideology*, London: Palgrave Macmillan.
James, Simon (1999), *Atlantic Celts: Ancient People or Modern Invention?*, London: British Museum.
Leerssen, Joep (1996), 'Celticism', in Terrence Brown (ed.), *Celticism*, 1–20, Amsterdam: Rodopi.
Löffler, Marion (2006), 'Celticism', in John T. Koch (ed.), *Celtic Culture: A Historical Encyclopedia*, Vol. 1, 387–9, Santa Barbara; Oxford: ABC-CLIO.
Mac Cana, Proinsias (1991), *Celtic Mythology*, New York: Peter Bedrick Books.
Mathews, Richard (2002), *Fantasy: The Liberation of Imagination*, London: Routledge.
Mendlesohn, Farah (2008), *Rhetorics of Fantasy*, Hanover, NH: Wesleyan University Press.
Rhŷs, John Sir (1892), *Lectures on the Origin and Growth of Religion as Illustrated by Celtic Heathendom*, London: Williams and Norgate.
Rolleston, T. W. (1911), *Myths and Legends of the Celtic Race*, London: G.G. Harrap & Co.
Sims-Williams, Patrick (1986), 'The Visionary Celt: The Construction of an Ethnic Preconception', *Cambridge Medieval Celtic Studies*, 11: 71–96.
Sims-Williams, Patrick (1998), 'Celtomania and Celtoscepticism', *Cambrian Medieval Celtic Studies*, 36: 1–36.
Sims-Williams, Patrick (2012), 'Celtic Civilization: Continuity or Coincidence?', *Cambrian Medieval Celtic Studies*, 64: 1–45.
Squire, Charles (1910), *Celtic Myth and Legend, Poetry and Romance*, London: The Gresham Publishing Company.
Stableford, Brian (2005), *Historical Dictionary of Fantasy Literature*, Lanham, MD: Scarecrow Press.
Sullivan III, C. W. (1989), *Welsh Celtic Myth in Modern Fantasy*, Westport, CT; London: Greenwood Press.
Sullivan III, C. W. (2004), 'High Fantasy', in Peter Hunt (ed.), *International Companion Encyclopedia of Children's Literature*, Vol. 1, 436–46, London: Routledge.
Tolkien, J.R.R. (1983), *The Monsters and the Critics and Other Essays*, ed. Christopher Tolkien, London: Allen and Unwin.
White, Donna R. (1998), *A Century of Welsh Myth in Children's Literature*, Westport, CT; London: Greenwood Press.

Part One

Celticity as fantastic intrusion

1

Mad, bad and dangerous to know: The Celtic fairy realm in Susanna Clarke's *Jonathan Strange & Mr Norrell*

K.A. Laity

Susanna Clarke's sprawling novel *Jonathan Strange & Mr Norrell* (2004) takes in the whole of the nineteenth-century battle to restore 'the ancient glories of English magic' to respectability (136). Readers are repeatedly warned in contrast that fairy magic is 'not respectable' – most often by the self-appointed Magician of England, Gilbert Norrell, who nevertheless stoops to its employment on at least one occasion as part of his relentless pursuit of the control of all magic in England. Why is fairy magic not 'respectable'? I will argue that it is because it is mostly Celtic rather than the more dour, upright and rather puritanical English magic that Norrell seeks to revive and rule over. Yet the celebrated medieval founder of English magic, John Uskglass, was trained in fairy magic and his troop, The Raven King's army, was specifically identified as the *Daoine Sidhe*, the fairies of Irish folklore, often popularly associated with the supernatural beings of medieval Irish Literature, the Túatha Dé Danann. Norrell's student and sometime enemy, Jonathan Strange, however, holds no such prejudice. In pursuing the Raven King's example, Jonathan Strange remains open to this Celtic influence and soon surpasses his teacher in skill and daring, but both Englishmen are unprepared for the full fury of the fight against the fairy that has become their enemy – The Gentleman with Thistle-Down Hair.

Defining 'Celtic' is notoriously problematic. As one of this volume's editors has written, authors 'rewriting and reimagining "Celtic" myth in contemporary fantasy is already an ideological act, depending on the perceptions of "Celticity" each fantasy author embraces' (Fimi 2017: 15). For Clarke's novel, the early nineteenth-century setting proves particularly important, for:

> Romanticism's fascination with nature and the exotic quickly configured the 'Celtic' countries and cultures as 'Other', perceived positively as ancient, mysterious, and wildly exciting. Wales and Scotland in particular were admired for their wild landscapes and the wistful echoes of their 'lost' cultures, expressed in the lore of the common 'folk'.
>
> (Fimi 2017: 11; see also Chapman 1992: 145; James 1999: 48–9)

This othering is key to the narrative. It sets up an unstable dichotomy between English and Celtic that falls apart by the end of the novel, but not without great struggles on the part of most of the characters. That primary division takes in a number of other dichotomies: human/fairy, rationalist/magical, empire/colony, hierarchical/chaotic, industrial/pastoral and quite pointedly male/female (this latter thread is further undone by Clarke's later stories in *The Ladies of Grace Adieu and Other Stories*, published in October 2006).

The 'Celts' broadly imagined can be defined within the narrative first by their *geography*. They dwell in the Other Lands, not England. On leaving England in 1434, the Raven King seems to have closed all the doors between England and these Other realms. The fairy folk can come to England once invited by a magician. But the designation 'Celt' goes beyond just the Other Lands. Any place that is not England can be suspect (of course that includes Ireland, Wales and Scotland). Yet the North of England comes under suspicion, too, because the home of the Raven King proves to be a liminal space. Not only is it a location traditionally porous for passage between realms but the people of the region keep their allegiance to that king; as Childermass explains, 'He is in our minds and hearts and speech' (914). From his first reappearance with command over three realms, the Raven King – 'who was not a fairy, but an Englishman' (35) – nonetheless opened access between the stability of England and the chaotic lands that bordered upon it in all directions.

The 'Celts' are also distinguished by *language*. While many of the Aureate and Argentine magicians use English terminology in their writings and spells, the use of (mostly) Irish vocabulary for fairy beings and magic clearly identifies them as Other. From using terms like the *Daoine Sidhe* to mentions of 'the language of the Scottish Highlands (which is like singing)' (753), the Celtic languages signal a difference from the English norm. In contrast Latinate terminology conveys the Enlightenment lack of sentiment and 'it reeks of musty antiquarianism, supercilious disdain, and the exclusivity of an earlier era' (Drexler 2004: 410). Like Norrell in his library, hidden from light and dusty with neglect, the language of the Friends of English Magic – his staunch supporters – reflects this carefully controlled and 'elevated' tone. It is mirrored generally in the split between *practical magicians*, dismissed as performers like Vinculus, and *theoretical magicians*, like the Learned Society of York Magicians, 'all rational beings' (24) and 'practical men [who] wished to apply the principles of reason and science to magic as they had done to the manufacturing arts' in 'Rational Thaumaturgy' (9). While Norrell's sympathies were entirely with the latter philosophy, his insistence on practising actual magic assures the explosive mix of the Celtic and English forces will be unleashed eventually.

Finally the 'Celtic' is identified by *affect*. English magic, at least as envisioned by Gilbert Norrell, is about logic, rationality and a lack of mysticism. His worst accusation against magicians and scholars is 'He is mystical!' (158). Magic should be cold, practical and thoroughly 'modern' in contrast to the usual image of magicians as lunatics, as 'any stark-eyed madman who stood upon the street corner screaming out that he was the Raven King' (22). Norrell's modern magic is an attempt to root out this Celtic emotionalism, fairy magic is 'not the sort of magic which civilized men wish to see practised in England nowadays' (154). Of course while Norrell may wish 'to maintain a lofty and magisterial silence' (158) in the face of various vexations, the truth is he cannot keep his composure when he is thwarted, for so many things vex him. All the attempts to clearly demarcate the 'Celtic' and the English soon collapse into chaos.

Geography

The geographies of magic are clearly delineated by custom and by naming in the novel. The development of English magic depends upon these clear demarcations. When the magic-hungry Mr Segundus reads Jacques Belasis's treatise of magic simply known as *The Instructions*, he discovers the clear distinction made between 'England, Faerie (which magicians sometimes call "the Other Lands") and a strange country that is reputed to lie on the far side of Hell' (17, n. 6), which suggests that there are at least four lands accessible within the isles. However, anyone but the English will notice the absence of the other realms of the kingdom, namely Scotland, Ireland and Wales. Indeed the reader soon discovers the Golden Age or Aureate magicians were fond of taking themselves to 'the most retired parts of England and Scotland and Ireland (where magic was strongest)' (7) 'whenever they had some seemingly impossible problem to solve' (6). Escape from England was a boon.

Norrell and the other proponents of a proper English magic desperately attempt to define and circumscribe the art distinctly, yet it continues to elude such compartmentalization. From its founding, 'English' magic is inextricably mingled with Celtic magic, and attempts to create a rationalist, Enlightenment-driven, sort-of-modern English magic are doomed to failure. Norrell and his confederates, in seeking to remove the objectionable influence of the Other Lands and those who dwelt there, unknowingly assured a return of that very magic and an opening of the realm to the wider world, ending the novel with one foot in fairy realms and the other in Venice. The French offer another opportunity to define Englishness by its opposite (especially through Strange and Norrell's military efforts during the Napoleonic Wars) but even there the opposition gets undone in ironic ways, such as when Christopher Drawlight advises Norrell to appoint his new London home with a rhetorical flourish to promote the cause of English Magic: 'the moral, as Mr Drawlight explained it, was that if Mr Norrell hoped to win friends for the cause of modern magic, he must insert a great many more French windows into his home' (68). England may be at war with the French, but that does not diminish the decorative superiority of that nation.

Yet Norrell attempts to make the Other Lands as much of an enemy territory as Napoleon's nation. The Raven King himself is the founder of English magic, yet Norrell 'cannot consider his influence upon English magic as any thing other than deplorable. His magic was of a particularly pernicious sort' (71) which is to say fairy-inspired or at least fairy-trained. Their influence on the English is seen as akin to racist notions of 'impurity' for the magician always speaks of them in those terms: 'A more poisonous race or one more inimical to England has never existed' (73). In the midst of Brexit fomenting hatred of 'foreigners', this sounds strikingly familiar. As Sarah Ahmed has argued about the constructed bodies of 'others' in *The Cultural Politics of Emotions*,

> These figures come to embody the threat of loss: lost jobs, lost money, lost land. They signify the danger of impurity, or the mixing or taking of blood. They threaten to violate the pure bodies; such bodies can only be imagined as pure by the perpetual restaging of this fantasy of violation.
>
> (44)

Like the country gentlemen who doubted Sir Walter Pole and the other ministers, and who 'had a strong suspicion that cleverness was somehow unBritish' (81), Norrell disdains the flashy magic of those from Other Lands, for the certain power contains a devil's bargain as far as he is concerned. As he berates the Gentleman with Thistle-Down Hair, 'all you want in return is to shackle English magic to your whims!' (212). Norrell would gladly set up more firm borders between England and Faerie, just as his magical beacons line the English coast against the French. He and Strange, when gazing into the silver dishes for visions, typically divide the four quadrants as 'England, Scotland, Ireland, Elsewhere' (966) as if the whole world were no more than that.

But the location of English magic proves rather more slippery than Norrell would like to believe: like the magic of the Other Lands, it is something that lies within the stones, trees, hills, wind and rain of England (977). Yet that physical geography which can be clearly marked on maps eludes a stable boundary. A clarifying note from the often disputatious narrator points out:

> When people talk of 'the Other Lands' they generally have in mind Faerie, or some other vague notion. For the purposes of general conversation such definitions do very well, but a magician must learn to be more precise. It is well known that the Raven King rules three kingdoms: the first was the Kingdom of Northern England that encompassed Cumberland, Northumberland, Durham, Yorkshire, Lancashire, Derbyshire and part of Nottinghamshire. The other two were called 'the King's Other Lands'. One was part of Faerie and the other was commonly supposed to be a country on the far side of Hell, sometimes called 'the Bitter Lands'. The King's enemies said that he leased it from Lucifer.
>
> (269)

While a monarch ruling many lands is nothing unusual in Britain, the lack of specificity regarding 'the King's Other Lands' suggests a blurring of boundaries that renders 'England' less than stable. The overlaps between 'the King's Other Lands' and Faerie also depict a mutability that calls into question the use of 'the Other Lands' more generally. As Mark Williams argues, 'the síd … is an elliptical and ambiguous concept' (2016: 89). When the roads between these lands are reopened by Jonathan Strange (see chapter fifty-nine), the borders become even more hazy and overlap, yet this mutability is suggested early on by the recitation of the Raven King ballad, which tells us:

> This land is all too shallow
> It is painted on the sky
>
> (36, n. 1)

The reflective image of the land celestially suggests both the unreal and the power of mirrors, used in the novel as doors between the lands.

The circumscribed geography of England is not as firmly demarcated as Englishmen had assumed (English women, it is hinted several times throughout the novel, know better but the men do not listen to them – cf. Lady Pole's comments, 937). This is to say nothing of the location of Hell between two of the King's realms. Near the end of the novel, despairing of the ability to communicate with John Uskglass, Norrell makes an offhand comment that rather than being nearby, the Raven King might be working his magic 'from a hundred worlds away – from the heart of Hell' (962). This expanding multiplicity of worlds lies behind the anxiety of controlling precisely what constitutes England, a desire for borders that uncomfortably reflects the Brexit era (see for example Aughey 2007). While 'nationalism in Scotland is Europhile in orientation' (Curtice 2013: 15), 'English*ness* was ... a significant driver of the choice for Leave', Henderson et al. argue in a recent study, 'Turning to the other measures of Englishness, each is initially a significant predictor of support for Leave, especially the view that English culture is not as valued as others' (2017: 641). The irony of this sentiment when all power rests in Westminster fits the Napoleonic era just as neatly, such as the ministers' fears of 'Johannites' attacking the factories in the north.

Yet even within the accepted boundaries of England, the North proves to be an unsettlingly liminal space compared to London and the South. Norrell makes use of the North/South split to his advantage, acknowledging that the South has gained prominence since the disappearance of the Black King of the North. He pursues the support of government officials in Westminster to authorize his particular definition of English magic. He rankles at his skill being dismissed as 'a Yorkshire gentleman's eccentricities' (78). Success comes in the South when he is acknowledged as 'the hero of the French Blockade' with the people of the capital 'cheering all the way, flinging their hats in the air and making up songs about him' (135). Respectability for magic depends upon Southern approval. Yet for all his disparagement of the Raven King, Norrell himself grew up in a 'house ... built upon the King's land, with stones from the King's abbey' (958). He retreats to his homeland in Yorkshire when Strange begins to unravel the carefully circumspect rules of magic that Norrell had devoted himself to maintaining and in the end, the two magicians unite to summon the lost Raven King.

Along with his preference for 'the society of clever women' (161), Strange also distinguishes himself from Norrell's more conventional Englishness by a fondness for the Raven King; after all his first book of magic is *A Child's History of the Raven King*. Strange shares many of the same provincial assumptions about the superiority of Englishness, yet growing up he spends half the year in

Scotland with his mother's family for he is half Scot (161). Like Wales, Scotland within the narrative seems to be situated on the periphery of England not only geographically but also magically, which thus renders it more 'naturally' porous and suspect, whereas Ireland is seldom mentioned – perhaps because it is assumed to be not in any way English (see the discussion of language below). When first entering Faerie, Lascelles muses that 'he had imagined it to be a fanciful, otherlandish sort of place; "But really ... it is very plain, like the castles of the Scottish border country"' (938), so there seems to be more than a passing resemblance between non-English Britain and the Other Lands. Lord Pole's butler, Stephen, who is well accustomed to the ways of fairies because he is so much in the company of the Gentleman, assumes when he sees 'a landscape so calculated to reduce the onlooker to utter despair in an instant' that it must be one of the kingdoms of his fairy companion, who assures him, 'Oh, no! This is Scotland' (604). Clearly it can be difficult to distinguish the non-English parts of Britain from the Other Lands.

In short, the anxiety about magic is about the porousness it brings – or perhaps reveals – to England. Jonathan Strange shares 'the commonly-held belief that all ruined buildings belong to the Raven King' (211, n. 1). When Strange opens the King's Roads, he doesn't just break down the border between England and the Other Lands. As Norrell affirms, 'The King's Roads lead everywhere. Heaven. Hell. The Houses of Parliament' (895). It's easy to see why the government would be anxious about that sudden lifting of border 'security'. Once Strange opens the doors to all English magic, the borders are less important to him; he has no anxiety because the Englishness of English magic is not a political identity, but one of the land itself. Drawlight gets a taste of this experience when he shares Strange's vision of the true magic that unites England with all nations:

> He lay beneath the earth, beneath England. Long ages passed; cold and rain seeped through him; stones shifted within him. In the Silence and the Dark he grew vast. He became the earth; he became England. A star looked down on him and spoke to him. A stone asked him a question and he answered it in its own language. A river curled at his side; hills budded beneath his fingers. He opened his mouth and breathed out spring.
>
> (861)

As Strange affirms to Norrell, 'One cannot be the conduit through which all English magic flows and still be oneself' (954). True English magic leaves the conduit no longer provincial but universal; Strange believes he has 'changed England ... the world' (957), but in the end, nothing essential has changed. What is English is not a political or cultural identification but part of the natural world into which one has been born – and to which one owes the allegiance for magic.

Yet still the enmity is there between the 'nations': when Strange restores the connection to all English magic, the Gentleman identifies the culprits by nationality: 'Thieves! Thieves! English thieves!' (949). However, what he fears most is a loss of the special position he has held for about a decade: the *only* fairy in England.

Language

While the geographical borders of English magic prove more porous than most of the characters would like to believe, the linguistic differences are easier to contain. The language of Faerie is mostly Gaelic, largely Irish. The overlapping of the Other Lands and the Emerald Isle seems to take place only in the linguistic realm: Ireland itself does not play much of a role in the novel. Since most of the fairy folk are not easily distinguished from the English (notable exceptions include those who are visibly more 'animalistic', e.g. Simon Bloodworth's fairy servant Buckler, 73, n. 5), the language offers a surer distinction. Norrell remarks on the slippage between human and fairy by mentioning the seventeenth-century scholar Richard Chaston, who wrote:

> men and fairies both contain within them a faculty of reason and a faculty of magic. In men reason is strong and magic is weak. With fairies it is the other way round: magic comes very naturally to them, but by human standards they are barely sane.
>
> (299, n. 2)

Of course the romantic association of the Celtic-speaking peoples with 'fairy' myth and lore is longstanding, popularized by nineteenth-century antiquarians like Child and Chambers as well as Walter Scott. In light of more recent work on the Irish in colonialist constructions of 'race' and difference, this distinction has added resonances. As Steve Garner argues, 'Ireland was the colonial setting for protoracism' and 'that the colonization and settlement of Ireland by English, and later Scottish, settlers constitutes the birth of "race" as a political category that inscribes inequality on the bodies and cultures of certain actors' (2009: 41). Under the Raven King, the Celtic/fairy folks were treated as valuable members of the wider community, but upon his departure English rule gradually established itself as the primary authority and highlighted the difference of Celtic/fairy folk as Other, and less desirable than English men. As Fimi argues, this perceived 'Celtic' nature 'gives more prominence to art, spirituality, inspiration, and emotion (but also unreliability and unruliness)' (60).

In his prologue to *The History and Practice of English Magic*, Jonathan Strange writes of how 'in the last months of 1110 a strange army appeared in Northern England' (637), then already a divided land with Saxon folk under Norman rule – a linguistic division that had political ramifications. After taking Newcastle and Durham, the host rested in the village of Allendale where the local folk feared that vulnerability might incline them to ravages from the troop. 'A company of brave Judiths' offered to 'make friends' with the soldiers, but arriving at the camp they found a strange host. The first woman to approach a soldier noted his Otherness:

> His skin was very pale (it shone in the moonlight) and entirely without blemish. His hair was long and straight like a fall of dark brown water. The bones of his face were unnaturally fine and strong. The expression of the face was solemn, His blue eyes were long and slanting and his brows were fine and dark as pen-strokes with curious flourishes at the end. None of this worried the girl in the least. For all she knew every Dane, Scot and Frenchman ever born is eerily beautiful.
>
> (638)

The girl however ends up 'entirely white and drained of blood while the snow around her was stained bright red. By these signs they recognized the *Daoine Sidhe* – the Fairy Host' (638–9). The specific identification of the Raven King's army as the *Daoine Sidhe*, coupled with their preternatural appearance and disregard for human life, situates the mythic and the Celtic as a dangerous other to the English. Yet the narrator is at pains to counter the general assumptions of the folk of the Other Lands maintained within the larger narrative, highlighting the fact that 'the fairies displayed very little of the cruelty for which their race is famed' and aligning them with the natural world (as opposed to English 'civilization') with the claim that 'the arrival of the Host at any new place was a cause of great rejoicing among animals both wild and domesticated as if they recognized in the fairies an ally against their common foe, Man' (639). Indeed birds in particular seem to frequently if accidentally traverse between the two worlds (158).

In this book-within-the-book, Strange lays out the accepted history of interactions which Clarke repeats circumstantially throughout the novel. In the reign of Henry I, 'fairies were not unknown in England … There were long-established fairy settlements in many places, some hidden by magic, some merely avoided by their Christian neighbours' (639). The uncivilized Otherness of the creatures was legendary, as was their indolence: despite mastering 'the arts of masonry, carpentry and carving ... most still preferred to live in places which they were pleased to call castles but were in fact *brugh* – earth barrows of great antiquity' (639). The underground dwellings suggest another link to the 'animalistic' nature of the creatures, again othering them from human and civilized English culture. In the brisk Protestantism of the Industrial Revolution, their indolence has a doubled distastefulness for the English. They also connect the fairies of this novel to the Túatha Dé Danann, who in early Irish texts inhabit *síde* (sing. *síd*), hollow mounds or hills. As Williams argues, '*Síd*-mounds are usually synonymous with the "otherworld" (in fact, rather various otherworlds), an intermittently accessible parallel dimension ... bigger on the inside' (2016: 30).

King Henry's men wonder at the success of the *Daoine Sidhe* in capturing the north, but rode north to meet them in battle. They feel the fairy effects before they can engage, embodied in 'a magic wind' and 'a sweet sound of pipe music', the beauty of which 'caused a number of the horses to break free and flee to the fairy side', re-establishing the link between the fairy folk and animals (640). Magic quickly disarms the king's troops and they surrender. Expecting a mighty king to step forward, they are nonplussed when their conqueror makes himself known:

> He was rather less than fifteen years old. Like the *Daoine Sidhe* he was dressed in ragged clothes of coarse black wool. Like them his dark hair was long and straight. Like them, he spoke neither English nor French – the two languages current in England at that time – but only a dialect of Faerie. He was pale and handsome and solemn-faced, yet it was clear to everyone present that he was human, not fairy.
>
> (640–1)

Clarke passes over this obvious recognition as if to suggest that the reader would surely know, too, but how such difference would be clear remains mysterious. The 'dialect of Faerie' receives a full footnote referring to aureate magician Martin Pale's *De Tractatu Magicarum Linguarum* which exists in the time of the novel only in 'a handful of borrowed words' of the language that Pale declared, 'related to the ancient Celtic languages' (640, n. 1). Clarke leaves enough wiggle room there to suggest that the borrowed words employed certainly do match up to known Celtic terms but there would also be the possibility of confusion even with a speaker of modern (that is to say, nineteenth century) Celtic languages.

The boy claims to have no name, though this information is not consistent. A woman in Lost-hope (the Gentleman's realm) pronounces the Raven King's prophesied return, naming him in what our narrator assumes 'John Uskglass' *Sidhe* name' though 'Strange could not make it out' (801). Norrell later claims that 'of course the fairies gave him a name after their own fashion, but he cast that off when he returned to England' (957). 'This muddle of names', as the older magician calls it, may have some practical use. In magic it is powerful to know the true name of a thing or person. No one knows the true name of so-called John Uskglass – and whether he was really the child of the Norman murdered by Hubert de Contentin.

If we accept Whorf's thesis that 'we dissect nature along lines laid down by our native languages' (2012: 212), we should not be surprised to find difficulties of understanding between the native folk and the fairies, to say nothing of their intercourse with nature, an ability the English appear to have lost altogether. When Henry and the Raven King negotiate, it seems fitting that the translator between the king and the conquering hero is a Norman knight, Thomas of Dundale (641). Thus England's surrender of the North comes via the tongue of the nation that has already subdued the Saxon language, and now subdues it further. Resentment of the Celtic powers seems to be of an altogether different nature than the hatred of the French, perhaps in part due to the Napoleonic wars. Direct battle with France has a satisfaction that the more guerrilla-like encounters with the fairy races lack.

An imprecise match between the two languages complicates interactions further. While the narrator informs us that the former 'nameless slave' abandoned the name before he returned to England, 'when he was a child in Faerie the *Sidhe* had called him by a word in their own language which, we are told, meant "Starling"' (641, n. 3). This offers a potentially concrete example of translation from the Celtic tongue, but the veracity of this equivalence is almost immediately challenged by a complementary example of translations 'we are told to be true' – by whom? When? And where? Clarke leaves us to guess whether this is the general narrator's comment or Strange's amplification to his own book. The young magician king (now crowned in both England and Faerie) claims to have been beholden to a king of the *Sidhe* whose name 'was particularly long and difficult' and 'traditionally he has always been known as Oberon' (642, n. 4). Is Oberon any more or less accurate than Starling? How much difference is there between words that sound sufficiently similar and those that approach the same meaning in the disparate tongues? Given the need for spells to 'require the magician to be most particular about names' as Gilbert Norrell advises (957), this inability to translate accurately sets up the distinct possibility of confusion and error, for the English magicians do not understand the true meanings of the Celtic terms and names.

Spaces where no precise common word exists, notably in the case of the Raven King himself, trouble the magical workings – how do you summon a person whose true name you do not know – but there are also a variety of specifically fairy beings and situations for which names are lacking or are suspiciously approximated, as if English cannot contain or cannot be bothered to replicate the 'long and difficult' nature of the names. The colourful names of the various fairy servants offer interesting instances of probable pseudonyms, names like Col Tom Blue, Coleman Grey, Buckler, Dick-come-Tuesday, Master Fallowthought. This mix of natural objects and various colours is also employed by fairy rules when they visit the other lands like England: Cold Henry, John Hollyshoes, Thomas Fairwood and of course the Gentleman with Thistle-down Hair. This close connection to the natural also imbues unusual colours with the mystery of fairy magic, like the box the colour of heartache and the women dancing in Lost-hope who wear dresses 'the colour of a winter sunset' (799) or 'a gown the colour of storms, shadows and rain, with a necklace of broken promises and regrets' (191). The richness of both Faerie language and fairy craft is suggested in the much-prized box that contained Lady Pole's finger, a token of the Gentleman's claim upon her:

> The box was small and oblong and apparently made of silver and porcelain. It was a beautiful shade of blue, but then again not exactly blue, it was more like lilac. But then again, not exactly lilac either, since it had a tinge of grey in it. To be more precise, it was the colour of heartache.
>
> (786–7)

The inability of English to convey concisely these concepts in translation speaks to the disparities between the two tongues and the otherness of the Celtic/fairy language(s).

As a specifically Celtic term, *brugh*, the term used for the fairy house or barrow, has interesting analogues, too. Scottish Gaelic *brugh* (= Modern Irish *brú*) derives from proto-Celtic *mrogi- 'territory, region', via Old Irish *bruig*, which is defined as 'land, cultivated land; holding; region, district, border; (farm-)house; abode, half, mansion, castle' (eDIL n.d.; Matasovic 2009: 280). This concept, therefore, can refer to both a single dwelling and a wider region or land, just like a single barrow becomes the kingdom of Lost-hope. In terms of the permeability of the Celtic/fairy world, it seems significant too that this multivalent word includes the concept of borders or border-country, as if to emphasize the openness of that border. As above, the connection to the mystic underworld of the *síd*, where the Túatha Dé Danann reside, remains: the *brugh* is never just a house, though it may wish to pass itself off as one (see for comparison Clarke's short story 'Mr Simonelli or the Fairy Widower' in *The Ladies of Grace Adieu* for a dissection of the brugh as house and how to see through the illusion). As Williams argues in the second chapter of his compendium, the concept of the *síde* in the Irish tradition is both significant and deeply problematic (30) because it can be at once synonymous with the whole of the Otherworld and at the same time indicate a specific dwelling. Clarke appears to prefer *brugh* as a way to indicate the latter, the home of a particular being. Yet the *brugh* remains a place of slippage, controlled by the power and imagination of its rightful 'owner'.

When Stephen kills the king of Lost-hope, the kingdom returns almost at once to its natural *brugh* form, though it carries the stamp of its new king. 'It was not simply that the house had become a hill, everything seemed to have undergone a revolution. The wood was suddenly possessed of a spirit of freshness, of innocence' (768). Otherworldly magic had sustained the primly decorative world of Lost-hope. When Stephen remarks on the change in the 'mansion' one of its denizens tells him with evident surprise, 'This is a *brugh*, grandfather! This is the world beneath the hill' (768). When the king changes, the magic changes with him and thus the glamour of the *brugh*.

While most of the suggestions of Faerie language definitely connect it to Celtic, there is also a suggestion of a multiplicity of fairy languages which may or may not be similar to Celtic tongues. Perhaps the best example of this alterity comes from one of the volumes reported to be in the auction of the Duke of Roxburghe's library which Norrell bought up during Strange's absence on the Peninsula with Wellington. The Duke's home in the Borders region brings us back to the possibility of an alternative Celtic connection, Scottish, though we are not privy to the language of the books directly. In particular one volume: '*The History of Seven* was a very muddled work, partly in English, partly in Latin and partly in an unknown fairy language' (362, n. 3). Given the similarity between Scots Gaelic and Irish (*síd* after all rendered as *sith* in the former, only a difference in orthographic habit), it seems unlikely that the knowledgeable readers consulting the book would not have been able to identify Scots within the macaronic text as so many medieval texts slip between tongues unconsciously. But it opens the door to the possibility of a much wider group of languages only some of which overlap with the Celtic tongues.

Affect

By far the characteristic difference Gilbert Norrell and the Norrellites wish to emphatically declare is the modernity of English magic upon its return. As a response offering to rebuke the sensibilities of the previous 'superstitious' ages, Norrell seeks to re-establish magic on his own terms. As he commands his man of business when moving to London to enact his scheme, 'You must get me a house, Childermass … Get me a house that says to those that visit it that magic is a respectable profession – no less than Law and a great deal more so than Medicine' (51). He is at pains to project an image of rational respectability distinct from 'mysticism' (his greatest criticism) and a rejection of all things Faerie is at the heart of it.

In her influential work *The Cultural Politics of Emotion*, Sara Ahmed argues how 'emotions work to shape the "surfaces" of individual and collective bodies' (2014: 1). The narrative othering those who 'cause' our uncomfortable emotions has grave effects in the political arena – as they do for the alternative nineteenth century in with Strange and Norrell live. Norrell's campaign to remove the 'pernicious' effect of the 'fairy race' masks his own failures and reveals the hidden emotions he tries so hard to disown. The disparity between the image he wishes to project and the truth of his actions cannot help but cause violence – a violence that affects directly those who have the least recourse to redress: women and people of colour (Arabella Strange, Lady Pole and Stephen Black). Norrell's attempt to construct a sort of universal truth without emotion fits what Ahmed describes:

> Such a tradition relies on a distinction between emotion and reason, which constructs emotions as not only irrelevant to judgement and justice, but also as unreasonable, and as an obstacle to good judgement. Indeed, it is the hierarchies established by such models, which allow women and racial others to be seen as less moral, as less capable of making judgements: it is such others, of course, who are often presented as being 'swayed by their emotions'.
>
> (195)

This is what Norrell projects onto Others especially women and fairies, that they are incapable of good judgement or rational behaviour.

His antipathy goes all the way back to the Raven King himself, of whom he says, 'his magic was of a particularly pernicious sort and nothing would please me more than that he should be forgot as completely as he deserves' (71). The fairies who gave the legendary king his training, he despises with even greater zeal, declaring 'A more poisonous race or one more inimical to England has never existed' (72–3). He later theorizes to Jonathan Strange that 'my own example makes it plain that almost all *respectable* sorts of magic are perfectly achievable without assistance from any one!' (300, emphasis original). Norrell believes that the Raven King made a habit of '*deliberately exaggerating the role of fairies in magic*' the better to bind his two nations together, England and his Faerie realm (299, emphasis original).

The Raven King's fairy magic is the locus of all Norrell's passionate ire. He intends to promote the rational nature of 'respectable' magic and endeavours to embody that rationality himself. Yet Norrell is constantly emotional. At his London debut he is 'all forlorn and ill at ease' (55). When he summons the fairy spirit referred to as the Gentleman with Thistle-Down Hair his voice is 'quavering', he 'stammered' and was 'extremely surprised … wavered and hesitated'; his voice goes hoarse and 'he looked a little ill … coughed and muttered' (109). All of these signs of distress make plain the pain he feels at dealing with the hated Celtic race. Norrell is unable to keep the 'rational' and 'respectable' façade he wishes to maintain.

Yet he projects all the emotionalism and irrationality onto the fairies – not entirely without reason, but certainly not without hypocrisy. As Ahmed argues, 'disgust is deeply ambivalent, involving desire for, or an attraction towards, the very objects that are felt to be repellent' (84). Norrell despises fairies consistently, speaks against them tirelessly, yet calls on one for his most famous magical work of all – then denies the fact. In the midst of the magical bargain with the Gentleman, with the thought that 'Sir Walter [Pole] might continue in office and lend his support to all Mr Norrell's plans for reviving English magic' he makes the agreement with the fairy, full of suspicion of course, for 'he knew well how deceitful they could be' but agreeing nonetheless (111–2).

However, when he schools his first and only student, Mr Strange, Norrell has so erased the knowledge from his conscious mind that he proclaims the achievement of reputable magic can be done entirely without the assistance of that 'poisonous race' for 'What have I ever done that has needed the help of a fairy?' (300). While he grudgingly admits there are 'some sorts of magic which are entirely impossible without fairies' the magician warns against engaging in such activities as they would put the whole of the realm in danger, as 'nowhere is the decline of English magic better understood than in the Other Lands' (300). The projected disgust has everything to do with fear. Norrell envies the knowledge and skill that the fairies have because it is the image of himself he wants to maintain. When Strange discovers the disparity between what Norrell wishes him to believe and what he knows to be true, he is understandably confused. As he tells Arabella, 'It was the queerest thing in the world! He was so frightened at having been found out, that he could think of nothing to say. It fell to me to think of fresh lies for him to tell me' (305). Likewise when a peevish Norrell suggests reviving the medieval Court of the Cinque Dragownes to punish Christopher Drawlight's magical grifting – an undertaking that would require the participation of a dozen magicians – Strange and Childermass have to remind him it is impossible because he has destroyed all magicians but his pupil. Norrell 'had the good grace to a appear a little embarrassed at contradicting all that he had maintained for seven years' (517).

Right up to the end, when he and Strange consider summoning the Raven King, Norrell is mostly attacked by fear any time he contemplates this man to whom 'the ways of the *brugh* were natural' – the English-born king of fairy magic. Strange is motivated by the need to restore his wife from the Other Lands, but Norrell resists employing this (self-)forbidden Other:

> Mr Norrell breathed hard. The very air seemed to quiver as if a deep note had been sounded. He was aware, to an almost painful degree, of the darkness surrounding them, of new stars above them and of the silence of the stopt clocks. It was one Great Black Moment going on for ever, pressing down upon him, suffocating him.
>
> (956)

When Strange persuades him to work the magic to summon the King, they encounter a variety of problems – not least of which is the problem of naming him – but summon him they do, so Norrell meets ever so briefly his greatest fear: utter vulnerability before the Celtic fairy king. In an instant he sees how tiny and insignificant he is when the seemingly giant eye of one of Uskglass's ravens looks in the window at Hurtfew Abbey:

> Mr Norrell thought of it as a hillside because it bore some resemblance to a moor where the heather is all burnt and charred – except that this hillside was not the black of burnt things, it was the black of wet silk or well-shone leather. Suddenly the stone did something – it moved or spun. The movement was almost too quick to grasp but Mr Norrell was left with the sickening impression that it had blinked.
>
> (990)

Having faced his greatest fear (not even directly but via metonymy) the Other whom he had set himself against all his life, Norrell begins to regard an eternity trapped in the Black Tower with his books and Mr Strange not as 'a destiny full of fear, horror and desolation!' but with something approaching equanimity (991). Having borne the burden of the whole of English magic on his back, perhaps Norrell can drop that burden now that he has seen (and the seeing seems important) how small he is in the scheme of things – all the things that comprise 'Heaven, Hell, Earth and Faerie' (966).

In the end the magicians fail. Norrell is unable to stop the opening of England to the Celtic/fairy magic and Strange is unable to control the magic once he opens the way to the King's Roads. In a possible embodiment of Ahmed's 'restorative justice', we might see the return of magic to the land and the opening of magical practice to those who had been denied the path by Norrell as 'a restoration of the community' (198). Thanks to Childermass they receive a gift, 'A book Norrell long desired, but never saw. A book Strange did not even know existed … John Uskglass's book' (1001). Magic has returned to its Celtic roots and the diverse community of magicians are left to untangle its mysteries while the warring magicians remain, 'Behind the sky. On the other side of the rain', (1000) having themselves become the Other.

References

Ahmed, Sara (2014), *The Cultural Politics of Emotion*, Edinburgh: Edinburgh University Press.
Aughey, Arthur (2007), *The Politics of Englishness*, Manchester: Manchester University Press.
Chapman, Malcolm (1992), *The Celts: The Construction of a Myth*, London: Macmillan.
Clarke, Susanna (2004), *Jonathan Strange & Mr Norrell*, London: Bloomsbury.
Clarke, Susanna (2006), *The Ladies of Grace Adieu and Other Stories*, London: Bloomsbury.
Curtice, John (2013), 'What Does England Want?', *Scottish Social Attitudes*, http://www.scotcen.org.uk/media/205435/wst-briefing-4-styled-final-7-.pdf, accessed 19 June 2021.
Drexler, Paul H. (2004), 'On Latin Quotation', *Sewanee Review*, 112 (3): 410–16.
eDIL: Electronic Dictionary of the Irish Language, 'bruig', http://www.dil.ie/search?search_in=headword&q=bruig, accessed 19 Jun. 2021.
Fimi, Dimitra (2017), *Celtic Myth in Contemporary Children's Fantasy: Idealization, Identity, Ideology*, London: Palgrave Macmillan.
Garner, Steve (2009), 'Ireland: From Racism without "Race" to Racism without Racists', *Radical History Review*, 104: 41–56.
Henderson, Ailsa, Jeffery, Charlie, Wincott, Dan, and Wyn Jones, Richard (2017), 'How Brexit Was Made in England', *The British Journal of Politics and International Relations*, 19 (4): 1369–481.

James, Simon (1999), *Atlantic Celts: Ancient People or Modern Invention?*, London: British Museum.
Matasovic, Ranko (2009), *Etymological Dictionary of Proto-Celtic*, Leiden: Brill.
Whorf, Benjamin (2012), *Language, Thought, and Reality: Selected Writings of Benjamin Lee Whorf*, ed. John B. Carroll, Boston: MIT Press.
Williams, Mark (2016), *Ireland's Immortals: A History of the Gods of Irish Myth*, Princeton, NJ: Princeton University Press.

2

The evolution of Alan Garner's Celticity in *Boneland*

Gwendolen Grant

Boneland is the long-awaited final book of Garner's *Weirdstone* trilogy, published in 2012, over fifty years after the first two instalments, *The Weirdstone of Brisingamen* (1960) and *The Moon of Gomrath* (1963). The first two books are considered children's books and are classic good versus evil intrusion fantasy stories, whereas *Boneland* is very much a book for adults. It is very different in tone from its predecessors and, as this chapter will show, it is heavily reliant on them for the reader to be able to understand the mythological references. Most strikingly, the overt fantasy of *Weirdstone* and *Gomrath* has become an introverted dream scape in *Boneland*, centring around Colin, while the fantasy elements are so tightly woven into the primary world that it is almost impossible to tease them apart. With this closeness of reality and fantasy, Garner explores two of the most important literary inspirations to him, the legend of the Sleeping Hero of Alderley Edge and 'Celtic mythology'.

Garner was first introduced to the legend of the Sleeping Hero of Alderley Edge as a child by his grandfather, as a last remnant of a truly oral tradition connected to his family and the place where they have lived for hundreds of years (the full legend as told by Garner's grandfather can be found in *The Voice That Thunders*, Garner 1997: 65–7). The young Garner's fascination with the mysterious old man of the story protecting the sleeping heroes and its basis in a landscape he already knew so well sparked a deep love and connection to the history and mythology of his home:

> So it is for a child born to the Edge. We know our place, and knowledge passed beyond the material, such as where a band of white clay was under the fallen leaves which could be used as soap to clean up with before going home. It passed

to the spiritual, too. I was bought up to respect both. They were there. Even the ghosts were those of relatives.

(Garner 1997: 13)

Garner has continued to be absorbed into the Edge by these ancestral ghosts his entire life, remaining immersed in its history and contributing to the study of the area's folklore, archaeology, anthropology and environmental preservation (see contributions to *The Story of Alderley*, Prag 2016). The Edge and its legend were both a fitting location and subject for *Weirdstone* and *Gomrath* as Garner's first two novels, where he worked on the premise that the legend was true, exploring the question of what it would mean for mortals to get tangled up in this world. The twin brother and sister, Colin and Susan, come into contact with the Otherworld of the Edge through Firefrost, the magical stone of the title of *Weirdstone*, which has come to Susan through their family. This stone holds the power to protect the sleepers from those who seek to destroy them and so Colin and Susan unwittingly become the focus of a battle between good and evil. Once they are involved and have seen the Otherworld of the Edge, there is no escape, with Susan taking the magic into herself and becoming part of the Otherworld in *Gomrath* and the object of the evil Morrigan's revenge. *Boneland* takes this story to its end and further than most writers of fantasy novels with child protagonists go, attempting to answer the question of what happens when the adventure is over. Colin is now an adult and suffers from severe mental illness as a result of his brush with the Otherworld, endlessly searching for his lost sister in the stars.

Both *Weirdstone* and *Gomrath* are heavily influenced by what is conventionally known as 'Celtic' mythology, with *Gomrath* containing almost exclusively Irish or Welsh names and references (for example, Celemon daughter of Cei is taken from the long lists of names in *Culhwch and Olwen* and Garanhir is associated with the Welsh poet Taliesin). Garner discovered mythological texts in Celtic languages through Welsh, the encounter with which he describes as an eye-opening experience of his youth:

> I felt that I understood the language without knowing what it was saying. I could not learn for lack of facilities, but the sensation was one more of remembering. It was as if I were hearing the knights, who lay in the cave with their king under the hill behind our house, talking in their sleep.

(Garner 1997: 196)

There was an instant connection for Garner on both a conscious and a subconscious level, that his own legends and the legends told in this ancient language from just across the Welsh border were somehow one and the same. It 'told its stories as I dreamed my dreams' (Garner 1997: 196). Celtic mythology from this first Welsh connection has become as personally important to Garner as the mythology of his own corner of land in Cheshire and has run a continuous thread throughout most of his books even though the original myths considered to be under the 'Celtic' umbrella are very different geographically. The strong Celtic influences of *Weirdstone* and *Gomrath* have been brought forward into the fantasy of *Boneland* through the interaction between place and characters in both the modern-day story of Colin and the concurrent story of the pre-historic Watcher, drawing a line through mythological and geographical history. It is this connection between place and person that I will be exploring in this chapter, looking at how Garner has used pan-Celtic elements in conjunction with his own private mythology and the wider mythology of Britain to create a world that is both local and universal.

Three primary features of *Boneland* will be examined and evaluated in terms of their Irish and Welsh mythological influences. Firstly, the Otherworld of the Edge is explored, looking at how Garner has used elements from the mythological source material to build an Otherworld local to the Edge while creating a place that is unique and yet universal for the setting of *Weirdstone* and *Gomrath*. This is brought forward into *Boneland* on the same principle, but we now see the extremes of the Watcher's complete immersion and Colin's isolation from the Otherworld. The theme of reincarnation is then explored and strong parallels drawn between the pre-Galfridian Myrddin Wyllt of the *Vita Merlini*, Colin and the Watcher. The wild man archetype runs through each of these characters, drawing them together to form a line of continuity through time which embeds Garner's trilogy into a wider pre-existing mythology. Lastly, the obvious Irish mythological character of the Morrigan is explored in her *Boneland* iteration of Meg the psychiatrist, who becomes a much richer and more subtle depiction of the Morrigan than in *Weirdstone* and *Gomrath*. Meg and Susan's characters are part of the same triple goddess and have become an exploration of female characteristics in Irish and Welsh mythology which speak directly to the universal, entering Colin's world from the outside.

As Catherine Butler remarks in *Four British Fantasists*, Garner sees the mythological source material he uses through the lens of traditional comparative mythology and its Jungian origins, including the work of mythographers such as Robert Graves (2006: 186). This tends towards a universalist and ahistorical approach and a free use of mythological elements from very different sources. Many of the features of *Weirdstone* and *Gomrath*, most notably the triple moon goddess, are not found in authentic mythological texts but in Graves's *The*

White Goddess. In the last section I will address the trilogy in terms of Garner's universalist approach to mythology and how he has used the Welsh and Irish source material, comparing *Boneland* with *Weirdstone* and *Gomrath* at either end of a fifty-year gap. In *Boneland*, Garner slots his own conscious fiction into the existing world of Celtic myth and then into a wider archetypal context in the pre-historic, communicating his personal affiliation with his own sacred place and with a pan-Celtic section of the mythological world.

Colin and the Otherworld of the Edge

The subjective experiences of the Otherworld that we see through the characters in this trilogy shift from the overt and tangible fantasy world of *Weirdstone* and *Gomrath* to the much more subtle psychological experience of Colin in *Boneland*. However, the manner in which the Otherworld interacts with the primary world throughout the trilogy remains consistent and is tied to the physical place of the Edge and to the author's view of the 'Celtic' Otherworld. There are no obvious boundaries between the two worlds and so the characters seamlessly pass from one into the other, often without realizing where they are. Garner describes the Otherworld in *Gomrath* as 'as near and unknown as the back of a shadow' (Garner 2014b: 18). This particular quality of the perilous and uncontrollable is prominent in Garner's Welsh mythological influences, where the Otherworld is not a place that you find, but a place that finds you. In the First Branch of the Mabinogi, Pwyll meets Arawn in the forest seemingly by chance when he becomes separated from his companions. There is nothing to indicate that he is no longer in his own world until he sees the fantastic hounds of Arawn (Davies 2007: 3). Every other feature of the forest is recognizable and familiar to him. This closeness of the Otherworld makes us question our view of the primary world and blurs the lines between the real and fantastic.

This stumbling into the Otherworld is experienced by Colin and Susan in *Weirdstone* in their first encounter with the svart-alfar. They only feel that something is not right when they step into the woods and are unnerved by a crow who seems to be staring at them (Garner 2014a: 36–7). This could be just a crow until the svart-alfar appear and they don't have time to question their reality, much like Pwyll suddenly seeing the white dogs with red ears in the *Mabinogion*. The crow is used as a bridging element between the real and the fantastic and is presented as a being which could be either, depending on one's perception. The first appearance of the Otherworld in *Boneland* works on the same principles, but Garner has refined the blend between the real and the fantastic which has now become much more subtle, to the point where we find ourselves questioning reality along with Colin. The introduction of Meg into Colin's life is completely integrated into the primary world as she is a professional recommended and seemingly known by his own doctor (Garner 2013: 18). The pairing of the first mention of Meg and the incident in the waiting room with the child's story of a witch's house are a strong indication for us that something isn't right (Garner 2013: 16–17). Colin's instinctive reaction to the story and his connection between crow, witch and Meg point us in the direction of who she really is, but we do not really know if this reaction is just Colin projecting or if it is a reality. Again, Garner is using the crow as a bridging element between reality and fantasy but in a very different tone. Rather than signalling the arrival of the Otherworld as it comes crashing through the forest in *Weirdstone*, in *Boneland* it is highlighting Colin's complex psychological relationship with the Otherworld and his forgotten childhood. We notice the disparity between what we remember and what Colin doesn't, adding a new psychological element to the tension between fantasy and reality.

To continue with the psychological tone of Garner's Otherworld in *Boneland*, we see an amplified use of dreams and visions as compared with the earlier books. Dreams and visions are a common connecting elements between the primary and the Otherworld in both Welsh and Irish mythological texts, for example in the *Dream of Rhonabwy* in the Welsh material (Davies 2007: 214) where the dreamer is an observer, or *Aislinge Oengusa* ('The Dream of Oengus') of Irish myth (Gantz 1981: 107) where the dreamer is actively invaded and put into a sickness by the Otherworld through the dream. Colin's most direct connection to the Otherworld is through the flashbacks and dreams that plague him from his forgotten childhood. We know that these dreams are of events that really happened in the first two books of the trilogy even though Colin is not sure himself (Garner 2013: 38). Returning to the events in the doctor's office, Colin's reaction to the story of the witch and his pressing of the doctor about whether or not Meg is a witch is treated as a symptom of his mental illness, even though we suspect he is right on the money. Garner uses this method of connection to the Otherworld to highlight the tension between reality and fantasy and how they can overlap both subjectively within a person's mind and objectively in the tangible world. The Watcher is a stark contrast to the way that Colin experiences the Otherworld through the medium of dream and also, despite the gap in time, brings us closer to the specific Otherworld of the Edge than Colin does. For the Watcher, there are no boundaries between fantasy and reality both subjectively and objectively. He interacts with an animistic Edge and takes an active role in its continually active mythology:

> The moon lifted into him and flowed from bone to bone; along his spine and every rib gleamed at his fingers, filled his skull, broke through his eyes, and brought pictures to his tongue.
>
> (Garner 2013: 8)

This is a description of the ritual dance to summon the seasons, the whole experience of which is later described by him as 'I dream in Ludcruck' (Garner 2013: 110). For the Watcher there is no unseen divide between the primary and Otherworld or even psychological divide between waking and dreaming.

At the beginning of *Boneland*, Colin and the Watcher are initially connected for us through dream. The first few alternations between the story of Colin and the story of the Watcher are presented as one being the dream of the other and vice versa. For example, at the end of the first part of the Watcher's story 'He lay for one day, He lay for two days. He lay for three days' is immediately followed by Colin waking up in hospital (Garner 2013: 2). At the next switch in narrative:

> Colin made a fire and sat at the table through the night until the day showed. Then he put out the lamp, sprawled on his bunk; and he slept.
>
> He woke, drank, blew a fire heap, ate meat, and left the lodge.
>
> (Garner 2013: 7)

This could be a continuation of the same story and it takes us a few sentences to realize that we have switched again into the Watcher and we realize the force of the contrast between Colin and the Watcher's interactions with the Otherworld. We could also interpret the world of the Watcher as being entirely a dream/fantasy world through this initial switching of the stories as we are more likely to accept Colin's world as primary, as it is the most like our own. As their stories separate and become more independent, the primary connection between Colin and the Watcher is the Edge and its Otherworld, and Garner brings this into tangible effect by intertwining the psychological with physical connections between the primary and the Otherworld.

Garner connects the Otherworld in the trilogy to the specific location of the Edge by introducing landscape features as markers of a subterranean world of fantastic beings that are able to emerge and interact with the primary world. Here Garner is blending the invisible boundary of the Welsh Otherworld with the physical boundary of the Irish mythological *síd*. A *síd* is a physical feature of the landscape, usually a mound, which harbours the Otherworld (see Williams

2016: 30). This element of the Otherworldly landscape is present from the beginning of *Weirdstone* as Colin and Susan go down into Fundindelve situated under Stormy Point, an actual place on the real Edge (Garner 2014a: 42). In *Gomrath*, the latent magic within the landscape is opened out in the ride of the Horsemen of Donn, which creates a new magical presence in almost every mound-like feature and is reminiscent of Echu's campaign to raise the *síde*. The most obvious connection with the subterranean Otherworld not only links us to the physical locality of the Edge, but to the local mythology of the Edge and the Sleeping Heroes who the wizard Cadellin is said to guard.

The Watcher's animistic landscape brings the Irish mythological theme of the subterranean Otherworld into *Boneland*. The Watcher's sacred spaces are within the cave of Ludcruck where he enacts the rituals that make the world (Garner 2013: 31) and the Hill of Life and Death where he leaves the woman and child to be taken to the next life (Garner 2013: 10). The Watcher is *of* the Otherworld and not just *connected* to it as he has free access to both the surface and subterranean spaces. He is responsible for the welfare of the outside world through the magic that he performs in these caves to bring the life out of the rocks, reminding us of the tendency in some Irish texts to align the Túatha Dé Danann with nature deities. The Túatha Dé Danann, although powerful and supernatural, are also considered to be humans of another race to the humans living above ground, only living in the *síd* mounds because they are the former defeated inhabitants of Ireland (see Williams 2016: 128–45). The Watcher similarly is both human and supernatural in his performance of the magic of creation within the earth and his direct interaction with an animistic landscape, but then he is also a mortal human who grows weak and dies. The active animism in the Watcher's story through the amplified form of the Otherworld conveys a latent animism to Colin's Edge which we only see glimpses of through Colin's eyes:

> Colin stood, pulled his hood about him, and breathed the wind. He saw the bright of spring. He smelt returning life. Then, in a moment that he knew, it was time to go. The Edge was waking to its other self.
>
> (Garner 2013: 25–6)

This unexpected connection between Colin, the movement of the seasons and a landscape being described as a conscious being awakening comes at a point in the narrative where the Watcher's story is suddenly stilled. But Colin's ritual is here reminiscent of the Watcher's more obvious ritual as the last time we were with the Watcher, he was singing the spring back into the world and freeing the year's new life from the rocks of Ludcruck. We may not overtly see the

Otherworld under the surface of the Edge in Colin's story, but Garner does not let us forget that it is there.

So far we have seen how Garner built his original fantasy landscape in *Weirdstone* and *Gomrath* through inspiration from both the Welsh and Irish Otherworlds, and then brought these elements forward into *Boneland* tightly interwoven into the story to create a unique place but one that is rooted in its sources. Garner also reverses the process in *Boneland* by taking objects back through to mythological references both within and outside of the story, as well as bringing them forward into the existing landscape. This is particularly important because Colin's experience of the Otherworld is so minimal, due to the curse of forgetfulness which has cut him off from direct interaction. It is through Colin that these backwards references are made, and they help to link the local to the mythological. There are significant sections of the dialogue devoted to Colin explaining areas of his vast knowledge and understanding of the landscape in his academic work. Garner chooses conversations that carry layers of meaning and connect back through the entire trilogy, becoming all the more powerful as referring to objects and places that exist in our primary world. An example is Colins's cellar with its Goblin Gold moss and light-producing quartz (Garner 2013: 76–7). Neither of these phenomena are Garner's invention and are already found in the real-world Edge as described in a study of its wildlife and geology, in an edited volume to which Garner directly contributed (see Edwards et al. 2016: 131). The ghostly effect of this shimmering plant and the sparkling light produced by the quartz pebbles brings to mind Colin's adit to Fundindelve as we have encountered it in *Weirdstone* and the shimmering blue light that shows the magic protecting the cave and the sleepers from the outside world (Garner 2014a: 47, 51). We are also reminded of the Watcher's reference to the sky as a cave and the stars which he is watching adorning the outer walls (Garner 2013: 44). These references to other elements of the story sparked in our memory remind us of the presence of the Otherworld at the Edge and how close Colin is to the magic he can no longer see. At the same time the mythological references already associated with the landscape discussed above connect the internal references to the local primary world of the Edge as well as the universal, mythological Edge.

A second example to note is the stone axe kept as sacred by the Watcher and found by R.T. under the place for the telescope at Jodrell Bank. There is a clear power in this piece of shaped rock felt by everyone who handles it, being described by R.T. as 'comforting' (Garner 2013: 109), and declared as 'alive' when Meg first touches it (Garner 2013: 114). Meg goes on to compare the axe with the Holy

Grail and its connections to the alchemical Philosopher's Stone, which bestows immortality, describing it with the alchemical maxim 'This stone is poor, and cheap in price; spurned by fools, loved more by the wise' (Garner 2013: 115).[1] The Stone as the Grail also relates to the personal healing properties that this object has for Colin as it focuses his mind to overcome his illness and come to terms with his past. This is one of the few overt mythological references made in *Boneland* and reminds us of the mythology of the surrounding lands of this area, forming another physical connection between the myth and the Edge through time, from pre-history to the present day. Garner himself owns an Acheulian axe kept on his desk (Mansfield 2012), but takes the axe of Boneland further back in time to the emergence of *Homo sapiens*. The myth reaches back to even before the emergence of our species as the Watcher is either *Homo erectus* or *Homo heidelbergensis*, 0.5 million years old (Garner 2013: 109), adding a tremendous sense of distant time.

The numinousity in the ancient is keenly felt by Garner in the landscape of the Edge and he has been involved in successfully proving the place as one of the oldest continuously inhabited places in Britain, reaching back to the Mesolithic era (see Prag and Timberlake 2016: 309). The story of his finding of a Bronze age shovel under the stage at his old school is well worth the read (Garner 1997: 184) and shows us the deep connection Garner feels to the history of life on the Edge. The Edge is presented in the trilogy as a stabilizing element of mythological thought across these vast amounts of time, and has been shown above to contain a pan-Celtic Otherworld that has been fully integrated with the local landscape and well as the local myths of the area. The universality of the Welsh and Irish influences is applicable and yet this place could be no other than Alderley Edge of the Cheshire countryside. While this area is in England, Cheshire is a historical borderland between ever-changing invading peoples going back to the Roman occupation of Britain. As Colin tells us:

> 'Boundaries aren't safe'.
>
> 'They occupy neither space nor time. Boundaries can change apparent realities. They let things through'.
>
> (Garner 2013: 131)

---

[1] The idea of the Grail as a Stone is found in Wolfram von Eschenbach's version of *Parzival* which is based on Chrétien de Troyes's *Perceval*. As this is not found in the Welsh material, I have not pursued this line of connection. However, it is worth mentioning that *Perceval* also thought to have inspired the Welsh legend of *Peredur* (Davies 2007: xi) and contains the Grail King/Fisher King who is heavily featured in Graves's *The White Goddess*, an enduring influence on Garner.

The complex and ever-changing history of Cheshire combined with Garner's feelings of personal connection to 'Celtic' mythology as mentioned above come together to form a space where the universal and the local can make sense with each other. As Butler points out in *Four British Fantasists*, Garner is not throwing whatever he feels to be magical at the place he wants to set his narrative in order to make it so, he 'perceives and communicates what is already latent … in the land itself' (Butler 2006: 46). Garner is not treating the Celtic Otherworld as a way of making his own locality magical, but bringing out what he perceives as a pre-existing Otherworld through other pre-existing mythological tools. The beginnings of this method seen in *Weirdstone* and *Gomrath* has had its volume turned down for *Boneland* resulting in a pan-Celtic Otherworld almost imperceptibly integrated into the local primary world.

Colin, Merlin and the Watcher

Colin has no memory of anything that happened to him as a child before his sister's disappearance, unless the memories come to him in flashbacks and dreams. He does not know why he must not leave the Edge and his deep knowledge of the area can be seen as a groping towards understanding in the only way he knows how. He is both entranced and comforted as well as oppressed by the place he must live in. Colin finally remembers at the end of *Boneland* that he is there as a punishment. He tried to wake the sleepers in his desperation to find his recently missing sister, so Cadellin cursed him to take on the role of protector of the Edge, and with forgetting everything in his past life but unable to forget anything new (Garner 2013: 135). Both Colin and Susan are therefore sucked into an eternity of living in the Otherworld after their perhaps ill-fated brush with the fantastic as children. As Susan is taken into her role as the third element in the triple moon goddess, Colin becomes the guardian wizard of the legend. Colin is taken into the High magic of the intellect represented by Cadellin, becoming part of the eternally changing mythology of the area to join a line of archetypal beings.

In *Boneland*, both Colin and the Watcher can be read as expressions of the wild man archetype but fulfilling this idea in different ways. They can be specifically related to Myrddin Wyllt of early Welsh poetry and Geoffrey of Monmouth's *Vita Merlini* as an example of this archetype from real world mythology. While Garner does not cite the *Vita Merlini* and associated poems as a source for these characters, I would argue that there is a very close connection which is present throughout the trilogy. This connection does not go so far as to map characters from Garner's stories onto mythological characters, a move which would be very un-Garner, but is intended to show how Garner uses traits from characters and story elements to enhance his own, emphasizing some and discarding others across the different expressions of this single archetype. Geoffrey of Monmouth claims to have constructed the story in the *Vita Merlini* from several old Welsh poems of which Myrddin was considered to be the author and narrator (Jarman 1995: 117–18). The *Vita Merlini* represents a specifically Welsh idea of the Merlin legend as opposed to the Merlin of Geoffrey's more popular work, *Historia Regum Britanniae*, in which he connects Merlin to the Arthurian legends for the first time.

The *Vita* begins with Myrddin's madness coming upon him during a bloody battle which has been identified from other sources as the Battle of Arfderydd in Cumbria (Jarman 1995: 118). The cause of Myrddin's madness is grief for the slaughter and loss of his companions with an alternative version stating that he saw a terrifying heavenly vision in the sky, laying the guilt of the slaughter upon him and punishing him with madness (Jarman 1995: 122). In *Scotland's Merlin*, Tim Clarkson argues that a particularly medieval European version of the Wild Man archetype combines the idea of the untameable wild savage with the solitary ascetic living in the wilderness from Christian tradition going on to narrow this further into a particularly 'Celtic sub-type' where the initial cause of the man becoming wild is guilt-induced madness for some terrible misdeed (Clarkson 2016: 92–4). This iteration of the wild man can be seen in the *Vita Merlini* and is also present in the Colin of *Boneland*. Both grief and guilt converge in the character of Colin and the nature of his curse as we come to learn that he has lost his entire family and guardians starting with the disappearance of his sister (Garner 2013: 62–3), and this seems to have triggered his desperate attempt to awaken the sleeping heroes guarded by Cadellin (Garner 2013: 135). He has also been in a terrifying and violent battle at the end of *Gomrath*, which took place to rescue him. We see Garner consistently emphasizing the violence and reality of death during this battle:

> The worst moment for Colin and Susan had come when the attack was seconds away, when they knew that they had to lift their swords and bring them down on living things.
>
> (Garner 2014b: 194)

We also see Atlendor of the lios-alfar laying blame for the battle directly at Colin's feet:

> 'I know that it has been a dear promise', said Atlendor. He looked at Colin. 'One life has cost thirty: it shall not take more'.
>
> (Garner 2014b: 202)

Whether the battle is really Colin's fault or not is secondary to the feeling of guilt being laid upon him by Atlendor as this guilt will remain with him nonetheless. This sense of loss and guilt drives him towards his attempt to wake the heroes and forms his punishment of forgetting as a precaution taken by Cadellin to prevent his knowledge of the Otherworld and, therefore, his access. The guilt in Colin is eventually directly expressed in *Boneland* when he tells Meg that he 'did so much wrong' (Garner 2013: 133) before remembering the specific wrong that he did. Colin's subsequent retreat from society into his present state reflects the mental distress felt by Myrddin from similar causes as described above and contains an element of the ascetic hermit in the un-modern way of life he adopts. As we shall see below, Garner draws on his own experience of mental illness for Colin's character resulting in a highly sensitive and realistic portrayal. There is a danger of Colin slipping into another romanticized portrayal of the 'mad professor' trope, but Garner's ability to convey the depth of pain within Colin does not hold back giving the book its emotional poignancy and avoiding this pitfall with a feeling of genuine depth of character. We are reminded of the approach to Myrddin's madness as written by Geoffrey in a time when mental illness was so misunderstood and in terms of the wild man archetype, as Garner brings a modern reality to this mythic idea.

The links between Myrddin and the Watcher are less about his story and more about his situation, relating exclusively to the personality Myrddin takes on when living in the woods. Myrddin settles himself at first on top of a mountain where he can oversee the whole forest which carries suggestions of governing or surveying the landscape and wildlife within it (Clarke 1973) just as the Watcher much more intensely must govern his landscape. Myrddin befriends a wolf who mirrors his hardship during the first winter as the Watcher is connected with a semi-supernatural wolf who defines the stages of his search (Garner 2013: 8). Myrddin therefore can be seen as providing a linking element between the Watcher and Colin. One trait which he shares with both is his association with the stars, a connection that all three express in different ways. Myrddin uses the stars to draw his prophecies from, seeing that his wife has been promised to another man and seeing political events in far off countries as they unfold. Towards the end of the story, he asks his sister to build him a house in the woods with 'seventy doors and as many windows, through which I can see fire-breathing Phoebus with Venus' (Clarke 1973: 81). The Watcher has a responsibility to keep the stars in the sky and oversee their turning through night and day and the seasons (Garner 2013: 31) and Colin continues his never ending search for his sister in the Pleiades through his work at the Jodrell Bank telescope (Garner

2013: 95). This connection between the characters mirrors the continuity that Garner portrays in the landscape discussed above as an element of permanence and immortality. Stars do not perceptually change to us or they only change very slowly over millennia so the Watcher, Myrddin and Colin are all looking at the same stars and drawing their energy from the same overarching force, creating a link that transcends the time between them.

Cadellin, as the other guardian of the Edge, is also included in this link and strengthens the Myrddin connection that is brought to the *Boneland* characters. Garner very deliberately did not want to equate Cadellin with Merlin in *Weirdstone* and *Gomrath* as the legend of the sleeping hero of Alderley Edge does not make the connection with Arthurian legend and does not name the wizard (Garner 1997: 66). The name Cadellin is taken from the long lists of names in *Culhwch and Olwen* (Davies 2007: 187) but this is as far as the conscious connection for Garner goes as so where many other names used for *Weirdstone* and *Gomrath*. However, due to Colin's connection with the pre-Galfridian Myrddin, it becomes tempting and fruitful to draw connections between Cadellin and the post-Galfridian Merlin. The connection again brings the wider mythology back to the local and highlights the connection between the wizard of the legend of the sleeping heroes and the legend that Arthur is himself sleeping on the isle of Avalon and will one day come back to Britain in its direst need. Garner's depiction of Cadellin is very much the guide, counsellor and friend that Merlin is to Arthur in the later iterations of the legend, behind whom is lurking a great power. Apart from the connection between Arthur and other legends of sleeping heroes from around Britain, Merlin is Arthur's protector during life, and therefore the protector of the land. Cadellin is also painted as the lofty and quick to anger wizard that we recognize in modern popular culture as a Gandalf-like character. Our first meeting of him in *Weirdstone* has Colin entranced:

> But Colin was staring at the old man, and seemed not to have heard. He saw an old man, but one whose body was as firm and upright as a youth's; whose keen, grey eyes were full of the sadness of the wise; whose mouth, though stern, was kind and capable of laughter.
>
> (Garner 2014a: 44–5)

Cadellin actually takes part in relatively little action in the stories of *Weirdstone* and *Gomrath* but remains a presence in the background through Colin and Susan's reliance on him and his central role in the legend of the sleepers. We are able to understand very little about him apart from one moment of humanity shown to us through Albanac in *Gomrath* when they are leaving for the battle with the Morrigan. This moment shines out from his otherwise sketchy personality:

> 'I have thought of this', said Cadellin. 'My duty is here, guarding the Sleepers. Only I can wake them. If I were killed, I should have betrayed my trust, and only in Fundindelve can I be certain of life …'
> As they went from Fundindelve, Albanac took Cadellin's hand, and so only he felt the wizard's grief, and saw the light that stood beyond his eyes.
>
> (Garner 2014b: 172–3)

This shows us the true task of Cadellin and connects him with the adult Colin, Myrddin, and the Watcher, to join the continuous line of mythological evolution of their personalities. We realize that he does care deeply and that he wants to help, but he is trapped in Fundindelve. This theme of being trapped in an environment is shown in Colin being unable to leave the Edge, Myrddin being so wedded to his life in the woods that he is unable to survive anywhere else, and the Watcher being duty-bound to stay in his home and keep the world afloat. In *Boneland* we learn that Cadellin's curse goes deeper as Colin remembers and tells us that Cadellin actually can't die, even though he should have long ago (Garner 2013: 135).

A further linking theme between these characters from both Garner's work and existing mythology is the relationship between knowledge and memory, explored in *Boneland* through Colin's illness. The history of this knowledge begins with the Watcher who uses the stories and dance of creation to keep the world turning by telling, retelling and re-enacting them over and over again. Myrddin gains his knowledge of the forest and thereby his prophetic powers by forgetting his life within society and interacting with the world as the Watcher enacts the world. The knowledge of the Watcher is then formalized by Garner into the High and Old Magic. Cadellin has a deep knowledge of both and uses them to protect the sleepers and contain the magic that they hold. As a supernatural being, Cadellin is here closer to the Watcher than to Myrddin or Colin, as he does not carry the choice between intellect and nature/high and old magic, he can know both. Colin then experiences a reverse of Myrddin's experience by being cut off from knowledge of the Otherworld and yet gaining the inability to forget any fact or occurrence in the real world, thereby gaining an encyclopaedic and yet surface understanding. But like Myrddin, Colin's healing process involves remembering his lost past and uniting the two halves of his personality. Interestingly this is directly related to Garner's own experience of healing, on which he draws for Colin, in the process of digging up and dealing with harmful memories hidden deeply from his consciousness with his own psychiatrist (Garner 1997: 113). It is noteworthy that Colin's knowledge of birds is emphasized throughout *Boneland* as part of the crow theme and that the *Vita Merlini* has Myrddin take us on a long explanation of the movements and migrations of birds.

We could imagine that the iterations of this wild man/wizard/guardian/shaman character are reincarnations of the same archetype sharing the same memories both within the reality of the story and within our reality as readers and creators of the stories. Each iteration is then remembering their former selves and this sense of responsibility is carried down through a sort of reincarnation and the mythology maintains its immortality. The connection between Colin and the Watcher at extreme ends of linear time is made obvious in *Boneland*, with Colin slipping into the world of the Watcher through his flashbacks as he remembers a deeper time than his own childhood (Garner 2013: 60). However, these reincarnations remain unique to their time and place and the Watcher is as much pre-historic man as Myrddin is ancient Welsh wild man and Colin is modern day professor. The combination of the universal and mythological versus the local and specific is as tightly woven into this line of characters as it is to the landscape as shown above. Taking the reincarnation theme out of the reality of the stories and into our own, Garner is also commenting on the nature of myth through the continuity of his characters with the existing mythological characters linked to the Edge and with the associated existing Welsh mythology. Colin and the Watcher are slotted into a pre-existing 'Celtic' framework while maintaining their unique characters which in turn is part of the mythological archetypes known the world over. The creation of the characters can also be seen as a remembering of an original archetype shaped by the memory of the land in which they are created. Their close connection with the continuity of the Edge sweeps the story into mythic time along with mythologies we already know.

The Morrigan, Meg and Susan

The character of the Morrigan in *Weirdstone* and *Gomrath* portrays a very stereotypical interpretation of her real world Irish mythological counterpart, the Morrígan. Garner initially homed in on her shrieking battle goddess aspect and made this her entire personality, shape-shifting between human and crow form (Garner 2014a: 82). In *Gomrath*, this character element is continued, but she is integrated into the triple moon goddess (maiden, mother and crone) at the centre of the story with Susan and Angharad (Garner 2014b: 138). The triple moon goddess is not a theme from the Irish or Welsh source material, but is a construct borrowed from Robert Graves's *The White Goddess* (Philip 1981: 151), and here Garner has bought together his own three goddesses for the purposes of his own story. Throughout these first two books the Morrigan is presented as the primary antagonist and condensed into a wholly evil character in contrast to the moral complexity of the Irish original. Garner completely transforms the Morrigan in *Boneland* into Meg, the ambiguously helpful psychiatrist, who reflects the Irish Morrígan's personality much more closely. Meg's relationship with Colin now contains all of the subtleties shown in the mythological Morrigan's relationship with Cú Chulainn in the Ulster cycle of Irish myth, as being antagonistic and cruel as well as helpful and protective.

The mythological Morrigan sometimes comes to the aid of Cú Chulainn and acts as a guardian. In the *Táin Bó Cuailnge* ('The Cattle Raid of Cooley') she appears at his call in the guise of Nemain and destroys hundreds of warriors to save him from an overwhelming battle. She also attempts to stop Cú Chulainn from going to the battle that she knows will kill him by breaking his chariot, but then appears on his shoulder once he is dead as a crow, as if to claim her own in the *Oidheadh Chon Culainn* ('The violent death of Cú Chulainn'). The guardian aspect of the Morrígan comes out in Meg's position as Colin's psychiatrist and supporter through his internal battle with his past. Meg's methods as a psychiatrist are modelled very closely on Garner's own psychiatrist (Garner 1997: 111), who forced him to dig up and confront the painful memories causing his illness. From the patients' perspective this can reflect the tendencies of the Morrígan to be antagonistic and cruel even though the aim is to heal, a part which Meg plays very well. The connection between the Morrigan and the crow is appropriated into *Boneland* but not as a physical transformation as in *Weirdstone* and *Gomrath*. Instead, the crow is internalized within Colin's fear of the Morrigan's previous form, now buried in his psyche and haunting him. The example of the doctor's office is again useful here as Colin instantly connects the crow with Meg on a sub-conscious level before he has even met her (Garner 2013: 18), as if his mind is already conjuring her presence. One of Colin's breakthrough sessions involves him remembering a traumatic encounter with crow as a child where he kills an injured bird out of an attempt at mercy (Garner 2013: 120–1). The horror of this event is relatable and can be seen as a symbolic banishment of the overtly negative aspects of the Morrigan from his childhood.

The Irish Morrígan's shape-shifting ability is creatively adapted into the trilogy: consistent with her connection with the Old Magic, the Morrigan is described by

Cadellin as being dangerous and untameable but not evil, 'it is a magic beyond our guidance: it is magic of the heart, not of the head: it can be felt, but not known' (Garner 2014b: 91–2). This kind of magic is exclusively connected with female characters in *Weirdstone* and *Gomrath* and comes through to *Boneland* in Meg and Susan, where the ability to shape-shift has been extended to an ability to alter the fabric of the universe. The association with the feminine is another Gravesian element that links directly to the triple goddess. Meg manipulates Colin's whole reality throughout *Boneland*, conjuring the house as an image of her lair from *Gomrath* that only Colin can interact with (Garner 2013: 141) and bringing Bert the taxi driver who seems to be fully integrated into the primary world but can be turned off like a switch when no longer needed (Garner 2013: 139). Parallels can be drawn here between her manipulation of Colin's reality and psychology, and the way that Caer manipulates Oengus in *Aislinge Oengusa* ('The Dream of Oengus'). Caer takes an active role in appearing to Oengus in his dreams from the Otherworld and making him sick. He must then seek her and is taken into the Otherworld by her when she is found, transforming him into a swan like herself (see Gantz 1981: 108–12).

The diversifying of the Morrígan's character through Meg in *Boneland* also sees her branch out of the Irish mythological influence and, as we have seen with the case of the Otherworld above, become a pan-Celtic blend of character elements. Meg's connection with Morgan le Fay becomes more obvious throughout the book, stemming from another Gravesian connection between the Irish Morrígan and Morgan le Fay detailed in *The White Goddess* (Graves 1999: 138). An early version of Morgan appears in the *Vita Merlini* where she is an enchantress and healer living on the Island of Apples with her eight sisters. She is described by Taliesin as being a shape-shifter who changes into birds and is connected to Arthur as the one who will cure his wounds in the Otherworld (see Clarke 1973). Morgan also appears in *Sir Gawain and the Green Knight* as the mover behind the story and enemy of Arthur, having enchanted Bertilak to appear in the form of the Green Knight. The healer in one story is causing mischief in another in order to test Gawain and the virtue of Arthur's court (see Tolkien 2006: 90–1), in turn recalling the changing loyalties and attitudes of the mythological Morrígan from her various stories in Irish texts. Garner gives us a definite clue to the link between Meg and Morgan by naming his taxi driver Bert. *Sir Gawain and the Green Knight* is deeply important to Garner as a writer, as it is a legend directly connected with his home and the language of his ancestors within that space and therefore the mythology of his past (Garner 1997: 49). In weaving this story into *Boneland*, he adds another layer of depth, local and regional significance, and another thread to the existing pan-Celtic mythological history that his stories are part of.

Susan is raised up to be much more of an equal counterpart and/or adversary to the Morrigan/Meg in *Boneland* as part of the Gravesian triple moon goddess and goes through a transformative experience mirrored in the mythological source material in order to get there. Parallels can be drawn between Susan's journey into the Otherworld and the journey of Étaín in *Tochmarc Étaíne* ('The Wooing of Étaín') (see Gantz 1981: 37). Étaín goes through a rebirth sequence where she is physically transformed by the jealous Fuamnach into a pool of water, into a larva, into a scarlet fly, then to be re-born as herself, during which process she acquires powers of healing and becomes a supernatural being by virtue of the transformation. Although Susan does not outwardly physically transform, she goes through a similar re-birth sequence at he hands of the Brollachan in *Gomrath*, where her spirit is separated from her to travel with Celemon. When Cadellin brings her back she is not the same person and begins her inevitable integration into the Otherworld. This is shown outwardly in her learning to use the magic of the bracelet given to her by Angharad and inwardly by her innate understanding in the confrontation with the Horsemen of Donn:

> Susan looked at him and was not afraid. Her mind could not accept him, but something deeper could.
>
> (Garner 2014b: 107)

The story of her final transformation and integration into the Otherworld is told in *Boneland* when Colin realizes he is right about her being taken through Angharad's island to the Pleiades, finally giving in to the pull of the Otherworld (Garner 2013: 103). As such, she appears in *Boneland* as crossing the boundaries of space and time to come back to Colin and communicating with him through manipulation of the spaces between reality in the parabolic dishes (Garner 2013: 55). It is significant that the only place she is able to physically manifest as an apparition is underground in Colin's adit, which was compared above with Fundindelve, as Colin has already crossed a boundary here between upper primary world and subterranean Otherworld.

Neil Philip in *A Fine Anger* notes that Garner's early female characters tend to consistently be one dimensional and passive to the detriment of the stories. Although it could be argued that Susan becomes more and more an active character as the story of the first two books goes on, the Morrigan and Angharad in *Weirdstone* and *Gomrath* fit Philip's assessment of a 'limiting image of women as either earth mother or world bitch' (Philip 1981: 154) portrayed as stereotypical good and evil characters. *Boneland* sees a move towards redressing this imbalance in the first two books of the trilogy as Meg and Susan are diversified and made active characters around the very passive Colin. Characters in mythology tend to be one dimensional compared with what we expect from a modern novel, but Garner has here used the diversification of mythological influences to flesh out the characters as shown by the wealth of sources that can be seen above. Garner also uses this diversification to make these characters more ambiguous in their motives and to convey the psychological perils of the Otherworld beyond Colin's illness. There is a constant tension between Meg and Susan throughout *Boneland* that plays on our previous knowledge of Morrigan = bad, Susan = good. Meg tries to convince Colin that Susan doesn't exist when he hears her through the parabolic dishes (Garner 2013: 64). We know that this is a move that is negative for Colin and yet she is the guise of psychiatrist who otherwise does all she can to help him heal. Susan is trying to reach out to Colin who she has lost as much as he has lost her and yet when she appears to him in the adit, she is a terrifying ghostly vision who mocks him and sings to him of death (Garner 2013: 88–90). Meanwhile Colin is the passive recipient in this tug of war, reversing the gender roles of texts such as 'The Wooing of Étaín' or the Second Branch of the Mabinogi where the female characters Étaín and Branwen are passively knocked from pillar to post by the male characters.

The female characters of *Boneland* do not form the same kind of line of reincarnation as is shown above with the Watcher, Myrddin and Colin. Meg is not a reincarnation of the Morrigan from earlier in the trilogy or from the source mythology, she *is* the same Morrigan, and is one of the defining examples of the connection of Celticity between all three novels. Similarly, Susan is not a reincarnation of any particular character or previous member of the triple goddess, but becomes a part of the Otherworld in her own right. The connection is formed directly with the universal and interacts with the local through Meg and Susan's parts in the story and interactions with Colin. This extends the confined space of Garner's story out into our own space bringing the mythological presence of the Otherworld with it.

Garner's Celticity

The discussion above has shown that throughout the *Weirdstone* trilogy, Garner has taken elements from both Welsh and Irish mythological texts and integrated them into the local landscape and mythology of the Edge to create a story which attempts to balance the local with the universal. He has adapted characters, situations and motifs from these mythologies and slotted them into his own representation of a local space, while keeping their universal appeal through the archetypes they represent. The Edge has taken on the mood and geography of both Welsh and Irish Otherworlds and interacts through its own mythology with recognizable characters who interlink with each other and real world mythological figures to form a sense of timelessness. We have seen how lines of continuity are drawn between The Watcher, Myrddin, Merlin, Cadellin and Colin of Garner's High Magic and then the Morrígan/Morrigan (both the Irish figure and Garner's), Étaín, Morgan le Fay, Caer and Susan of Garner's Old Magic. Garner thereby expresses his own ideas of Celticity through this interweaving, creating a response to his influences that is both personal and universal.

Although *Boneland* seems so far from the tone of *Weirdstone* and *Gomrath*, I have attempted to show how it could be considered a much more in-depth exploration of the Welsh and Irish source material that engages with the archetypes rather than just inserting them into a story. However, it can be seen as problematic that Garner has chosen to do so by removing the mythologies completely from their places of origin and combining them with tangentially related local material. In *Four British Fantasists*, Butler discusses Garner's use of 'Celtic' mythology in terms of cultural appropriation and the abuse of a romanticized view of the 'Celtic' to inject Otherness into fantasy literature (Butler 2006: 152). I do not believe that this was Garner's intention when writing *Weirdstone* and *Gomrath*, but Butler's comment on the 'Celtic Disneyland' can be applied to these books in their undiscriminating use of names, characters and motifs from across mythological systems and cultures that are lumped together as if they are one (Butler 2006: 154). This is symptomatic of the universalist approach taken by Garner as discussed above, and of his combining elements that he personally felt deeply connected to in the same way. Butler also notes his growing restraint in the use of overt mythological references over time and a tendency for references to become more tightly integrated into the primary story with each new novel (Butler 2006: 201). We can see the extreme effects of this in the contrast between *Boneland* and its predecessors of the same trilogy which shows not only the other end of the tendency towards restraint but also a long process of refinement that avoids the 'Celtic Disneyland' while still integrating influences from pan-Celtic source materials. Garner speaks of this kind of syncretistic approach in his 1983 lecture 'Achilles in Altjira':

> The story is the medium though which the writer interprets the reality; but it is not the reality itself. The story is a symbol, which makes a unity of the elements, hitherto seen as separate, that combine uniquely in the writer's vision.
>
> (Garner 1997: 41)

This essay has attempted to demonstrate that Garner has achieved this unique vision in *Boneland* through his methods of seamlessly integrating the local with the universal through the lens of Welsh and Irish mythology. To return to the two main characters as primary examples, Colin is both himself, the person who experienced a brush with the Otherworld as a child and came out of it the worse off, but he is also the reincarnation of the guardian of the sleeping heroes as well as the wild man archetype expressed through Myrddin Wyllt. Meg is a psychiatrist of the primary world with all of the usual techniques, connections and procedures but she is simultaneously the Morrigan, an Otherworldly being with a complex set of motives that stem from both her incarnation and her mythological self.

This process of restraint, refinement and integration has lead to another issue with Garner's use of mythological material, in essence the opposite of the problems of the universalist approach discussed above. More than once, his later books have been criticized as being too obscure for the average reader to pick up on the myths behind the story, even in *The Owl Service* which is the most closely tied book to a single Welsh myth (Sullivan 1989: 24–5). *Boneland* is heavily reliant on *Weirdstone* and *Gomrath* for the reader to be able to understand the mythological references, which I believe would be completely lost if the book was read on its own. Even then, many of the themes brought into the characters and place of the Edge as discussed above would be lost on the reader without a prior knowledge of the source material. But perhaps Garner does not intend for us to be able to pin-point his sources as we read in this kind of formalized, academic manner. If Garner is aiming for a seamless integration of the universal and the local, then it could be considered unnecessary. In Garner's 1996 lecture 'The Voice That Thunders', he describes the writing process of *Strandloper* (1996) as a kind of absorption of facts by the intellect and then allowing his subconscious do to the work of organizing, making connections and writing (Garner 1997: 226). This is a very Jungian approach which leads to the idea that the archetypes will speak for themselves from the collective unconscious. This writing process is projected forward onto the reader as a recipient of the archetypal symbols encoded into the story. Garner also turns this around on the reader in expecting a certain amount of creative participation in the reading of his books in order to make the story work to its full effect (Garner 1997: 27), although this is not to say that Garner expects his readers to do the kind of background research necessary to dig out the references. In terms of this very personal approach, the reader's direct experience of the mythological source material has become secondary to the surface story, but the mythology as source material has remained of the utmost importance in Garner's writing methods.

Garner has described his own sense of deep responsibility to his source material and expresses this by whole-heartedly diving into research before putting pen to paper (Garner 1997: 225–6). He has also described his dislike for both *Weirdstone* and *Gomrath*, describing *Weirdstone* as little more than a 'fairly bad book' (Garner 1997: 60). *Boneland* feels like Garner reconciling himself with his first two novels as he has fully absorbed the Celtic mythological inspirations that he feels resonate with him on a level as deep as that of his ancestral home at the Edge. It is this resonance and depth that comes across to the reader, so that, rather than Garner telling us what he thinks Celticity is, he is showing us through the trilogy what Celticity means to him.

References

Butler, Catherine (2006), *Four British Fantasists: Place and Culture in the Children's Fantasies of Penelope Lively, Alan Garner, Diana Wynne Jones, and Susan Cooper*, Lanham: Children's Literature Association and Scarecrow Press.

Clarke, Basil, trans. (1973), *The Life of Merlin by Geoffrey of Monmouth*, Cardiff: University of Wales Press.

Clarkson, Tim (2016), *Scotland's Merlin: A Medieval Legend and Its Dark Age Origins*, Edinburgh: Birlinn.

Davies, Sioned, trans. (2007), *The Mabinogion*, Oxford: Oxford University Press.

Edwards, Sean R., Timberlake, Simon, and Guest, Jonathan (2016), 'The Vegetation of the Edge', in A. J. N. W. Prag (ed.), *The Story of Alderley: Living with the Edge*, 120–43, Manchester: Manchester University Press.

Gantz, Jeffrey, trans. (1981), *Early Irish Myths and Sagas*, London: Penguin.

Garner, Alan (1997), *The Voice That Thunders*, London: Harvill Press.

Garner, Alan (2013), *Boneland*, London: Fourth Estate.

Garner, Alan (2014a [1960]), *The Weirdstone of Brisingamen: A Tale of Alderley*, London: HarperCollins.

Garner, Alan (2014b [1963]), *The Moon of Gomrath*, London: HarperCollins.

Graves, Robert (1999), *The White Goddess*, London: Faber & Faber.

Jarman, A. O. H (1995), 'The Merlin Legend and the Welsh Tradition of Prophecy', in Rachel Bromwich, A. O. H. Jarman and Brynley F. Roberts (eds), *The Arthur of the Welsh: The Arthurian Legend in Medieval Welsh Literature*, 117–45, Cardiff: University of Wales Press.

Mansfield, Susan (2012), 'Interview: Alan Garner', *The Scotsman* (15 Sep.), https://www.scotsman.com/arts-and-culture/books/interview-alan-garner-2461506, accessed 19 Jun. 2021.

Philip, Neil (1981), *A Fine Anger: A Critical Introduction to the Work of Alan Garner*, London: Collin.

Prag, A. J. N. W., and Timberlake, Simon (2016), 'The Archaeology of Alderley Edge', in A. J. N. W. Prag (ed.), *The Story of Alderley: Living with the Edge*, 303–41, Manchester: Manchester University Press.

Sullivan III, C. W. (1989), *Welsh Celtic Myth in Modern Fantasy*, Westport, CT; London: Greenwood Press.

Thomas, Neil (2000), 'The Celtic Wild Man Tradition and Geoffrey of Monmouth's *Vita Merlini*: Madness or *Contemptus Mundi*?', *Arthuriana*, 10 (1): 27–42.

Tolkien, J.R.R., trans. (2006), *Sir Gawain and the Green Knight*, ed. Christopher Tolkien, London: HarperCollins.

Williams, Mark (2016), *Ireland's Immortals: A History of the Gods of Irish Myth*, Princeton, NJ: Princeton University Press.

3

Woman as goddess in the Irish fantasies of Jodi McIsaac

Kris Swank

Jodi McIsaac's heroines are goddesses, although they don't realize it yet. When Cedar McLeod's daughter is abducted by 'fairies' and Nora O'Reilly's father and brother are murdered in the Northern Irish Troubles (1968–98), both women are set on paths which will change their ideas of reality, history and themselves. Canadian author Jodi McIsaac self-published her first novel, the contemporary fantasy *Through the Door* (2013), which became a bestseller after being picked up by Amazon's speculative fiction imprint, 47North ('Jodi' 2013). That novel grew into *The Thin Veil* series which centres upon Cedar McLeod's encounters with the Tuatha Dé Danann, the supernatural race from Irish mythology who inhabit Tír na nÓg, the Otherworld or 'Land of Youth'. The series also includes the novels *Into the Fire* (2013) and *Among the Unseen* (2014), and the novella, *Beyond the Pale* (2014). While Cedar and her daughter Eden travel between parallel worlds, another heroine, Nora O'Reilly, travels through time in McIsaac's *Revolutionary* series, comprising the novels *Bury the Living* (2016) and *Summon the Queen* (2017). Nora is sent to the past by a relic of the Christian Saint Brigid to help save Ireland from its enemies. She hopes that by changing history, she can also change the fates of her father and brother. Like Cedar, Nora encounters figures from Irish mythological texts, particularly the mercurial Brigid.

Aspects of McIsaac's own life are woven into the lives of her characters. When she penned *The Thin Veil* series, both McIsaac and Cedar McLeod were thirty-something mothers of young girls, and both were from Canada's Maritime Provinces. McIsaac's experiences as an aid worker and living in Belfast helped to shape Nora O'Reilly's background as well. The infusion of the Tuatha Dé Danann into McIsaac's fiction is also partially a result of the author's background. She writes, 'I was trying to come up with my own magic system ... and failed miserably. So I turned to mythology for some ideas, and came across Celtic mythology. My family heritage is part Irish (like most families on the east coast of Canada), but I didn't know anything about the mythology until I started digging into it' (Mills 2016, ellipses original). It was a fortunate encounter, for her Irish sources are particularly ripe for McIsaac's brand of feminist-oriented fantasies. Powerful, clever and resilient goddesses like Brigit/Bríg, mother-protector and keeper of the sacred fire, or Medb and Macha, queens regnant and military leaders, were just the sort of strong female role models McIsaac needed to inform her own heroines, Cedar and Nora. In the course of their stories, both of McIsaac's leading ladies discover they possess supernatural gifts which connect them to these Irish supernatural figures. Yet, in the end, it is their human qualities of bravery, self-sacrifice and love which ultimately prove to be their true 'goddess' powers.

The Thin Veil

In McIsaac's *The Thin Veil* series, some of Ireland's most enduring mysteries are resolved by a modern mother and her six-year-old daughter, Cedar and Eden McLeod, when the pair learn of their close connections to the ancient Tuatha Dé Danann. In *Through the Door*, the first book of the series, single mother Cedar McLeod is trying to make ends meet as a graphic designer in Halifax, Nova Scotia, and to provide stability for Eden. Eden's father, Fionbharr 'Finn' Donnelly, had abruptly disappeared before he learned Cedar was pregnant, but when Eden suddenly manifests the ability to open portals to distant locations, Cedar is forced to contact the Donnelly family for answers. She learns they are members of the Tuatha Dé Danann, ancient exiles who 'had ruled Ireland before the coming of the Celts, but had lost a great battle and had been relegated to Tír na nÓg, the Otherworld' (McIsaac 2013b: 89). The Donnellys are, in fact, double-exiles. They were first exiled from Earth and more recently from Tír na nÓg when they lost a battle to a murderous usurper, Lorcan. Forced to flee back to Earth, they now hide in plain sight, disguised as humans. In McIsaac's series each of the Tuatha Dé Danann possesses unique 'gifts' or powers which appear magical to humans. For example, a woman named Nuala has the power of hypnotic persuasion. Finn can transform into animal shapes. The power to open portals, or *sidhe*, was last wielded by the deceased High King Brogan. Upon

Brogan's death, the Halifax exiles had no way to re-open a *sidh* to Tír na nÓg. The discovery of Eden's gift renews the hope that they may be able to return home and defeat Lorcan.

McIsaac mines a variety of medieval Irish texts to create the history of her exiles. The late ninth-century *Scél Tuáin meic Cairill* ('The Tale of Tuáin son of Cairell') relates how the Gaels invaded Ireland and displaced other groups who already lived there, including the Tuatha Dé Danann, 'whose origin the learned do not know; but they think it likely that they belong to the exiles who came from heaven' (Koch and Carey 2000: 224). An eleventh-century version of *Lebar Gabála Érenn* ('The Book of the Takings of Ireland') also depicts them as descending from the heavens: 'The Tuatha Dé Danann from afar. They landed, a splendid savage troop, on stern Sliab Conmaicne Réin', a mountain in Connacht (Koch and Carey 2000: 249). The version of *Lebar Gabála* found in the *Book of Fermoy*, dated to around the fifteenth century, euhemerizes the Tuatha Dé Danann as human descendants of the biblical Noah. They were said to have arrived in Ireland on ships from four great island-cities in the north where they learned 'knowledge and lore and devilry' (quoted in Williams 2016: 149). Later, the Tuatha Dé Danann were defeated at the Battle of Tailtiu by the Gaels, the ancestors of the modern Irish, and forced to retreat from Ireland. McIsaac weaves all of these mythic strands into her history of the exiles, including their origins in four magical cities, their resemblance to humans and their defeat by the Gaels. McIsaac then invents a later war in which Lorcan, a dark mage who absorbs the gifts of others by killing them, deposed the high king and queen, Brogan and Kier, and forced survivors like the Donnellys to take refuge back on Earth.

Cedar no sooner learns that her child belongs to a magical race, then Eden is abducted by the Tuatha Dé Danann woman, Nuala, who wants Eden to open a *sidh* to Tír na nÓg so that she can join forces with Lorcan. The motif of the human child stolen by fairies is popular in Irish folklore. Tom Peete Cross in his *Motif-Index of Early Irish Literature* lists a number of examples where '[f]airies carry people away to fairyland' and 'fairy steals child from cradle' (1952: 259). In the classic *Fairy Faith in Celtic Countries*, Walter Evans-Wentz relates one of the earliest literary accounts of such a 'taking' when the grandson of the King of Leinster 'was enjoying a game of hurley with his boy companions near the *sídh* of Liamhain Softsmock, two of the *sídh*-women, who loved the young prince, very suddenly appeared, and as suddenly took him away with them into a fairy palace and kept him there three years' ([1911] 2010: 294). Perhaps the most recognizable Irish fairy-abduction story today is from William Butler Yeats's poem, 'The Stolen Child', first published in 1889. The fairies call enticingly,

> Come away! O human child!
> To the woods and waters wild,
> With a fairy hand in hand,
> For the world's more full of weeping than
> you can understand.
>
> (Yeats [1918] 2011: 77–8)

In Yeats's time, the promise of life in a paradisiacal fairyland may have been more attractive to an Irish child than life under English rule. However, Yeats's 'stolen child' will never again be seen in mortal lands. To be 'away with the fairies' was to be deranged or dead. In William Allingham's poem, 'The Fairies', both outcomes are presented. The old King has 'nigh lost his wits' in the mist-covered fairy-hills, while little Bridget dies:

> They stole little Bridget
> For seven years long;
> When she came down again
> Her friends were all gone.
> They took her lightly back,
> Between the night and morrow,
> They thought that she was fast asleep,
> But she was dead with sorrow.
>
> (Allingham and Färber [1849] 2008)

Purkiss observes that 'Bridget's sojourn with the fairies is a form of death, as is her return to the mortal world' (2000: 298). McIsaac convincingly adapts the parental horror of the stolen-child motif to a contemporary setting. Cedar alternates between disbelief, despair and frantic activity in her pursuit of Nuala and Eden before they disappear forever through a *sidh* to Tír na nÓg. Eden would be killed there by Lorcan so that he could absorb her gift to open *sidhe*-portals and thereby secure for himself the ability to invade Earth.

When Cedar asks if the Donnellys are ancient Celtic gods, Finn's mother replies, 'We're not gods … although we were once worshipped as such. We're a different race, you might say' (McIsaac 2013b: 90). Finn's sister jokes, 'They say we're fairies now!' (McIsaac 2013b: 90). Cedar recalls, 'Over the centuries, the Tuatha Dé Danann had developed into the "little folk" of Irish folklore' (McIsaac 2013b: 89–90). Yet, the idea of the fairies of modern Irish folklore as remnants of the medieval Tuatha Dé Danann, as McIsaac portrays them, did not become popular until the nineteenth century. At that time, Irish writers such as Yeats and Lady Augusta Gregory, who sought to uncover (or create) a specifically Irish mythology to distinguish their national identity from that of their British rulers, promoted the idea of continuity between the Tuatha Dé Danann and the Irish fairies (see Williams 2016: 278). Yeats, for example, 'tried to connect [Irish folklore] with the Irish epics of Cúchulain and Fionn, and with the pantheon of Celtic deities' (Purkiss 2000: 295). Historian Diane Purkiss interrogates this theory, noting that the identification between the medieval sagas and the Irish fairy-folk did not occur until Micheál Coimin's *The Lay of Oisín in the Land of Youth* in the late eighteenth century. She writes, 'The assumption that the spirit-women of the Otherworld of the hero sagas have anything to do with the *sidhe* who infest nineteenth-century folklore is just that: an assumption. The same applies to the Tuatha dé Danann, Tir na nÓg, and all the rest' (2000: 294). Nonetheless, McIsaac employs the popular belief that the Tuatha Dé Danann and the Irish fairies are one and the same, and that they steal human children to whisk them away to the Otherworld.

On the other hand, McIsaac subverts a related motif of the 'changeling child'. If Eden is the 'stolen child', then flashbacks in *Through the Door* and its companion novella, *Beyond the Pale*, reveal her mother, Cedar, to be a 'changeling', the fairy substitute left when a human child is stolen from its cradle (Cross 1952: 259). Cedar discovers she is not the natural child of the human woman who raised her, the druid Maeve. Instead, she proves to be the long-lost daughter and heir of the Tuatha Dé Danann king and queen, Brogan and Kier. Maeve and the fatally injured Kier hid the newborn Cedar from the usurper Lorcan by casting a spell which transformed her into a human. Thus, in McIsaac's series, it is the fairy child who is taken from the cradle and replaced with a human child, although both here are, in fact, one and the same child. The abduction itself is performed by the child's own mother for the child's protection.

Cedar's story is also somewhat reminiscent of a tale preserved in the *Book of Fermoy*, known as *Altromh Tige Dá Medar* ('The Nurturing of the House of Two Milk Vessels'). The same tale may also have been the source for the name of Cedar's boyfriend, Fionbharr. In *Altromh Tige Dá Medar*, Finnbarr is the brother of the Tuatha Dé Danann god, Oengus Mac ind Óc (i.e. Aengus). While visiting Oengus's palace to ogle his beautiful foster-daughter, Eithne, Finnbarr makes such a lewd remark that Eithne spontaneously transforms from Tuatha Dé Danann to human. Unable to remain in the Otherworld, she departs for the mortal world, converts to Christianity and subsequently dies (Arbois de

Jubainville 1903: 157–8). Cedar was also transformed from Tuatha Dé Danann to human, lived as a mortal in the mortal world, and dies. In the climactic action of *Through the Door*, Cedar and the Donnellys follow Nuala and Eden through a *sidh* to Tír na nÓg, where they discover Lorcan attempting to kill Eden. Cedar offers herself in Eden's stead. When Lorcan kills Cedar, he unwittingly absorbs her gift – humanity – which in turn makes him mortal and vulnerable. Lorcan is then killed by Finn, and all those whom Lorcan had murdered are restored to life, including Cedar. Now knowing that she is actually a member of the Tuatha Dé Danann, and Brogan's heir, Cedar opts to stay in the Otherworld, help repatriate the exiled Tuatha Dé Danann, and rebuild Tír na nÓg.

The second volume of the series, *Into the Fire*, concerns the restoration of order. As Brogan's daughter, Cedar's ascension to the throne should begin to heal the wasteland Lorcan left behind. Yet, the sceptical Council doubts that someone raised by humans, as a human, could successfully rule Tír na nÓg. As a test, they task Cedar with finding the lost *Lia Fáil*, or Coronation Stone of Tara. The *Lebar Gabála* from the *Book of Fermoy* tells how the Tuatha Dé Danann brought four magical treasures from their four mystical cities: a spear, a sword, a cauldron, and '[f]rom Falias was brought the Stone of Fál [the Lia Fáil] which is in Tara, which used to cry out beneath every king who used to take control of Ireland' (quoted in Williams 2016: 149). Conflicting legends claim the Stone remains in Tara or was given to the Scots in AD 500, from where it was seized by Edward I of England in 1296. Alternately, it has been posited that the Stone of Scone given to Edward was not the same stone as the Lia Fáil, the latter of which was hidden away and then lost (Bonwick 1894: 313–20). If the medieval writers of the *Acallam na Senórach* ('Dialogue of [or with] the Old Men') knew the true fate of the Lia Fáil, their answer is lost to history, for that text breaks off just as the Lia Fáil is carried out of Ireland (O'Grady 1892: vol. 2, 265). The Council gives Cedar one week to find the Stone. As the frantic search begins, the scheming Nuala attempts to kill Cedar and take the Stone (and crown) for herself. But Cedar finds it first. When she steps on the Stone it cries out, signifying that she is the rightful heir. Cedar then begins burning from within, 'The sensation was almost unbearable … Every nerve and fiber in her body felt like it was on fire, but it was strangely painless. She felt stronger, more energized than she had ever felt in her life. She felt like she could do anything. She felt like a *goddess*' (McIsaac 2013a: 227, emphasis added).

Through her encounter with the Stone, Cedar unlocks the supernatural gift of fire, a trait which links her to a pre-Christian goddess and an early Irish saint both named 'Brigid'. In McIsaac's fictional space, the character is both the goddess and the saint. Finn Donnelly's mother says,

> She is one of our Elders, one of the first who came to this world. However, she chose to leave Tír na nÓg many years ago; I think it was around the fifth century of your time. She said she preferred the company of humans to the company of gods. And she's lived here ever since, under various guises, of course, including a saint.
>
> (McIsaac 2013b: 96)

While the historical relationship between goddess and saint is a contested one, both figures appear to have been affiliated with the element of fire. An early Irish glossary ascribed to Cormac mac Cuilennáin (d. 908), the scholar-bishop-king of Munster, describes 'Brigit' as a poetess and female sage, 'very famous for her protective care' (Cormac 1868: 23). According to the entry, her sisters were also named 'Brigit': 'Brigit the female physician ... [and] Brigit the female smith' (Cormac 1868: 23). Cormac states that 'Brigit' was simply the Irish word for 'goddess' (1868: 23). Others speculate that Brigit was a tripartite deity. Kim McCone notes evidence for 'an intimate ideological connection, apparently with pagan roots, between fire and the tripartite arts of medicine, craftsmanship, and learned insight' (McCone 2000: 165). Healers heat their cauldrons for brewing medicaments. Blacksmiths fire their forges. An eighth-century Old Irish text known as 'the Caldron of Poesy' [sic] illustrates that fire-imagery has long been employed to describe poetic inspiration (see McCone 2000: 166). Thus, the three goddesses named 'Brigit' are connected with three aspects of fire. McCone also finds it plausible that the Romano-Celtic goddess Minerva, whose temple housed a perpetual sacred fire, 'is a partially syncretized native Celtic *Briganti*' (McCone 2000: 164), that is, Brigit. Saint Brigit, a legendary Christian abbess believed to have lived in the fifth century, was also said to have tended a perpetual fire at the convent she founded at Kildare. According to twelfth-century historian Giraldus Cambrensis (Gerald of Wales), the fire was never allowed to go out due to the constant attentions of the nuns and holy women, including Brigit herself (Giraldus 1905: 96). Saint Brigit's connection with fire and the hearth extends into the modern era. Séamas Ó Catháin describes 'raking the fire', a Scottish Gaelic ritual for preserving the hearth embers until morning, which is accompanied by a prayer invoking Brigit and Mary (1992: 13). Thus, when Cedar acquires the power to emanate fire, she not only *feels* like a goddess, in essence, she *is* one.

Cedar also resembles legendary goddess-queens in her role as mother. Anne Connon writes, 'motherhood constituted another major element of Irish queenship', as royal marriages, along with the children they produced, were visible symbols of political alliances (2005: 393). The name of the pre-Christian Brigit in her aspect as a goddess of healing would have been invoked in relation to pregnancies and childbirth (Ó Catháin 1999: 244). Donál Ó Cathasaigh notes the pagan Brigit's other maternal traits include 'connections with symbolic riverine waters (life fluids)', her role as 'household protector', and her festival of Imbolc, 'the spring rite celebrating the lactation of ewes' (1979: 317). The Christian Brigit, while eternally virginal, was nevertheless similarly associated with maternal activities. She is depicted in Gaelic folklore as the foster-mother of the infant Jesus (Carmichael 1900: vol. I, 235). Many of the rituals performed on or around her feast day, such as churning milk into butter, bees and honey-making, and the weaving of Saint Brigit's crosses, 'concerned agricultural, pastoral and human sexual fertility' (Cusack 2007: 92). The *Carmina Gadelica*, a collection of traditional poems and songs gathered from the Scottish Gaels and reworked by nineteenth-century folklorist Alexander Carmichael, invokes 'the lovely Bride' (i.e. Brigit) in blessings for sheep and cattle (1900: vol. I, 297 & 315). Cedar McLeod, as mother-protector of both her own daughter and her newly discovered people, the Tuatha Dé Danann, ushers in a rebirth of the war-wasted Tír na nÓg.

Cedar is also a queen regnant. Her lover, Finn Donnelly, is her consort, but he is not the king. Historically, Irish queens did not rule independently of their husbands. Yet, in Irish mythological texts such situations were possible as illustrated by tales of the pre-Christian queens Macha and Medb. In *The Annals of the Four Masters*, a chronicle of the history of Ireland, Macha Mongruadh, daughter of Áed Rúad, is the only queen in the List of the High Kings of Ireland. It had been customary for Áed to rotate the kingship every seven years with his cousins Díthorba and Cimbáeth, yet after Áed drowned, Macha claimed her father's next turn for herself. Díthorba and Cimbáeth would not be ruled by a woman and raised their armies against her. Macha won. She expelled Díthorba and married Cimbáeth, ruling with him until his death. Macha then ruled alone for seven years until she was slain by another rival (Ryan 2002: 72–5). The Irish mythological queen and king of Connacht, Medb and Ailill, have a similar relationship dynamic to that of Macha and Cimbáeth. Medb has equal property and power with Ailill, but it is she who leads their great army to invade Ulster in the famous epic, *Táin Bó Cuailnge* ('The Cattle Raid of Cooley') (Simms 2005: 520). John Koch writes, 'In general, the most notable attribute of the couple is that Medb is usually dominant and prone to aggressive action, both military and sexual' (2006: 1282). And, like Macha, Medb's character may have originated as a sovereignty figure (Koch 2006: 1282). For these reasons, Koch contends, 'Medb has had particular appeal for modern readers and her personality has lent itself in recent times to feminist interpretations and semi-popular ideas about the liberated Celtic woman' (Koch 2006: 1282). Cedar McLeod illustrates just such a feminist interpretation of Celtic mythology. Not only is she a queen regnant, she leads the Tuatha Dé Danann warriors into battle against Nuala and her druids. Cedar also reflects the sovereignty motif. The popular conception of the lady of sovereignty is that she chooses her own mate and their union fructifies the land (see Williams 2016: 508–9). Cedar chooses Finn as her mate and their union begins the healing of a Tír na nÓg blighted by Lorcan's ill rule.

Throughout *The Thin Veil* series, Cedar's personal history proves to be a continuation of Irish legendary history as she becomes the impetus to solving a series of ancient mysteries, each one involving the self-sacrifice and subsequent metamorphosis of one or more 'goddesses'. In *Through the Door*, Cedar solves the mystery of what became of the Tuatha Dé Danann after they were defeated by the Celts in pre-Christian Ireland: they were exiled, first to Tír na nÓg and then back to Earth where they had to live disguised as humans. When Cedar, also living on Earth disguised as a human, sacrifices her human life to save her daughter and destroy the evil Lorcan, she also empowers the exiles to finally reclaim their homeland, Tír na nÓg. In *Into the Fire*, Cedar solves the mystery of the fate of the Lia Fáil, and by doing so she is reborn again as a Tuatha Dé Danann queen who can open *sidh*-portals and emanate fire. The six-year-old Eden is also (temporarily) reborn as her adult future-self in order to defeat the scheming Nuala. In the third novel of the series, *Among the Unseen*, Eden once again calls forth her adult future-self to battle the Norse god Odin, though in doing so she risks sacrificing the child-Eden forever. Meanwhile, solving the mystery of the fate of magical creatures in Ireland, Cedar forces the Tuatha Dé Danann Elder, Brighid, to face the consequences of her role in the curse devastating the merrows, pixies and other magical folk. Consuming the last of her powers to break the curse, Brighid is forced to shed her physical form and become a pure white light. Cedar, Eden and Brighid each employ their goddess powers to resolve some of Ireland's greatest ancient mysteries. And yet, they cannot prevail with their goddess powers alone. Ultimately, it is their human qualities of mother-love, courage, compassion for others and self-sacrifice, fused with their Tuatha Dé Danann goddess powers, which save the Earth and Tír na nÓg. Although the series is mainly concerned with Cedar's journey through the discovery and exploration of her goddesshood and her connections to Irish history and legend, Cedar's paramount discovery is that her own humanity remains a potent gift, one which, combined with her magical abilities, makes her an unstoppable force.

Revolutionary

In Jodi McIsaac's historical time travel series, *Revolutionary*, Nora O'Reilly is sent back in time to help save Ireland. These novels compare well to Diana Gabaldon's *Outlander* series which likewise deals with themes of family, oppression, war and freedom, as well as love that crosses time. McIsaac's voice has matured in this second series. Her characterizations have deepened, and her already complex plotting has evolved even further, thanks in no small measure to her extensive research on Ireland's history. Nevertheless, once again, hidden goddess-power emerges as a central theme. During Nora's adventures, the character Brigid is key, bringing this series squarely into conversation with McIsaac's *Thin Veil* series. And like Cedar McLeod, Nora O'Reilly turns out to be more than she at first appears.

In the first volume, *Bury the Living*, Nora O'Reilly joins the Irish Republican Army following the deaths of her father and brother during the 'Troubles', the religious-political conflict in Northern Ireland of the late twentieth century. After years of fighting, Nora decides to become a protector and healer instead, working for Catholic Relief Services in disaster zones like Haiti, Afghanistan and Zimbabwe. She thinks, 'There was always a humanitarian emergency somewhere in the world. Always someone who needed help' (McIsaac 2016a: Kindle Location 495). And Nora feels compelled to help, particularly the affected children. In 2004, she finds herself in a refugee camp filled with orphans of the Sudanese civil war. An orphan herself, 'she ached for these kids. The ongoing war in Sudan had already created tens of thousands of orphans, and each day the camp was flooded with more tiny survivors' (McIsaac 2016a: Kindle Locations 490–1). Nora begins dreaming of a white-haired man who pleads with her, 'Go to the church at Kildare and ask for Brigid … She'll explain everything and lead you to me. *You must come*' (McIsaac 2016a: Kindle Locations 547–8, emphasis original). Surprising even herself, Nora travels to Kildare, Ireland, where she meets Mary, a member of a secret order of Brigidine Sisters, 'committed to service and harmony in the spirit of Saint Brigid' (McIsaac 2016a: Kindle Locations 956–7). Mary tells Nora that Brigid wishes to bestow upon her 'a very special gift' and that she, Nora, is 'the bane of Aengus Óg' (McIsaac 2016a: Kindle Locations 928, 986–7). Nora accepts the gift, a sacred relic of Saint Brigid with the power to transport her back through time, seeing it as a chance to prevent her brother's death and assist the man from her dreams. Nora is first transported to the middle of the Irish Civil War (1922–3) where she joins the Republican cause and meets the legendary Fionn mac Cumhaill (i.e. Finn mac Cool), an 1800-year-old warrior cursed to eternally battle Ireland's enemies, and Nora's mystery man.

Finn (or Fionn) mac Cumhaill is one of the most recognizable names from Irish legend and McIsaac mines multiple sources for his portrayal. From the thirteenth-century *Acallam na Senórach* ('Dialogue of [or with] the Old Men'), McIsaac derives Fionn's white hair, his sentient wolfhound, Bran, and much of the character's backstory. From oral folklore comes the conception that Fionn, like King Arthur, will rise again to defend his country in time of need (MacKillop 1986: 31). In McIsaac's imaginative space, Fionn was a second-century man cursed by the Tuatha Dé Danann god, Aengus Óg, to live until he has saved Ireland from her enemies. The trick, of course, is that Ireland has had a lot of enemies, so Fionn is condemned to an interminably long and lonely life. Over the years, Fionn has received Brigid's help. He tells Nora, 'She's always been fond of me. But she can't interfere directly. Not with the curse' (McIsaac 2016a: Kindle Locations 3741–3). And so, Brigid sent Nora in her stead.

Brigid in the *Revolutionary* series is the same character who appears as Brighid in McIsaac's *The Thin Veil*. As in those novels, she is the last Tuatha Dé Danann Elder on Earth and the source of legends concerning both the ancient Irish goddess and the early Christian saint. Among scholars, the connection between the two figures remains contested. Carole Cusack, for instance, concludes 'Brigit was part of the old Irish religion that continued into the new Christian culture' (2007: 96). Alternately, Mark Williams states that the precise nature of the connection between Brigit the goddess and Brigit the saint is 'impossible to unravel, and debate continues as to whether it actually exists at all' (2016: 162). However, as in *The Thin Veil*, McIsaac makes the connection explicit in *Revolutionary*. In Kildare, Mary tells Nora, 'The church you see now was built in the thirteenth century, but it rests on the site of the church Saint Brigid herself had built in the fifth century. Before that, it was a site of worship to the pagan goddess Brigid' (McIsaac 2016a: Kindle Locations 920–3). Brigit's attributes of fire and water are further suggested by the proximity of Saint Brigit's Fire Temple and Saint Brigit's Well.

Nora functions throughout the *Revolutionary* series as Brigid's representative. Nowhere is this more evident than in Nora's frequent encounters with Saint Brigid's crosses, small woven objects believed to safeguard a house and its occupants (see Figure 3.1). Nora's mother had 'hung a Saint Brigid's cross above their doorway in Belfast' (McIsaac 2016a: Kindle Location 864). In 1923, the Gillies family has '[a] Saint Brigid's cross made from reeds hung above the doorway, just like the one that had hung in her childhood home in Belfast' (McIsaac 2016a: Kindle Location 1912). Nora remembers weaving 'Saint Brigid crosses out of rushes with her classmates every February 1 while their teacher told them stories of Brigid's miracles' (McIsaac 2016a: Kindle Locations 1917–18). Ó Catháin recounts the tradition from County Leitrim of weaving crosses on Saint Brigid's feast day, February 1: 'These were made of green rushes and chips of timber and in the making of the cross a piece of the food … was inserted … The cross and board were then placed over the door … and her assistance was invoked for the protection of the family from sickness, sin, and scandal for twelve months' (quoted in Ó Catháin 1992: 23–4). Cormac described 'Brigit' as 'very famous for her protecting care' (1868: 23). Likewise, Ó Catháin writes that the old people of Donegal 'had great belief in Brigid in this district and any time they would be in danger or in difficulty they would place themselves under her protection and patronage' (Ó Catháin 1999: 234). Nora herself prays, at the sight of the cross over the Gillies' doorway, 'Saint Brigid … I need your help. I don't know why you sent me here, or even if you were truly the one who sent me. But if it was

Figure 3.1 Saint Brigid of Ireland's Cross (Knott 2006).

you ... it was a mistake. This isn't where I belong. Please, help me get back home' (McIsaac 2016a: Kindle Locations 1914–16, ellipses original).

The cross symbolizes Brigit's guardianship, but for Nora, it is also a means of communicating with the saint, and a connection between her past and present, her journey and fate. These are, in fact, also traditional symbols associated with the Saint Brigit's cross. Ó Catháin identifies the cross as symbolic of the 'tree of life' or *axis mundi*, which 'achieves communication between ... subterranean space, earth and sky. The tree provides access to the invisible world' (Ó Catháin 1999: 258). Other symbolism relates the cross to space and time. Its four arms represent 'the four cardinal points, the four elements, the four celestial beings (sky, sun, moon and stars) and the four divisions of time (day, night, month, year)' (Ó Catháin 1999: 259). The crossed arms also reproduce the mast and yard arm of a ship, representing navigation, while the plaited rushes signify weaving, which 'is closely bound up with attempts to determine what the future held and with fate' (Ó Catháin 1999: 259). It is not hard to see Nora's journey entwined with such symbolism. She, too, communicates with a powerful being from another realm, navigates through time and space, and attempts to weave new fates for her brother, for Fionn and for Ireland, all under the patronage of Brigid.

Nora is further connected to Brigid through her role as a healer. One of 'Brigit's' aspects in *Cormac's Glossary* is as a physician, and McIsaac employs this particular role. When Nora is shot, Brigid places 'her smooth white hand over the gunshot wound in Nora's leg, and immediately the pain disappeared' (McIsaac 2016a: Kindle Locations 4182–3). As Brigid's representative, Nora, too, is a healer. In the second novel, *Summon the Queen*, Nora and Fionn travel back to 1587 to join forces with the historical Granuaile, that is, Grace O'Malley, the pirate queen of Connaught, against the English lords colonizing Ireland for Elizabeth I. When Nora and Fionn are caught in a shipboard explosion, Nora 'pitched in as best she could, helping to treat the wounded men' (McIsaac 2017: 157). Later, when a Spanish ship wrecks off the coast, everyone else goes for the plunder while Nora rescues and treats the half-drowned sailors, despite the fact that such an act has been declared treasonous (McIsaac 2017: 247). Brigid's patronage 'often directly involved children or young adults and was frequently directed in particular towards the welfare of children and of females, both younger and older' (Ó Catháin 1999: 234). Nora has a similar affinity for aiding women and children. In *Bury the Living*, she tries to free the female prisoners of Kilmainham Gaol. In *Summon the Queen*, she establishes a school for the children of Granuaile's clan, including the girls. The pirate queen tells

Nora, 'It was the greatest gift my father ever gave me, and I want every young girl in this túath to have the same opportunity I did' (McIsaac 2017: 228). Nora could not agree more. She knows how important it is for women to be self-reliant. One cannot always count on ancient goddesses to save the day.

For, although Brigid is a guardian, she does not always intervene on cue. When Nora's father is shot and killed by an unknown assailant at their front door, Nora thinks, 'The Saint Brigid's cross that had hung over the doorway for as long as Nora could remember had failed in its promise to protect them' (McIsaac 2016a: Kindle Locations 46–7). Granuaile tells Nora, '[Brigid] makes you think you can rely on her, and then one day you find out you can't. You're on your own. It's a lesson, see, and a hard one, to learn one can only rely on oneself' (McIsaac 2017: 143–4). Fionn concurs, 'I've needed – or wanted – her help many times in my life. Turns out I can handle most problems myself' (McIsaac 2016a: Kindle Locations 4060–6). Later he tells Nora, 'It would be just like her to make you believe she was the one orchestrating everything, when in reality you had it in you all along' (McIsaac 2017: 282–3).

This indeed proves true when Nora learns she has the power to traverse time on her own, without Brigid's relic. Yet, like Cedar McLeod in *The Thin Veil* series, Nora's most potent goddess-powers turn out to be essentially human. Before she ever met Brigid of Kildare and learned she could travel in time, Nora felt her purpose was to protect others. As a humanitarian relief worker, Nora points out, 'I've spent the last several years of my life helping complete strangers' (McIsaac 2016a: Kindle Locations 990–2). When called in her dreams to aid a mysterious man, she travelled through time to find him. Nora wades in to rescue the injured even at the risk of her own life. If one could describe Nora O'Reilly with a single word, it would not be 'goddesslike' but 'humane'.

Conclusion

McIsaac was initially attracted to Irish mythology because of her own heritage and the system of magic she could use to undergird her fantasy novels. But the powerful supernatural female characters she found there proved to be ideal models for her own heroines. In *The Thin Veil* series, Cedar McLeod learns she is a member of the Tuatha Dé Danann race who can open trans-dimensional portals and wield fire. Yet, it was neither of these powers which freed Tír na nÓg from Lorcan's tyranny, nor saved Earth from the same threat. It was Cedar's gift of mere humanity. Despite possessing the power to traverse time, humanity is also Nora O'Reilly's greatest gift. She pursued humanitarian work in the wake of her own traumatic youth, and her humanity continues to drive her concern for helping the less fortunate, be they Sudanese orphans, Spanish sailors, or Irish rebels. Feminine-empowerment forms the sacred centres of both *The Thin Veil* and *Revolutionary* series, where ordinary women discover they have hidden gifts like those of the ancient Irish goddesses Brigit, Macha and Medb. These powerful mythological beings serve as role models for the potent female agency that both Cedar and Nora claim, and this is McIsaac's greatest debt to the Irish tradition. Yet, her stories are also about very modern, very human women, as both Cedar and Nora discover that their 'goddess-powers' are not sufficient by themselves to prevail against evil; these must be fused with the human and humane qualities of courage, self-sacrifice and love.

References

Allingham, W. ([1849] 2008), 'The Fairies', in *Poems by William Allingham*, compiled B. Färber, Cork: University College, CELT: The Corpus of Electronic Texts, https://celt.ucc.ie//published/E850006-001.html, accessed 26 Jun. 2021.

Arbois de Jubainville, H. d' (1903), *The Irish Mythological Cycle and Celtic Mythology*, trans. R. I. Best, Dublin: Hodges, Figgis & Co, https://catalog.hathitrust.org/Record/100333760, accessed 26 Jun. 2021.

Bonwick, J. (1894), *Irish Druids and Old Irish Religions*, London: S. Low, Marston, https://catalog.hathitrust.org/Record/006809278, accessed 26 Jun. 2021.

Carmichael, A. (1900), *Carmina Gadelica: Hymns and Incantations with Illustrative Notes on Words, Rites, and Customs, Dying and Obsolete*, Edinburgh: T. and A. Constable, https://catalog.hathitrust.org/Record/100001349, accessed 26 Jun. 2021.

Connon, A. (2005), 'Queens', in S. Duffy (ed.), *Medieval Ireland: An Encyclopedia*, 393–4, New York: Routledge.

Cormac, King of Cashel (1868), *Sanas Chormaic. Cormac's Glossary*, ed.W. Stokes, trans. J. O'Donovan, Calcutta: Irish Archeological and Celtic Society, https://catalog.hathitrust.org/Record/100218342, accessed 26 Jun. 2021.

Cross, T. P. (1952), *Motif-Index of Early Irish Literature*, Bloomington: Indiana University, https://catalog.hathitrust.org/Record/006929790, accessed 26 Jun. 2021.

Cusack, C. M. (2007) 'Brigit: Goddess, Saint, "Holy Woman", and Bone of Contention', in V. Barker and F., Di Lauro (eds), *On A Panegyrical Note: Studies in Honour of Garry W. Trompf*, 75–97, Sydney: University of Sydney.

Evans-Wentz, W. Y. ([1911] 2010), *The Fairy-Faith in Celtic Countries*, Glastonbury: Lost Library.

Giraldus Cambrensis (1905), *The Historical Works of Giraldus Cambrensis*, ed. T. Wright, London: George Bell, https://catalog.hathitrust.org/Record/011718182, accessed 26 Jun. 2021.

'Jodi [McIsaac] Interview on CBC Radio Calgary' (2013), [Radio programme] CBC Radio Calgary (2 May), youtu.be/sr29LjThBXw, accessed 26 Jun. 2021.

Knott, T. (2006), 'Saint Brigid of Ireland's Cross', [digital illustration] *Wikimedia Commons* (29 January), https://commons.wikimedia.org/wiki/File:St_Brigid.png, accessed 26 Jun. 2021. License available: https://creativecommons.org/licenses/by/2.5/deed.en, accessed 26 Jun. 2021.

Koch, J. T. (2006), 'Medb and Ailill', in John T. Koch (ed.), *Celtic Culture: A Historical Encyclopedia*, Vol. IV, 1282–3, Santa Barbara, CA: ABC-CLIO.

Koch, J. T., and Carey, J., eds (2000), *The Celtic Heroic Age: Literary Sources for Ancient Celtic Europe and Early Ireland and Wales*, 3rd ed., Andover, MA: Celtic Studies.

MacKillop, J. (1986), *Fionn mac Cumhaill: Celtic Myth in English Literature*, Syracuse, NY: Syracuse University Press.

McCone, K. (2000), *Pagan Past and Christian Present in Early Irish Literature*, Maynooth: Department of Old Irish, National University of Ireland.

McIsaac, J. (2013a), *Into the Fire*, Seattle, WA: 47North. Kindle ed.

McIsaac, J. (2013b), *Through the Door*, Las Vegas, NV: 47North. Kindle ed.

McIsaac, J. (2014a), *Among the Unseen*, Las Vegas, NV: 47North. Kindle ed.

McIsaac, J. (2014b), *Beyond the Pale: A Thin Veil Novella*, Calgary, AB: Inkwood Communications. Kindle ed.

McIsaac, J. (2016a), *Bury the Living*, Seattle, WA: 47North. Kindle ed.

McIsaac, J. (2016b), Jodi McIsaac [official web site], http://www.jodimcisaac.com, accessed 26 Jun. 2021. Kindle ed.

McIsaac, J. (2017), *Summon the Queen*, Seattle, WA: 47North. Kindle ed.

Mills, J. S. (2016), 'Interview with Jodi McIsaac, author of *Bury the Living*', *SFFWorld* (4 Nov.), http://www.sffworld.com/2016/11/interview-with-jodi-mcisaac-author-of-bury-the-living, accessed 26 Jun. 2021.

Ó Catháin, S. (1992), 'Hearth-Prayers and Other Traditions of Brigit: Celtic Goddess and Holy Woman', *The Journal of the Royal Society of Antiquaries of Ireland*, 122: 12–34.

Ó Catháin, S. (1999), 'The Festival of Brigit the Holy Woman', *Celtica*, 23: 231–60.

Ó Cathasaigh, D. (1979), 'The Cult of Brigid: A Study of Pagan-Christian Syncretism in Ireland', *Mankind Quarterly*, 19 (4): 311–28.

O'Grady, S. H. (1892), *Silva Gadelica: (I–XXXI); A Collection of Tales in Irish; with Extracts Illustrating Persons and Places*, London: Williams and Norgate, https://catalog.hathitrust.org/Record/001725758, accessed 26 Jun. 2021.

Purkiss, D. (2000), *At the Bottom of the Garden: A Dark History of Fairies, Hobgoblins, and Other Troublesome Things*, New York: New York University Press.

Ryan, E., ed. (2002), *Annals of the Four Masters*, trans. J. O'Donovan, Cork: University College, CELT: The Corpus of Electronic Texts, https://celt.ucc.ie/published/T100005A/index.html, accessed 26 Jun. 2021.

Simms, K. (2005), 'Women', in S. Duffy (ed.), *Medieval Ireland: An Encyclopedia*, 520–2, New York: Routledge.

Williams, M. (2016), *Ireland's Immortals: A History of the Gods of Irish Myth*, Princeton, NJ: Princeton University Press.

Yeats, W.B. ([1918] 2011), *Irish Fairy and Folk Tales*, New York: Fall River Press.

Part Two

Celtic fantasy worlds and heroes

4

The heroic biographies of Cú Chulainn and Connavar in the *Rigante* series

Alistair J.P. Sims

David Andrew Gemmell (1948–2006) was regarded by his peers and the UK fantasy community as one of Britain's most accomplished heroic fantasy authors. Even posthumously he continued to influence and inspire new authors of the genre with the Gemmell awards.[1] His engagement with the Celtic past, therefore, is significant within the context of modern fantasy.

There are two clear forms of 'Celticity' that influence Gemmell's *Rigante* series novels, *Sword in the Storm* (1999) and *Midnight Falcon* (2000): the image of the 'Celts' taken from classical writers, and early Irish texts such as the Ulster Cycle. The chapter by Anthony Smart later in this volume focuses on Gemmell's engagement with Classical ethnography, which gives Gemmell's Keltoi the image of the 'Celts' as portrayed by Roman and Greek writers. As I have discussed elsewhere (Sims 2018), Gemmell used at least two classical sources directly: Caesar's *Gallic Wars,* and *De Re Militari,*[2] but I argue in this chapter that the Irish medieval tradition is at the heart of the 'Keltoi' of Gemmell's series. To create the character of Connavar – on whom this chapter will focus – Gemmell seems to have blended the figures of Cú Chulainn and Vercingetorix. The backdrop of Gemmell's two novels is the defence of the 'good' Keltoi heroic society against the all-consuming and 'bad' empire of Stone, which, evidently, stands in for the Roman Empire. It is, therefore, pretty clear that the Keltoi, the people to whom the main protagonists, Connavar and Bane, belong, are in

---

[1] The Gemmell awards were a highlight of the UK Fantasy community's calendar from 2009, until their closure in 2018. Winners of the awards have included many well-known authors of the fantasy genre, such as John Gwynne, Brandon Sanderson, Andrzej Sapkowski and Patrick Rothfuss.

[2] Gemmell quotes verbatim from the *De Re Militari,* and specifically the translation by Lieutenant John Clarke in 1767 (Anne Nicholls, personal communication; Sims 2008).

these novels based on the historical Iron Age peoples of Britain and Western Europe, under the catchment term 'Celts' (Sims 2018). Nevertheless, Gemmell may have used classical ethnography for the worldbuilding element of the novels (including peoples, nomenclature, material culture, etc.) but for the supernatural components and the creation of heroes, he relies on 'Celtic' mythology, and specifically the Irish tradition.

The novels *Sword in the Storm* (1999) and *Midnight Falcon* (2000) have two main protagonists: Connavar, and his estranged son, Bane. *Sword in the Storm* is a classic fantasy narrative of a boy marked for greatness, eventually becoming a king. Connavar grows up amongst the Seidh,[3] a magical race of being as old as time, who take note of him. While looking specifically for the father Seidh, the Thagda (Gemmell's spelling of a figure who is rather obviously a version of the Irish Dagda), Connavar saves a fawn in the woods, and he is gifted with a fine Seidh-forged dagger (Gemmell 1999: 47–9). Soon after, the Morrigu[4] comes to him to grant a wish (Gemmell 1999: 80). After asking for glory from the Morrigu, a bear attacks Connavar while he is carrying the crippled Riamfada. Connavar refuses to leave and fights to protect his friend. Terribly injured, he survives with the help of Vorna the witch (Gemmell 1999: 106–24). After surviving, Connavar leaves on a journey across the water with his mentor Banouin, who is later murdered on the order of the King of the Perdii. Connavar joins General Jasaray and aids the Stone Armies conquer the Perdii to gain revenge. Sickened by what he experiences, and after killing the King of the Perdii, Connavar goes back home to face the invasion that will certainly come and prepares to defend the Rigante against the Vars (Sea Raiders) and then subsequently the armies of Stone at the battle of Codgen field.

Midnight Falcon follows a similar narrative, although, instead of starting as a young boy at the opening of the novel, Bane is already a man, an outlaw, hunted by his father's men. Bane goes on a journey to Stone with the foreigner Banouin's son, also named Banouin. Bane is almost killed by a Knight of Stone while trying to defend a family he was staying with. Bane is close to death, but the Morrigu heals him (Gemmell 2000: 120–30). After his recovery Bane continues his journeys to the city of Stone and trains to be a gladiator to gain his revenge. After killing the Knight of Stone, he returns home and joins with other outcastes to defend his home village against a raid by the Vars (Gemmell 2000: 453). Bane gains some reconciliation with his father and grandmother, before Connavar

---

[3] Gemmell uses Seidh, an variant spelling of the *síd* in the Irish tradition, an alternative name for the Tuatha Dé Danaan (Williams 2016: 360).

[4] Gemmell uses the second, shorter variant spelling Morrígu rather than Morrígan, for his version of this Irish supernatural female figure (Williams 2016: xxviii).

is then murdered by his own step-brother. Bane takes the place of Connavar in the last, deciding battle against Jasaray and the Armies of Stone, where they are victorious (Gemmell 2000: 517).

Gemmell's novels explore honour, loyalty and redemption, and his protagonists tend to be flawed. But importantly they are still heroic and larger than life. This is how, at the beginning of *Sword in the Storm*, a young boy sees Connavar, at that point the heroic King of the Keltoi:

> At his side was the legendary Seidh sword, with its hilt of gold. He rode into the Circle and sat his stallion staring at the men. They seemed to be tense, almost frightened by his presence.
>
> (Gemmell 1999: 12)

Nevertheless Connavar, like many heroic characters in *Sword in the Storm*, is flawed, and his flawed heroic ethos mirrors Irish texts such as the *Táin Bó Cuailnge* ('The Cattle Raid of Cooley'), especially in the earliest incarnation of these tales which portray heroes breaking promises and prone to betrayal (Edel 2015: 15–26). Instead of the stereotypical image of the barbarian, as portrayed by Classical writers, Gemmell moulds Connavar as a romanticized hero, closely hewn from characters the Irish medieval texts, with close affinities to Cú Chulainn.

Cú Chulainn is an iconic hero, who had been already appropriated in earlier texts of fantasy and speculative fiction, such as Patrick McGinley's *The Trick of the Ga Bolga* (1985), Gregory Frost's *Táin* (1986) and *Remscela* (1988), and Morgan Llywelyn's *The Red Branch* (1989). To take Edel's rather apt metaphor of bandwidth, due to a multitude of translations, there are different oscillations of the character of Cú Chulainn, all overlapping with each other to some degree (Edel 2015: 15). This is prime material for fantasy authors, also illustrated by a number of chapters in this volume (see Grant; Smart; Sneddon). In regard to Connavar in *Sword in the Storm* and *Midnight Falcon*, Gemmell presents us with his own version of Cú Chulainn, creatively adapted and re-shaped to suit his own narrative and imagined world.

Connavar the Keltoi (Irish) hero

In medieval Irish tradition there are two heroic models: the hero of the tribe, such as Cú Chulainn, champion and defender of his people; and the hero outside the tribe, the wanderer and outlaw (see Ó Cathasaigh 1977: 11; McCone 1986: 9; Sjoestedt 2000; Carey and Koch 2006: 908–9). This binary separation has also been challenged: rather than having two separate categories of a hero, it is possible to read those as two aspects of a single figure. McCone has suggested that 'outlaws' may have been adolescents waiting for an initiation into society (see Carey and Koch 2006: 908–9). This can be linked to the hero's perilous nature and his association with boundaries, either defending a boundary (e.g. of a settlement) or raiding outside it. In the case of Cú Chulainn this boundary is symbolized by the dog (Irish *cú*), an animal separated by only a thin line from a wolf, *cú allaid* (literally, wild dog) (McCone 1990: 213; Carey and Koch 2006: 908–9).

Sétanta, later named Cú Chulainn, is a hero in whom this duality is expressed fully. He is given the name 'Culann's hound' after he slays the smith Culann's monstrous guard dog (Kinsella 2002: 84; Edel 2015: 36; Freeman 2017: 66). It is significant that in the *Táin Bó Cuailnge* Cú Chulainn guards the border (boundary of Ulster) on his own, beating warrior after warrior in single combat. Cú Chulainn's ties to the hound imagery go further with one of the many *gessi* that bind him. A *geis* (pl. *gessi*) is a specifically Irish cultural concept, usually translated as a taboo, prohibition or obligation, predominately given at birth, or when taking on a new role in society. As a literary motif, it is a means of motivating seemingly senseless and heroic actions, which can be destructive to the protagonist (Sjöblom 2006: 796–7). Heroic figures continually break theirs *gessi* and in doing so create conflict and narrative drive. One of Cú Chulainn's gessi bans him from eating dog flesh, highlighting once more his affinities to the symbolic functions of the dog or hound.

One more aspect linking Cú Chulainn with the threatening, rather than the protective, aspects of the hound is an infamous episode in the *Táin* in which, after he returns from a raid across the border, Cú Chulainn is so full of the heat of battle that he goes into his shape-shifting *ríastrad* (a physical distortion of his body when in the midst of blood lust) and threatens to kill his own people, a situation only resolved by a ruse (Carey and Koch 2006: 909). The idea that the hero loses his ability to distinguish friend from foe, or restrain his blood lust, is a genuine flaw that contributes to the blurring of the hound/wolf dichotomy.

This idea of a hero having two aspects, inside the boundary and outside the boundary, is something that can be seen in Gemmell's *Sword in the Storm* and *Midnight Falcon*. The two protagonists, Connavar in *Sword in the Storm* and Bane in *Midnight Falcon*, fulfil each of these roles respectively. Connavar, like Cú Chulainn, is the hero who is inside the boundary (the settlement of Three Rivers) and sets out to protect it from invaders (Gemmell 1999: 337). He learns at an early age about the people of Stone through the teaching of the foreigner Banouin. After taking part in Stone's conquest of the Perdii, Connavar becomes obsessed with protecting his people, specifically his own tribe, the Rigante, but also all Keltoi with whom he feels kinship, such as when the Vars invade the lands of the Pannones (Gemmell 1999: 450). The boundary for Connavar becomes larger than just his own lands: it expands to the land of all the Keltoi.

Bane, on the other hand, takes on the role of the 'outlaw'. As the son of Connavar, Bane is marked for greatness, but is self-exiled and one of a band of outlaws, the wolfshead (Gemmell 2000: 453). McCone mentions Wolfskins, who he describes sometimes as adolescent capable warriors, or criminals, or robbers (McCone 1990: 213; Carey and Koch 2006: 908-9). This seems to mirror Bane and the wolfshead. With Bane are men such as Wik, who were once of a different tribe such as the Pannones. Wik tells Bane that many of those who defended the Settlement of Three Rivers were just poor folk with nothing to eat, not really outlaws, but from many different tribes such as the Novii and Cenii (Gemmell 2000: 433). The group also consists of older warriors who have been ostracized, such as Grale, who had fought and was named a hero at Cogden Field, where Connavar first defeated the armies of Stone (Gemmell 2000: 423).

This symbolism of the wolf and boundary is particularly clear to see with Bane and the group of outlaws (the wolfshead), who, in the end, come inside the boundary and defend the settlement. They thus eventually become accepted by those who they protected, so much so that later, when Connavar comes pardoning them all, he gives Wik a commission into his horse archers (Gemmell 2000: 438). Therefore, Bane in this story conforms to the very idea of the adolescent waiting for initiation into society. At the end of *Midnight Falcon* we see his grandmother accepting him at last, and the villagers welcoming him and his fellow outlaws (Gemmell 2000: 428). This is followed by the ultimate conclusion where Bane, after the murder of his father, takes the place of, and impersonates, Connavar in the final battle (Gemmell 2000: 517).

Just like the *gessi* in the Irish tradition, in Gemmell's *Rigante* series, every Keltoi child is given a geasa (as Gemmell spells this) at birth. The witch Vorna explains to Banouin that a geasa is not a curse, but a protective prophesy of a pivotal moment in a person's future, and that these geasa mostly do not foretell death but success or happiness (Gemmell 1999: 178). Nevertheless, most of the principle characters of *Sword in the Storm* have a death geasa just as many heroes of the Irish tradition.[5] Similar to Cú Chulainn, Connavar's geasa is associated

---

[5] Ruathain is given the geasa 'be not the Kings Shield' (Gemmell 1999: 180), Banouin is given 'drink no wine when you see the lion with eyes of blood' (Gemmell 1999: 178), Carac is told 'if any royal blood were spilled he would not live past his fortieth birthday' (Gemmell 1999: 295), and Fisher Laird is given 'let not one of your deeds break a woman's heart' (Gemmell 1999: 429). All these geasas are broken. Banouin drinks wine in front of a shield with a lion embossed with ruby eyes, and is then murdered by Carac, who in turn murders his family to the throne, spills his own royal blood and dies by Connavar's hand. The Fisher Laird's sons kill Connavar's bride Tae with an arrow in the heart, and they are all killed by Connavar.

with dogs: that he will die the day he kills the hound that bites him (Gemmell 1999: 179), a geasa he violates and which leads to his death.

Apart from breaking his geasa, though, Connavar also breaks a promise (something he is warned against by the Seidh) to his youthful wife Tae (Gemmell 1999: 434). Connavar sleeps with his old flame with disastrous consequences and does not ride with Tae, leading to her death by an arrow in a blood feud, in which the Fisher Laird breaks his own geasa (Gemmell 1999: 424). In rage, Connavar destroys an entire village single-handedly (Gemmell 1999: 420–31), his uncontrolled blood lust very much comparable to Cú Chulainn's *ríastrad* and threat to his own people. Bane also – like his father – has a rather threatening temper, killing two men for insulting his dead mother (Gemmell 2000, 17), but Connavar does display a rather chilling monstrous side when he destroys and kills uncontrollably at the Fisher Laird's village, a scene very vividly portrayed:

> Walking to a nearby hut he splashed oil to the wooden walls then set it alight. The wind fanned the flames, and burning cinders flew from one thatched roof to the next. Soon a number of fires were blazing. People began to run from their homes. Connavar moved among them, slashing left and right with his sword. Behind him flames licked out of the open doorway of the Long Hall, then broke through the roof. Panic swept through the settlement as Conn strode through the flames, killing anyone who came within the reach of his sword. Two young men ran at him, carrying hatchets. He slew them both. The villagers began to stream from the settlement.
>
> (Gemmell 1999: 430–1)

Cú Chulainn and Connavar share one more important element that fits in with the ambivalent figure of the hero: their association with the Morrígan/Morrigu. In the Irish texts, the Morrígan is a supernatural female figure who incites war, heralds death and is associated with prophesy, fertility, valour, heroism and the encouragement for glory in battle for heroes (Davidson 1988: 92–101; Lysaght 1996: 152–65; Kinsella 2002). In the *Táin Bó Cúailnge* in particular, she can change into an animal, appear as beautiful woman, or old hag (Lysaght 1996: 152–65). This Morrígan of the Irish texts is clearly analogous to the Morrigu in the *Rigante* series, who continually interacts with the main protagonists for both good and ill. She is seen by the characters themselves as bringer of death and mischief (Gemmell 1999: 35), but also one who grants wishes and particular in regard to Connavar, glory (Gemmell 1999: 80). There are many descriptions of her, not least showing that she appears in more than one form, sometimes an old woman and other times, a crow (Gemmell 1999: 82). This is similar to the Morrígan's interaction with Cú Chulainn, coming to his aid and acting as a guardian, but also as foe, just as the Morrigu is certainly there in the shadows of Connavar's life. She is there at his birth, she brings the storms that destroy the sword that would save Varaconn's life, and she is there when Meria, his mother, tells awful things to his step farther, Ruathain, and thus begins their separation which then leads to Connavar searching for the Thagda (Gemmell 1999: 82). She appears later as an old hag and grants Connavar the wish of glory, sending the bear to attack him. She is there when he kills Carac (Gemmell 1999: 294), and at that point she also prophesies there will many more things to sadden Banouin if he was still alive, insinuating that Vorna and Banouin's baby will die in childbirth. Connavar asks for a wish to save the child, and the Morrigu grants it (Gemmell 1999: 297, 397). The Morrigu again acts in aid when, as Connavar is dying, she goads Vorna to perform an act that is dangerous to her to heal him, unknown to either of them, the Morrigu holds Connavar's soul in place (Gemmell 1999: 399). Thus Vorna loses her powers, which in turn leads to her marrying Banouin and having a child.

The relationship between the Morrigu and Connavar, and the Keltoi people in general, is a profound and complex one. The special status of Connavar is clearly shown in a conversation between Vorna and the Morrigu:

> The Seidh avoid humankind. But not Connavar. You gave him his first knife, you healed him in the lands of Perdii. You warn him of the dangers to his lady. You took his friends spirit to live among you, rather than let it roam the dark. Why is he special to you?
>
> (Gemmell 1999: 399)

The Morrigu replies:

> Such a clever girl, Vorna. It is why I have always liked you. Connavar is important to us. Not just for what he is, but for what he represents. More than that I will not say.
>
> (Gemmell 1999: 399)

This same importance can be seen in *Midnight Falcon*, in which once again she takes on a similar role with Bane and his friend Banouin, the son of Vorna. Her many interactions with Bane in *Midnight Falcon* are more overtly indebted to the relationship between Cú Chulainn and the Morrígan. At the battlefield of Codgen field, the Morrigu appears and threatens Bane's life (Gemmell 2000: 48) and then later she heals Bane (Gemmell 2000: 121). It is here that the Morrigu tells Banouin that the reason Connavar and Bane are so important to the Seidh is that she and the world around them are fed by the 'energy' generated by their actions:

> where does it come from, this life-giving energy? It comes from men like Connavar and Ruathain, from women like Vorna and Eriatha and Meria. People who know love and warmth, people who will risk their lives for all they believe in.
> (Gemmell 2000: 123)

The Morrigu continues telling Banouin:

> Yes, Bane is violent, and some of his deeds do him no credit. But when he risked himself to save the horse he added to the spirit of the world. He fed the earth. And when he came into this house to save the innocent he fed it again – this time with his blood. You did not remember my warning, did you, Banouin? No man conquers fear by running away from it.
> (Gemmell 2000: 123–4)

Throughout the *Rigante* series both Connavar and Bane are special to the Morrigu (Gemmell 2000: 439), and it is perhaps this shared relationship that squarely points to Cú Chulainn as the inspiration for Connavar.

Connavar's heroic biography

Central to any comparison of Connavar and Cú Chulainn is an exploration of the hero and the heroic career as they appear in Irish literature, tracing how they may have been shaped to fit with *Sword in the Storm* and *Midnight Falcon*. The hero (as a character) and the hero's journey (as a narrative pattern) is a common trope of fantasy literature and is clearly an important facet of early Irish literature and scholarship. Epic poems such as *Beowulf* or the *Odyssey* are often considered the forerunners of modern fantasy literature (Mathews 2002: 1), and the hero's journey is central to these works. Generally, a hero achieves personal fame in struggle against the odds. He is usually short lived, his fame being ever-lasting. Heroes are liminal characters, being immensely powerful but vulnerable at the same time, due to their place in-between the divine and the mortal world. The gods cannot help but meddle with them – in some cases life-threateningly so (see de Vries 1963: 180–8; Renehan 1987; McCone 1990: 189; Kavanagh and O'Leary 2004: 119–21). The scholarly concept of the heroic biography as it applies to early Irish literature goes back to the nineteenth century with Edward Taylor's work in 1871 (Ní Mhaoileoin 2015: 11), whose work was later expanded by von Hahn in 1876. Alfred Nutt amended von Hahn's pattern in 1881, thus allowing greater flexibility. Unlike Ó Cathasaigh (1977), who uses the de Vries 1963 pattern in his examination of Cormac Mac Airt, the best fit for my examination of Cú Chulainn, Connnavar and Bane is von Hahn's model, with Nutt's additions (in italics), as combined by Ní Mhaoileoin (2015: 148) and as presented in Table 4.1.

Connavar is born a hero, or what is described as a 'great man' (Gemmell 1999: 13). Son of Meria and Varaconn, he is born in supernatural circumstances (Table 4.1, 1.c.) during a storm brought down by the Morrigu, who, as discussed above, frequently interacts with Cú Chulainn and Connavar for both ill and good (see also Sims 2018). The storm shatters an iron sword that has been blessed by four druids, owned by Connavar's father (Gemmell 1999: 20). Connavar is given the soul-name Sword in the Storm. This soul-name could be compared to heroic names, however, there are other that better fit him during the course of the novel. There are several versions of Cú Chulainn's conception and birth, but the best-known one places him as the son of King Conchobar's sister, Deichtine, and fathered by Lug, a divine figure (see Ó hUiginn 2006: 507). As with their births, both Cú Chulainn and Connavar share extraordinary deaths (Table 4.1, 13).

Table 4.1 The Heroic Biography Pattern as outlined by von Hahn, with Nutt's additions in italics, as combined by Ní Mhaoileoin.

1. Hero born
    a Out of wedlock
    b *Posthumously*
    c *Supernaturally*
    d One of twins
2. Mother, princess residing in her own country
3. Father
    a God from afar
    b Hero from afar
4. Tokens and warnings of hero's future greatness
5. He is in consequence driven from home
6. Is suckled by wild beasts
7. *Is brought up by a: childless (shepherd) couple, or widow*
8. Is of passionate and violent disposition
9. Seeks service in foreign lands
    9a Attacks and slays monsters
    9b Acquires supernatural knowledge through eating a magic fish (or other animal)
10. Returns to his own country, retreats and again returns
11. Overcomes his enemies, frees his mother and seats himself on the throne
12. Founds cities
13. The manner of his death is extraordinary
14. He is accused of incest. Dies young
15. He injures an inferior who takes revenge upon him or upon his children
16. He slays his younger brother

Source: Patricia Ní Mhaoileoin, *The Heroic Biography of Fergus Mac Róich: A Case Study of the Heroic-Biographical Pattern in Old and Middle Irish Literature* (PhD Thesis: University of Galway, 2015).

Cú Chulainn at his death scene ties himself to a standing stone to keep himself upright, while Connavar is killed among standing stones. Also, Cú Chulainn is betrayed by his foster brother Fer Diad (Kavanagh and O'Leary 2004: 117), just like Connavar is betrayed by his half-brother Braefar. Cú Chulainn slays Fer Diad, while Braefer commits suicide, therefore both half-brothers die at consequence of their heroic kin (Table 4.1, 16).

Fostering (see Table 4.1, 7) is an important cultural concept in early Irish texts (McCone 1990, 194) and it is clearly a significant element of Cú Chulainn's heroic biography, as he is fostered with multiple characters of Irish tradition (Kinsella 2002: 24–5). Like Cú Chulainn's fosterage by King Conchobar, Connavar is fostered with Ruathain, the First Sword of the Rigante tribe, who marries Meria, Connavar's mother, after his father Varaconn dies in battle (Gemmell 1999: 116). Comparable to the druid Cathbad in role in Cú Chulainn's case, in *Sword in the Storm* we have the foreigner Banouin, who lives with the Rigante, becoming Connavar's teacher and instructing him in the language of the Stone, about tactics, and the great writers of his people (Gemmell 1999: 39). We also have a third fatherly figure through Connavar's marriage with Tae, the daughter of the Long Laird. This becomes more pronounced where the Laird sets Connavar to be his successor. Lastly, the Thagda can be compared to Cú Chulainn's immortal father Lug (Table 4.1, 3a). The Thagda first gifts Connavar with the Sidhh dagger (Gemmell 1999: 47–9), and later heals him (Gemmell 1999: 244). This latter scene mirrors the healing of Cú Chulainn by Lug (Kinsella 2002: 142–3).

Connavar, just like Cú Chulainn, receives many tokens and warnings of his future greatness (Table 4.1, 4) which are remarkably similar in tone. The first hint of greatness is repeated throughout the novel. It is first noted just after his stepfather Ruathain and mother Meria separate, when Connovar goes searching for the Thagda, the father Seidh, to bring the 'big man' (as he names Ruathain) and his mother together, where he rescues a fawn in the brambles. He is then gifted with a Seidh dagger (Gemmell 1999: 47–9). He is later told by Vorna the Witch that the fawn was the Thagda (Gemmell 1999: 85). This token and the warning by Vorna recurs throughout the novel, as, for instance, when the druid Solstice meets Connavar and sees the dagger, and feels that there is something about him and has a physical reaction to Connavar's prophesied greatness (Gemmell 1999: 161). In the case of Cú Chulainn, stories about his supernatural strength at childhood, including the story of his killing Chulainn's hound while playing (see above), are part of his early signs of greatness.

When Connavar meets an old woman who tells him that his destiny is calling him, she asks Connavar what he would wish for. He asks for glory, and the cool wind buffets him and a light blinds him (Gemmell 1999: 80). This is obviously a momentous scene, foreshadowing Connavar's greatness. Following this incident, the witch Vorna tells Connavar that the old woman was in fact the Morrigu. Connavar is unfazed, and tells Vorna that there is no price he wouldn't pay for the gift of glory and that Banouin has promised him an iron sword to take into battle. This is to be his destiny (Gemmell 1999: 83). This is remarkably similar to Cú Chulainn taking up weapons after the prophesy by the druid Cathbad (Kinsella 2002: 84) that if he took up arms on that day, his name would be greater than any name in Ireland, but ignoring the part of the prophesy that mentions he would die early because of it. Like the choice Cú Chulainn was faced with, it is in *Sword in the Storm* that Connavar has a choice to make: he could be just another warrior hero whose fire burns bright and short, or he can be something greater (Gemmell 1999: 83). This warning continues in this scene, and a second token is given, when the witch Vorna tells Connavar of Calavanus, a hero of the past, and says she knows something of Connavar's destiny, enough to warn him. That he must seek a higher purpose or just be another lesser hero like Calavanus. Vorna then gives Connavar a talisman to protect him from the Morrigu (Gemmell 1999: 83). This idea of destiny and being more than just a hero reoccurs later in the novel. Connavar through the course of the narrative is more than just Cú Chulainn and is perhaps a progression of the Irish hero as Gemmell imagined him.

Continuing to mirror Cú Chulainn, in order to protect his friend, a crippled silversmith, Connavar fights a monstrous bear, similar to Cú Chulainn fighting the monstrous hound (see Table 4.1, 9a). The fight with the bear marks Connavar apart from his own people. The fact that he should be dead but is not is significant here (Gemmell 1999: 107). As Connavar lays dying, the Morrigu tells Vorna that Connavar now has fame and honour, as the 'boy who fought the bear'. He is now famous across other Keltoi clans and even across the water (Gemmell 1999: 113–22). This tale of Connavar and the bear takes a life of its own, and instead of a cripple, he is said to have saved a princess and to have descended from noble blood of Rigante heroes (Gemmell 1999: 139). In some ways, like Cú Chulainn taking his heroic name from killing the hound of Culann (Kinsella 2002: 83; Freeman 2017: 65), Connavar, as the 'boy who fought the bear', does the same. This is conceivably a better fit for a heroic name than his soul-name.

Perhaps though, the name Demonblade (Gemmell 1999: 262) is more significant and this yet again stems from a token of the Seidh, when Connavar is gifted with clothing and a sword (Gemmell 1999: 249). Mirroring the episode of Cú Chulainn's time learning the skill of arms with Scáthach, Connavar leaves his home to study the armies of Stone, and fights with them against the Perdii

(Gemmell 1999: 232–97) (see Table 4.1, 9). Cú Chulainn and Connavar by choice leave their home for similar reasons, to better themselves. Cú Chulainn leaves to train with Scáthach in order to win Emer (Kinsella 2002: 26–31; Freeman 2017: 73). Connavar leaves Three Rivers with Banouin to learn about the world outside his own (Gemmell 1999: 181–219), ends up fighting with the army of Stone (Gemmell 1999: 232–97) and in doing so becomes famous for his skill of arms. Like Cú Chulainn gaining his spear, Connavar gains his sword. Both Connavar and Cú Chulainn come home to acquire a wife (Table 4.1, 10). Connavar, after coming back from across the water, goes at the biding of the Long Laird to see the defences of Seven willows, he then rescues the Laird's daughter Tae from the Sea Wolves and wins her hand (Gemmell 1999: 372).

There are numerous examples of Cú Chulainn's passionate and violent nature (Freeman 2017: 71, 75) exemplified by his *ríastrad* during which he takes on a monstrous form (Table 4.1, 8). Cú Chulainn is often considered unstable and has a Jekyll and Hyde personality (Moore 2009, 154; see also discussion above). This personality comparison is very apt not just for Connavar but for other prominent characters in the series, such as Fiallech, who has a vicious temper and will resort to violence in his jealously regarding Tae (Gemmell 1999: 323). Connavar too is passionate and has a violent disposition. This begins even as a young boy, where he gets into fights with a number of boys, including the smith's son Govannan (Gemmell 1999: 24). This violent disposition is also shown in his time away from home, where he sets out to have revenge over Banouin's death, and vows to kill Cardic, king of the Perdii, and destroy the whole tribe (Gemmell 1999: 223, 234). The last and most significant moment of *ríastrad* for Connavar is after he has broken his promise to Tae to go riding, and tribesmen from the Fisher Laird's village attack Ruathain, and end up killing Tae (Gemmell 1999: 424). As we saw above, on finding out about this, to his great shame, Connavar goes berserk and kills the Fisher Laird, his sons, and everyone in the village, child, woman and all (Gemmell 1999: 429–31). During it all Connavar doesn't really know what he is doing and comments about it to the Earthmaiden Eriatha[6] (Gemmell 1999, 436):

> I burned the village. And worse. I can scarce remember how I felt as I rode to the Fisher Laird's hall. It was as if all the anger and the hurt, the loss and the shame turned me to winter. I went into the hall and killed the Laird and his sons. Flames were all around me. The hall was burning. I cannot remember

---

[6] An Earthmaiden is a prostitute in the Rigante world.

how it started. But when I left I carried a lantern and set fire to nearby houses. There was a roaring in my head, and then there were people running around me, screaming and shouting. I lashed out at them. I killed them, Eriatha. When dawn came I walked through the ruins. I saw the bodies. Two were children. But there were women too.

(Gemmell 1999: 436-7)

As it has become clear through the course of this examination of heroic biographies, Connavar and Cú Chulainn are very similar. Connavar follows many of the same the biographical patterns as Cú Chulainn: he is born a hero (Table 4.1, 1), his birth is supernatural (1c), he is given tokens and warning of his greatness (4), is fostered (7), is of a passionate and violent disposition (8), seeks service in a foreign land (9), attacks and slays monsters (9a), returns home (10), his death is extraordinary (13), and he is responsible for the death of his younger brother (16). The one element that Connavar has in his heroic biography (11) that Cú Chulainn does not is that he overcomes his enemies and seats himself on the throne. Connavar does have some markers missing from the table, mainly regarding birth, such as being born out of wedlock (1a), his mother being a princess and residing in her own country (2), and father is a God (3a). However, tentatively even these elements are roughly comparable, as Connavar's mother is a person of influence and power in the Rigante tribe, and there is father-like connection between Connavar and the Thagda, reminiscent of Cú Chulainn and Lug.

Bane's biography is an extensions of his father's, ending up with posing as him in the final battle due to Connavar being slain by his younger half-brother (Table 4.1, 14), which is alluded to in the prologue of *Sword in the Storm* and played out in *Midnight Falcon*. Bane is also comparable to Cú Chulainn in that he shares with Cú Chulainn elements of the heroic pattern that Connavar does not, regarding his birth: Bane is the son of a hero and was born out of wedlock as was Cú Chulainn (see Table 4.1, 1a, 3b; Kinsella 2002: 21-5). Unlike Bane, Connavar and Cú Chulainn share a fuller biography going from birth to death.

Connavar, the High King of the Keltoi: The story as it ought to have been

As we saw, demonstrating that clear Cú Chulainn parallels are very much present from the earliest stages of Connavar's heroic career is not a difficult task. Nevertheless, as Anthony Smart argues in this volume, Gemmell's world of the Rigante can also be read via the lens of classical ethnography. The use of the term

'Keltoi' itself alludes to classical ethnographical influence. It is the Greek term for 'Celts' and was first used by Herodotus (Bridgman 2004: 156). This classical label tells the reader that these 'barbarians' belong to Iron Age British 'Celts', as do their individual tribal names, such as Rigante, Norvii, Cenii and Perdii. The term Rigante, from whom the series takes its name, could be derived from the Brigantes, not mentioned by Caesar, but by another Roman writer, Tacitus (Tacitus 1999: 14). Regarding the other tribes mentioned in the novel, they seem to originate from historical tribes in the continent: the Norvii possibly from the Nervii, and the Perdii perhaps from the Parisii. These are mentioned in Caesar's *Gallic Wars* (Caesar 1996). The similarities as seen in this nomenclature are hard to ignore. Gemmell is clearly also utilising a classical ethnographical Celticity, and that can be claimed to be the case for Connavar too: unlike Cú Chulainn, who is a heroic warrior, Connavar is something more as he becomes High King of the Keltoi, analogous to figures such as Vercingetorix.

There are many similarities between Connavar and Vercingetorix in their high status and actions, and in defying parallel empires. Not only do they both create tribal alliances, but also fight using the same tactics.[7] However there are significant differences. Connavar succeeds in defeating Jasaray and the armies of stone, not just once, but twice (Gemmell 2000: 10, 527). There is no Alesia[8] and total defeat for the Keltoi and Connavar. There is also little to compare to in regard to each figure's heroic biography, as we know very little about Vercingetorix's early life. I would, therefore, argue that Connavar is Vercingetorix as he *should* have been through Gemmell's romanticized imagination by blending him with heroic figure of Cú Chulainn, allowing him to imagine the Iron Age 'Celts' as victorious. In Gemmell's version of their fantastic alternative history, their various tribes have been banded together by a charismatic leader against a shared threat, but the outcome is different to the historical Vercingetorix's alliance.

Gemmell's novels combine opposing sides of perceptions of the 'Celts' (classical ethnography, and Irish medieval texts), therefore adhering to a linear history of the 'Celts', linking Iron Age tribes of Britain with the culture and texts of medieval Ireland, despite a gap of centuries and a difference in geographical

---

[7] In *Sword in the Storm* and *Midnight Falcon*, Connavar's prized Calvary are named the Iron Wolves (Gemmell 1999: 405). The Iron Wolves harry the baggage train of the armies of stone, a tactic that Vercingetorix also used (Malleson 1889: 8).

[8] The siege of Alesia was the final engagement between Vercingetorix and Julius Caesar. It was a regrouping of all the Gallic tribes under Vercingetorix control and in the end was the precursor to defeat and led to the conquest of Gaul.

locations. This narrative, though, was already being dismantled by scholars around the time of the publication of Gemmell's *Rigante* series by archaeologists (see Mallory 1992), but also from the perspective of Irish medieval literature (see Aitchison 1987; McCone 1990; also the Introduction to this volume). As mentioned above, Gemmell engaged with specific classical sources and was aware of historical debates between scholars.[9] Moreover, Gemmell was known to be well read, and in an interview regarding *Lord of the Silver Bow* (2006), the first novel of a series set in Troy, he displays his fascination with, and hunger to learn more on, a subject he was researching:

> We have scores of research books detailing bronze-age Greece. It is actually amazing to discover how little is known about the period! I am constantly coming upon odd little facts that remain baffling to experts. I am still trying to find out why ostrich eggshells were so valuable.
>
> (quoted in Penguin Random House n.d.)

It is, therefore, entirely possible that Gemmell was not unaware of the scholarly debate that challenged the linear narrative of the 'Celts', from Iron Age tribes to medieval Ireland. Nevertheless, combining classical sources and the Irish tradition gave him the opportunity to present an alternative narrative to Vercingetorix's crushing defeat, and challenge the perception of mighty Rome in favour of the underdogs – a prime heroic narrative trope, with a 'eucatastrophic' (in Tolkienian terms) ending. As a fantasy author, he was not constrained by historical accuracy, but rather more interested in a compelling story, and characters one can empathize with.[10] At the same time, by infusing the Iron Age 'Celtic' tribes with supernatural elements from the Irish tradition (deities such as the Morrígan/Morrigu and the Dagda/Thagda; the importance of warnings, tokens, and the role of *gessi/geasas*) and with the heroic biography of Cú Chulainn, straddling the hero/outlaw boundary, he has turned a vaguely historical world into a magical one, making *Sword in the Storm* and *Midnight Falcon* unequivocally epic fantasy novels, and a key contribution to Celtic-inspired fantasy.

---

[9] For example, in the Foreword to his novel *Ghost King*, set in Roman Britain, he shows awareness of opposing views among historians (Gemmell 1998: 7).
[10] See Cox's chapter in this volume, regarding fans' perceptions of Celticity and their reactions to accurate research.

References

Aitchison, N. B. (1987), 'The Ulster Cycle: Heroic Image and Historical Reality', *Journal of Medieval History*, 13: 87–116.

Bridgman, Timothy P. (2004), *Hyperboreans: Myth and History in Celtic-Hellenic Contacts*, New York: Routledge.

Caesar, Julius (1996), *Seven Commentaries on the Gallic War, with an Eighth Commentary by Aulus Hirtius*, trans. Carolyn Hammond, Oxford; New York: Oxford University Press.

Carey, John, and Koch, John T. (2006), 'Heroic Ethos in Early Celtic Literatures', in John T. Koch (ed.), *Celtic Culture: A Historical Encyclopedia*, Vol. 3, 907–12, Santa Barbara; Oxford: ABC-CLIO.

Davidson, H. R. Ellis (1988), *Myths and Symbols in Pagan Europe: Early Scandinavian and Celtic Religions*, Syracuse, NY: Syracuse University Press.

Edel, Doris (2015), *Inside the Táin: Exploring Cú Chulainn, Fergus, Ailill, and Medb*, Berlin: curach bhán.

Freeman, Philip (2017), *Celtic Mythology: Tales of Gods, Goddesses, and Heroes*, New York: Oxford University Press.

Frost, Gregory ([1986] 2015), *Táin*, Cedar Crest: Book View Café.

Frost, Gregory ([1988] 2015), *Remscela*, Cedar Crest: Book View Café.

Gemmell, David (1998), *Ghost King*, London: Legend.

Gemmell, David (1999), *Sword in the Storm*, London: Random House.

Gemmell, David (2000), *Midnight Falcon*, London: Random House.

Gemmell, David (2006), *Lord of the Silver Bow*, London: Corgi Books.

Kavanagh, Donncha, and O'Leary, Majella (2004), 'The Legend of Cú Chulainn: Exploring Organization Theory's Heroic Odyssey', in Yiannis Gabriel (ed.), *Myths, Stories, and Organizations: Premodern Stories for Our Times*, 116–30, Oxford: Oxford University Press.

Kinsella, Thomas (2002), *The Táin: From the Irish Epic Táin Bó Cuailnge*, Oxford: Oxford University Press.

Llywelyn, Morgan (1989), *Red Branch*, New York: W. Morrow.

Lysaght, Patricia (1996), 'Aspects of the Earth-Goddess in the Traditions of the Banshee in Ireland', in Sandra Billington and Miranda Green (eds), *The Concept of the Goddess*, 152–65, London; New York: Routledge.

Malleson, G. B. (1889), 'Vercingetorix', *Transactions of the Royal Historical Society*, 4: 1–40.

Mallory, James P. (1992), 'The World of Cú Chulainn: The Archaeology of *Táin Bó Cúailgne*', in James P. Mallory (ed.), *Aspects of the Táin*, 103–59, Belfast: December.

Mathews, Richard (2002), *Fantasy: The Liberation of Imagination*, New York; London: Routledge.

McCone, Kim R. (1986), 'Werewolves, Cyclopes, *Díberga* and *Fíanna*: Juvenile Delinquency in Early Ireland', *Cambridge Medieval Celtic Studies*, 12: 1–22.

McCone, Kim R. (1990), *Pagan Past and Christian Present in Early Irish Literature*, Maynooth: An Sagart.
McGinley, Patrick (1985), *The Trick of the Ga Bolga*, London: Cape.
Moore, Elizabeth (2009), '"In t-Indellchró Bodba Fer Talman": A Reading of Cú Chulainn's First Recension Ríastrad', *Proceedings of the Harvard Celtic Colloquium*, 29: 154–76.
Ní Mhaoileoin, Patricia (2015), *The Heroic Biography of Fergus Mac Róich: A Case Study of the Heroic-Biographical Pattern in Old and Middle Irish Literature*, PhD Thesis: University of Galway.
Ó Cathasaigh, Tomás (1977), *The Heroic Biography of Cormac mac Airt*, Dublin: Dublin Institute for Advanced Studies.
Ó Huiginn, Ruairí (2006), 'Cú Chulainn', in John T. Koch (ed.), *Celtic Culture: A Historical Encyclopedia*, Vol. 1, 507–8, Santa Barbara; Oxford: ABC-CLIO.
Renehan, R. (1987), 'The Heldentod in Homer: One Heroic Ideal', *Classical Philology*, 82 (2): 99–116.
Sims, Alistair (2018), 'Celtic Obsession in Modern Fantasy Literature', in R. Karl and K. Möller (eds), *Proceedings of the 2nd European Symposium in Celtic Studies. Held at Prifysgol Bangor University from July 31st to August 3rd 2017*, 21–35, Hagen/Westf.: curach bhan.
Sjöblom, Tom (2006), 'Geis', in John T. Koch (ed.), *Celtic Culture: A Historical Encyclopedia*, Vol. 3, 706–7, Santa Barbara; Oxford: ABC-CLIO.
Sjoestedt, Marie-Louise (2000), *Celtic Gods and Heroes*, Great Britain: Dover Publications.
Penguin Random House, 'Author Q&A: Interview with David Gemmell author of *Troy: Lord of the Silver Bow*', https://www.penguinrandomhouse.com/books/59023/troy-lord-of-the-silver-bow-by-david-gemmell/, accessed 6 Oct. 2021.
Tacitus (1999), *Agricola and Germany*, trans. Anthony R. Birley, Oxford; New York: Oxford University Press.
Williams, Mark (2016), *Ireland's Immortals: A History of the Gods of Irish Myth*, Princeton, NJ: Princeton University Press.

5

Classical ethnography and the world(s) of the Rigante

Anthony Smart

His beard was red gold in the dying sunlight. He was wearing a winged helm of bright silver, a breastplate embossed with the Fawn in Brambles crest of his House, and the famous patchwork cloak. At his side was the legendary Seidh sword, with its hilt of gold. He rode into the Circle and sat his stallion staring at the men. They seemed to be tense, almost frightened by his presence.

These are the words of a Rigante child, upon seeing his king, a hero to his subjects, and the most fearsome warrior of the land in David Gemmell's *Sword in the Storm* (1999: 12). Connavar, the king, called Demonblade, is riding to his doom, fully aware that those waiting for him are planning his death. There is a certain sense of familiarity here, with moments from 'Celtic' mythology, and in the image that is being created. A noble warrior, a king and lord, facing his enemies in combat, fearless and undaunted. The strong focus on nature, the presence of a magical blade and the backdrop of a stone circle tell the reader in the opening pages that this is a Celtic world.[1] Figures recognizable as the Dagda, the Morrígan and the Túatha Dé Danann from Irish medieval literature can be found in David Gemmell's *Sword in the Storm*.[2] So too can deliberate allusions to heroes of Celtic myth, most notably Cú Chulainn. At first reading, the book and its characters belong firmly to the expected mythological backdrop of Irish literature and folk-lore. Alistair J.P. Sims provides an excellent examination of the connection between Connovar and the *Táin Bó Cuailnge*

---

[1] By the 'Seidh' Gemmell is alluding to the *síd* from Irish mythology, the sense of otherworldly power, visible within the lived landscape. See Williams (2016: 30–71).
[2] The Morrígan (Morrigu) and the Dagda (Thagda) play a crucial role throughout Gemmell's *Rigante* series. Williams describes the Morrígan as 'a gruesome war-goddess, shapeshifting between woman and crow, eel and wolf' and the Dagda as the 'good god' (2016: xiii; 10).

('The Cattle Raid of Cooley') (see Sims 2018: 21–35).[3] This is however only one layer in the worldbuilding that Gemmell has undertaken, and when we move beyond the familiar fantasy tropes of Celtic myth and legend, we see a rather different world. The names of the tribes of this land bear remarkable similarity to Roman writings of Gaul and Britannia. The physiology and appearance of these tribes reflects Roman images of barbarians (e.g. Tacitus 1970: 17; Gemmell 1999: 159–70, 285–7, 300). The political structure and the levels of aristocratic power belong not to Celtic myth; but instead classical ethnography, and how barbarians were understood by Roman and Greek writers. It will be argued in this chapter that the Celtic identity of the Rigante world comes not from the actual Celtic peoples of antiquity, but their image given in ancient writings by classical authors. The world of the Rigante that Gemmell creates does not belong to familiar Celtic myths, but instead represents the ancient world of Rome, and its own interaction with Barbarian Europe. In so doing, Gemmell reinforces the Romanized perspective of Celtic history, which itself repeated the ideas found in ancient Greek texts. Although there are clear and powerful allusions to Celtic myth and heroic tales here, as Sims argues in this volume, the world of the Rigante is fundamentally a Roman construct. Classical ethnography presents a fixed and immutable image of the barbarian world. Although later classical writers had direct experience with peoples beyond Rome's borders, they sought to place them into a received literary tradition, harking back to Herodotus and the Greek world of the fifth century BCE. Even Tacitus, who gives us Calgacus, and the battle of the Graupian mountains, and Caesar who writes of his own conquests in Gaul and Britannia, categorize the non-Roman peoples into pre-existing patterns of ethnographic thought. In *Sword in the Storm* David Gemmell presents a heroic world deeply enmeshed in classical history. Here there are peoples whose culture, society and heroism echo the words found in the Roman writings. Here too there is a fixed boundary between Celtic and Roman, shaped heavily by ethnographic perspectives, and drawing upon real moments of interaction (Gemmell 1999: 268–73 and 285–7). In this chapter the debt to the classical material will be explored, showing how strongly the world of the Rigante belongs to the Roman discourse on otherness and self-identity. First, we shall investigate how barbarians were written about by Greek and Roman authors, beginning with Herodotus and Thucydides, before looking at Caesar

---

[3] Sims notes both the wider literary influences and the importance of classical learning in shaping some of David Gemmell's ideas. This is achieved through a study of direct references in Gemmell's writings, as well as recorded interviews the author gave. See also the essay by Sims in this volume: 'Heroic Biographies of Cú Chulainn and Connavar in the Rigante Series'.

and Tacitus. Second, we shall look at how Romans depicted the Celtic tribes within their artificial understanding of barbarian identity. Third, this shall be applied to the world of the Rigante that Gemmell creates, by focusing on the political landscape and the character of Connavar.

Classical ethnography: Greek and Roman

Philip Freeman asks an important question concerning ancient sources and Celtic identity: '[c]an we trust these classical sources to give us a true picture of the ancient Celts?' (Freeman 2000: 22). This question casts a large shadow over the study of ancient writings, and can govern the methods of interpretation and value of the available evidence. There is an immediate temptation to either dismiss the ancient writings out of hand, as speculative efforts, or trust them too much and follow them too closely as genuine windows into the Celtic world. We either 'believe everything they say or […] believe nothing' (Freeman 2000: 22). The reality governing ancient Greek and Roman ethnographic studies is rather more complex and nuanced. While ethnographic studies are often found in ancient historical works, rather than in items specifically focused solely upon ethnography, they can serve a variety of different purposes, and can be found in other forms of writing as well. Carol Dougherty for instance has viewed Homer's *Odyssey* as an ethnographic study (2001: 3-16), and recent writings have applied ethnographic ideas on for instance Greek *polis* histories (Tober 2017: 460-84; Thomas 2019: 39-51), or widen the parameters of study beyond the established 'set-texts' (Derks and Roymans 2009; Bonfante 2011; Woolf 2011; Almagor and Skinner 2013). Skinner observes that ethnographic ideas can be found even in the Greek archaic period, and that ethnographic study 'found order and expression via a complex array of structures incorporating everything from epithets and stereotypes to amulets and the images stamped on coins' (Skinner 2012: 255). In recognizing these complexities, we can view the classical writings on others as forming a crucial component not just in describing different peoples, but by its very nature creating a sense of embryonic identity. The crucial connection lies not only with identity politics, but rather the historical method, and the creation of complex narratives in the ancient material. While physical artefacts, and poetic works, undoubtedly present ethnographical perspectives, the most familiar examples are found as digressions within wider historical works (e.g. Ford 2020: 29-39). These can help create the sense of otherness, and in one sense tell us as much about the writer themselves (their preconceptions), and the literary form itself. When approaching classical ethnography we must draw upon the ancient historians, and recognize how and why they provide these moments of digression, and the wider objectives they can serve (see Dench 2005; Woolf 2011; Maas 2012: 60–91). They are bound by tradition, and yet that does not devalue their usefulness, it simply means, as Freeman tells us, that we 'must be careful not to treat all the classical sources on the Celts equally' and that we must consider the 'background, motives, and sources of each author' (2000: 28).

The Greek world was a divided one. Although the various *poleis* shared cultural connections, religious practices and spoke the same language, they were often deeply divided and found themselves in conflict with their neighbours. The *poleis* were 'involved in an unrelenting cycle of high-stakes poker games' where they sought '*proteion* (first place) in a wider narrative of rank, and that rank was formed by a quest for prestige and honour' (Smart 2020a: 256). Christian Meier writes of the Greek world as a 'unified whole', recognizing the shared social practices, architectural style and pursuit of excellence in all things: '[f]rom the Crimea to Africa, from Marseilles to Cyprus, the Greeks were one people' (1999: 115, 116). This shared identity only ever manifested itself when placed in opposition to other peoples. The sense of Hellenism could only overcome the many different rivalries and quarrels of the *poleis* when forced, by war, to see up close a non-Greek enemy. While scholars have rightly challenged a simplistic teleological narrative of identity, it is difficult to ignore the changes wrought upon Greece by the Persian Wars.[4] In part because of the joint efforts made to defend Hellas from their enemies, we begin to see a much greater recognition of some kind of shared identity, Panhellenism. This built not just on facile acknowledgement of similarities between *poleis* (which could still be, and often were, divided by constitutional variances), but instead on the gulf that separated their world, their way of life, and that of the barbarians. The Persians gave the Greeks an opportunity to see their world anew, and to reform pre-existing stereotypes and attitudes. Initially, the separation had been focused on linguistic grounds, those who spoke Greek and those who did not. The word itself in Greek is meant to imply nonsense sounds, for instance *barbarophonoi* in the *Iliad* (Isaac 2014: 117–37). The success in the Persian wars, against the odds, embellished this, creating a sense of political and military superiority over the Persians, and branding them as a hostile people. This elevated wider

---

[4] Skinner's final chapter is particularly useful here, and as he writes: 'It has been argued both that there was a significant quantity of ethnographic activity prior to the Persian Wars and that the information thus generated was actively employed in discourses of identity and difference' (2012: 242). See also Hall (1989).

Greek culture, at the expense of the barbarian world. It is here that we find the indication that to be Greek is 'good' and a part of laudable civilized landscape, and to be a barbarian is to be lesser, weaker and inferior. This was grounded further in a celebration of Greek freedom and law.

Herodotus and Thucydides are the two most important Greek historians, and they allow us a window into contemporary attitudes towards ethnography and thoughts on barbarians. Herodotus writes of the Persian Wars, while Thucydides, his younger contemporary, focused on the Great Peloponnesian War between Athens and Sparta.[5] Both writers include crucial insights into how the Greek world imagined and understood the barbarians beyond their lands. Herodotus makes a determined effort to write about not just Greeks, but the barbarians as well. Although regarded as the 'father of history' in one sense he is a travelling ethnographer, depicting for his audience the many peoples and lands he has visited. He provides impressionist sketches, fast-moving vignettes, that suggest and reinforce the difference between the Greek world and the barbarian. He is not naturally dismissive of, or derogatory towards the Persians, but in reality each of his discussions provides reflections of the Greek world. This has been very well explored by Hartog (1988). Scholars have tended to see impartiality or neutrality in his depiction of Greek and barbarian, and certainly later Greek writers thought he was too kind to the barbarians. He recounts one episode that demonstrates cultural difference, but also the ignorance of the barbarian king Darius, who asks first the Greeks and then the Indians what it would cost to perform each others' burial rights at 3.38 (burning or eating the dead, respectively). The sense of freedom and divine justice emerge quite strongly (Herodotus 1972: 8.142–4, 7.139), when the Athenians, for instance, react so strongly at the Persian messenger (and the doubting Spartans), when the Spartans refuse to bow upon the floor before Xerxes (*proskynesis*). It is the same two Spartans, willing to die for their *polis*, who when speaking to Hydarnes, a Persian satrap, say that he understands only slavery, and not freedom, and that he cannot know whether it 'tastes sweet or bitter', and it is the Spartan Pausanius who refuses to imitate the brutal violence that the Persian meted out upon the body of Leonidas after victory at Plataea (7.135.6, 9.78–9). Finally, even though Herodotus is providing depictions of the *erga* (great deeds) of both Greek and barbarian, he makes it clear that the barbarian world can be, and should be, placed into the pattern of Greek thought and in particular Greek myth. There are moments

---

[5] The scholarship on both Herodotus and Thucydides is vast. A useful starting point for Herodotus is Dewald and Marincola (2006). For Thucydides, see Tsakmakis and Rengakos (2006).

in his ethnographic surveys and historical recollections that demonstrate how the world of the barbarian can be absorbed by the great Greek concept of the past. When the leaders of Argos are considering whether to fight alongside the Spartans against Persia, Xerxes sends them a letter suggesting a shared heritage (Herodotus 1972: 7. 150–2). When he recounts the origins of Scythia, Herodotus gives the audience two competing narratives (before he offers his own historical interpretation), first the Scythian perspective, and then the Greek. What is so arresting here is that in both it is the Greek mythological framework that provides the foundational narrative, for the Scythians it is Targitaus, the son of Zeus that is their progenitor; for the Greeks it is Heracles (Herodotus 1972: 4.5–4.8). Kostas Vlassopoulos has noted instances of shared morality between the Greek and barbarian worlds (2013: 200). It is worth recognizing, however, that this is still favourable towards the Greek sensibility and moral compass; and, if anything, suggests some surprise that it can be found beyond Hellas.

Thucydides is reacting in part against the style of history that Herodotus pursued, and his focus is the great conflict between leading Greek powers of their age: Athens and Sparta. Nonetheless he speaks of barbarians throughout his work, most often presenting them in a derogatory and dismissive manner. He recognizes that in the time of Homer there was no distinction between Greek and barbarian but his narrative very quickly presents a sense of alterity and polarity (e.g. Thucydides 1972: 1.3). He suggests that there are similarities between the archaic (read less civilized) way of life and how barbarians still behaved. This of course carries with it a pejorative and prejudiced preconception (Thucydides 1972: 1.6). When he writes of the Eurytanians, he notes that of all the local (non-Greek) dialects it is the most incomprehensible, they live in unfortified villages and they 'are said to eat raw flesh' (Thucydides 1972: 3.94). Each of these is a sharp opposite of Greek norms, and carries a strong sense of cultural superiority. Later, he singles out the Thracians for their bloodlust, because they slaughtered not just the enemy soldiers, but women, children and any living creature that could be found, including the beasts of burden: '[t]hese Thracians are as bloodthirsty as any other barbarian race' (Thucydides 1972: 7.29). They may in fact be the most murderous of all barbarians; but they are just an example of a wider foreign body that behave in ways that undermine Greek *nomos*, and elevate the Greek way of life. Thucydides builds upon the perspective found in Herodotus of polarity and difference; but also, because of the nature of the war that is his focus, the dissonance and erosion of societal norms. A reading of Thucydides *The Peloponnesian War* can allow for an awareness of the barbarization of Greek society; this was a conflict where Athenians and

Spartans began to ignore the norms of Greek warfare, and act in a manner the writer expects of Thracians and other barbarians. The ethnographic attitude of the Greeks created a homogeneous unity through seeing the perceived abject differences to be found in barbarian culture. Moreover, they interpreted the world beyond their borders through the lens of their own myth and history, and with Thucydides a focus ever more on the depravity and violence of the barbarian peoples. This was the backdrop against which Roman writers were working; and it is from the Greek concept of historical writing and ethnographic observation that the Romans viewed their own barbarians.

It can be difficult to think of Rome without the barbarians, so integral did they become in shaping ancient attitudes of political dominance and rule. In one sense the relationship of Rome and the barbarian world beyond determined its political survival, and its ultimate demise. For Rome to shine so bright in the writings of ancient authors and nineteenth-century historians, there needed to be a counterweight, a darkness; and this was of course to be found in the barbarian world. The core essence of Roman ethnographic writing is the difference between themselves and their sometime allies and often enemies. Time and again the Latin writings provide a nuanced interpretation of Roman identities, but in so doing create an image of the outside world that is stark, simple and grey. They induce homogeneity in peoples where there was none, and they interpret this world through the expected prism of classical ethnography, namely who and what the Greek writers before them had written. Thomas Burns surmises: '[a]ncient ethnographers, like ancient historians, employed a dichotomy between civilized and uncivilized, urban civilization and barbarians, as a basic tool in their analyses' (2003: 3). This dichotomy was simplistic, and designed to reveal the greater complexity and nuance of Roman civilization. It played against the rhetorical backdrop of the conquered and conqueror; but it was a crucial part of Roman political authority. In Virgil's *Aeneid*, the Romans are entrusted with *imperium sine fine*, an empire without end. This in turn was built upon the command to rule, to bring order, and to 'battle down the proud' (Virgil 2008: 6).

Caesar provides one of the most extensive depictions of a barbarian world gradually taken under the Roman banner. One of the great self-promoters of the dying years of Roman republican government, Caesar recorded his own account of his victories in Gaul; and thus gives us the most complete Roman perspective on the world of barbarian Europe (see for instance Krebs 2017). In his *Germania*, Tacitus refers to Caesar as 'the greatest of authorities' on Gaul (1970: 28), and Suetonius also speaks of *De Bello Gallico*'s great acclaim (56). Andrew Riggsby notes that '[t]he role of a propagandistic text like the *De Bello Gallico* [...] is, then, not so much to legitimate particular campaigns as to reinforce the worldview in which their legitimacy will be taken for granted' (2006: 45). The image of barbarians in Caesar's writing presents the favoured juxtaposition of Roman and non-Roman seen so often in historical and ethnographic writings. It contains familiar tropes that echo both his own immediate literary environment, and the deeper historical backdrop. Johnstone writes that 'both the barbarian other and the Roman self are subject to the author's power of (re)presentation' (2017: 81). Moreover, '[t]he Gauls and the Germans become integral parts of his own image and his own world view' (Smart 2019).

Caesar's image of the barbarians begins with a falsehood that adds rhetorical flavour to his piece and weight to the many great victories that he and his forces pursue: he speaks of Gaul as one, divided between three peoples (see e.g. Riggsby 2017). This, it becomes almost immediately clear, is an artificial sense of unity, not realized until much later in his conquests, under the leadership of Vercingetorix (1982: 1.1). In the opening lines he also presents a familiar Roman moral reading: '[t]he Belgae are the bravest of the three peoples, being farthest removed from the highly developed civilization of the Roman Province, least often visited by merchants with enervating luxuries for sale, and nearest to the Germans across the Rhine, with whom they are continually at war' (1982: 1.1). The barbarians can be both primitive and pure, but behind it all is Caesar's awareness of Rome's absolute dominance and mastery. In all interactions with non-Romans, Caesar operates from a position of strength and dominance, victor and arbiter, commander and conqueror (Burns 2003: 116).[6] In book 2, Caesar demonstrates the superiority of the Roman military machine, and the gulf between the Gauls and the Romans. The Belgae, regarded as great warriors and intimidating fighters, are defeated through their own inability to match Roman discipline. They break camp just before midnight 'amid great uproar and confusion, without any proper order of discipline' (1982: 2.11). Expecting a trick, Caesar waits until his scouts tell him that it is a genuine flight, and then he dispatches his forces; the rear-guard fight with courage, while the rest of the Belgae flee to their death: '[t]hus our troops were able, without any risk, to kill as many of them as there was time to kill'. After this bloody deed is done, the Roman soldiers 'returned to camp in accordance with their orders' (1982: 2.11). This is a celebration of some gallantry shown on the part of the barbarian forces, but serves as mirror on Roman strength and order.

[6] In writing of those barbarians who do surrender a particular formula is used time and again: '*traditis in deditionem accepit*'. This reinforced Roman notions of power and authority, and the integration of barbarians into the Roman world.

Caesar paints an image of varying shades of barbarian identity and leans heavily on pre-existing genre expectations. In freeing a Roman captive (Valerius Procillus), Caesar learns that his German captors had chanced fate in deciding whether he should be burned to death or executed at a later date (1982: 1.53). This violent undertone marries uncomfortably with a barbarian focus on freedom. The battle that sees Caesar rescue his friend also allows him to witness the wives of those enemy warriors 'who as the men marched to battle stretched out their hands and implored them with tears not to let them be enslaved by the Romans' (1982: 1.51). Much later, in a moment of *oratio recta*, Critognatus delivers a powerful rhetorical performance that Caesar believes should be documented 'for its unparalleled cruelty and wickedness' (1982: 7.77). Here the barbarian speaker discussed Rome as envious, keen to enslave them all, and that 'this is how they have always treated conquered enemies' (1982: 7.77). The focus on freedom is a point of separation; but even here in a speech that Caesar derides as malicious, in reality it just stressed the dominance of Rome. For Caesar, then, the barbarians are enemies *and* friends, lesser figures who exist both in the reality he sees around him, and the imagined literary world of ethnographic treatise.

Tacitus is one of the most significant Roman historians, and one who had an interest in people beyond the Roman world. In both the *Germania* and the *Agricola* he paints an image of the non-Roman world. He also celebrates the fraught nobility and primitive virtues that he witnessed in these lands. The *Germania* is unique as the only surviving Latin piece devoted to a single non-Roman body of people (see Thomas 2010). Victoria Pagán has shown that there are elements in the *Germania* that reflect the 'more latent concerns about the erosion of Roman identity' (2017: 81). The *Germania* tells us just as much about Rome as the barbarians Tacitus is writing about: '[t]he identity of the Other [...] is developed through a carefully crafted series of antitheses with the Romans' (Pagán 2017: 82). Tacitus identifies their gods as Roman; Mercury is the god they worship above all others, with human sacrifice. Hercules and Mars feature too, and the Egyptian cult of Isis is seen in one tribe. The origins of the Germans are speculated to belong to the travels both of Hercules and Odysseus. Tacitus places his discussions of these people within a pre-existing framework of classical repertoire and understanding. Their land is unforgiving and hard, which in turn breeds warriors of skill, and inspires a purity that he admires greatly (Tacitus 1970: 9). This, of course, is an attack upon the vices that he sees crippling the Roman world of his own day; the audience are expected to recognize the moral failings around them (e.g. Tacitus 1970: 18–20). This is not however an idyll or utopia. Some of the peoples he describes are 'savage and disgustingly poor', and he is unafraid of criticizing their customs and way of life (Tacitus 1970: 46). Tacitus also reinforces the sense of homogeneity in the world beyond Rome: 'their physical characteristics, in so far as one can generalize about such a population, are always the same' (Tacitus 1970: 4). The people thus tend to have 'fierce-looking blue eyes, reddish hair, and big frames', and '[t]hey are less able to endure toil or fatiguing tasks and cannot bear thirst or heat, though their climate has inured then to cold spells and the poverty of their soil to hunger' (Tacitus 1970: 4). Although providing an important window into the lands of the Germans, this is not an eyewitness account. Instead, it is based on pre-existing writings, rather than travel, and echoes the models found in the earlier Latin and Greek writings. It reinforces the sense of 'us' and 'them'; a dichotomous relationship that ignores the realities of ancient inter-state relationships. Although the best of Roman historians, Tacitus is still unable to break away from the pre-existing models of ethnographic thought.

Both Tacitus and Caesar, therefore, are representing the derivative nature of Roman ethnographic discourse within historical writing. Tacitus uses Caesar, as Caesar uses earlier pieces (see e.g. Shuttleworth Kraus 2017: 282–8). There are similarities in language, most tellingly in their opening lines (*Germania omnis/Gallia est omnis divisa*), but also in how they frame the peoples beyond the Roman world. Tacitus is rather more subtle and gifted a writer, using barbarians as a way to attack the excesses of imperial rule, but both draw upon a standard toolkit of ancient ethnography. They are seeking to create an 'other', in opposition to their own world and their own people. Herodotus separated people between *ethnē* and *genē* (people and tribes), and this was grounded in specific geography (see Geary 2002: 43–9; Rood 2006). In the Latin writings they use *populus* and *gentes*, placing people within specific spatial constructs. Ethnographic digression became an established component in wider historical writings, when those writings discussed non-Roman peoples. Sallust, the great historian of the first century BCE, interrupts the narrative of *The Jugurthine War* to provide 'a brief exposition of the geography of Africa and some mention of those peoples with whom we have fought wars or made alliances' (2010: 17.1). Both Tacitus and Caesar pause in their narratives to digress upon the geography and culture of peoples: Caesar at 6.3 and 6.4 and Tacitus at 10–13 of his *Agricola*. All three make use of speeches or the words of Roman enemies, which of course may be nothing more than the imaginings of the Romans rather than reflecting any genuine barbarian voice.[7]

---

[7] Sallust (2010: 4.69) (Letter of Mithridates); Caesar (1982: 7.77) and Tacitus (1970: 30.5). On this as a wider area of study, see Adler (2011).

Patrick Geary has shown that even later Roman writers who had dealings with, and personal knowledge of, the barbarian groupings still used the same language and ideas of their Greek and Latin forebears. He discusses Ammianus Marcellinus, Procopius and Priscus, who 'sensed the contradictions between the received tradition and their own personal experiences with the barbarian peoples', and yet 'could not free themselves from the assumptions of classical ethnography' (Geary 2002: 56, 57). They simplified and homogenized, writing for an audience that expected certain tropes and descriptions. The weight of intellectual tradition thus restricts the nature of classical ethnography.

The Celts in the Roman histories

The Celtic tribes loomed large in the weight of Roman historical memory, well before Caesar's conquests. Around 390 BCE, a vast army marched upon Rome. These warriors were filled with rage, on the quest for vengeance, and destroyed all who stood before them (see Livy 1967: 5.37). They smashed aside the Roman forces arrayed beside the Allia, sending the Romans fleeing for their lives. They reached the city by night-fall, their voice and songs like the cry of wolves in the hunt (Livy 1967: 5.39). The population still in the city retreated to the Capitol, to save their lives before the barbarian onslaught. Some of the more august senators and nobility returned to their homes, to die as models of Roman virtue. Livy tells us that those Romans watching from the relative safety of the citadel 'could hardly believe their eyes or ears as they looked down on the barbaric foe roaming in hordes through the familiar streets' (5.42). This became a defining moment, a crucial foundation stone upon which the Romans would develop their sense of historical identity. The sack of the city by barbarian forces created an image in Roman minds of the Gauls, and through them the Celtic tribes, as the most fearsome of barbarians: '[t]he Romans of the Republic carried with them the memory of the Gallic sack of the city in the fourth century BCE, and their own near demise at the hands of their enemies' (Smart 2020b: 314).

There is an issue here regarding historical definitions of people. The modern terminology of Celt and Celtic comes from the Latin *Celti* and through that the Greek *Keltoi* (Sims-Williams 1998: 21–9; Fimi 2017: 7–15). Ancient writers referred to various peoples we might consider part of a shared Celtic culture as *Galli*, *Galatai* and *Celtiberi*. The division between *Celti* and *Germani* can appear both vast and negligible, with the two belonging simply to a wider barbarian world separate from Rome. Dimitra Fimi has noted that '[t]here is no evidence that the people for whom the classical authors used these terms ever called themselves "Celts" or even saw themselves as one people or ethnic group' (2017: 9). Sims-Williams writes that the actual Latin and Greek words reflect 'a map of the distribution of classical terms' rather than the self-perception of those discussed (1998: 25). This chapter will use 'Celtic tribes' and will be sensitive to the distinctions between them.

Caesar and Tacitus provide detailed depictions of the Celtic tribes. If we focus on Tacitus' *Agricola* we are given a stirring examination of barbarous nobility, freedom and the costs of opposing Rome. Tacitus provides speculative origins for the Britons based on their physical characteristics. Those Caledonians to the north, because of their red hair and large build, must be German, and those he calls the Silures because of their hair style and skin colour (and that they live opposite Spain) must in turn mean that they are Spanish in origin. Finally, those he is most familiar with (in the south), he argues, are very similar (if not the same) to those tribes found in Gaul. This image is unimaginative, descriptive and erroneous. However, very quickly, it becomes clear that the Celts of Britain are superior to others; the most noble of the barbarians. Although their language is similar to the Gauls, with similar courage in facing adversity, in the *Agricola* it is the Britons who 'show more spirit' (Tacitus 1970: 11). For they are still willing to make war, and they have not become enervated by luxury and peace. Of the Gauls Tacitus writes that 'their valour perished with their freedom' (Tacitus 1970: 11). Militarily they are strong and courageous. They are in the main infantry forces, although certain aristocrats fight from chariots. They are divided, lacking in unified leadership, and as willing to fight against one another as they are the invading Romans (Tacitus 1970: 12). His depiction of the landscape laments the rain and mists, but there is no harsh winter that we find in his depiction of Germania. The Britons appear then both more noble than their Celtic kin on the continent; and yet less fearsome than the German tribes beyond the Rhine. These are figures Tacitus is comfortable describing, albeit in part erroneously, and a people he celebrates for their virtues and their failings. He recognizes in them willingness to submit to certain governmental pressures (e.g. military service and payment of tribute), but will not countenance any form of abuse: 'they are broken in to obedience, but not as yet slavery' (Tacitus 1970: 13). In his discussion of the Boudicca revolt, he paints an image of Roman excess, and Celtic unwillingness to bow to yet further injustices. In an odd *oratio recta* from an unnamed Briton, the speaker compares his people with the Germans who successfully beat back the Romans: '[s]uch thoughts prompted the Germans to throw off the yoke; and they have only a river, not the Ocean, to shield them'

(Tacitus 1970: 15). This is a heavily Romanized rhetorical speech that serves to invite comparisons between Rome and the 'other', rather than speaking to true Celtic anger at the attack upon Boudicca and her daughters. Tacitus' father-in-law restores order, brings law and justice, and pushes the Celts further north, deep into Caledonia. The tribes of the north coalesce around one of the leaders, Calgacus, a man of great courage and conviction (Tacitus 1970: 29). He delivers a stirring speech to the assembled warriors (Tacitus imagines they are 30,000 strong). He speaks of the 'dawn of liberty', and refers to all those around them as the 'last of the free'. The Romans are avaricious, greedy and violent, 'they make a desert and call it peace' (Tacitus 1970: 30).[8] The strength of the Roman army is found in the weakness of their enemies, not the strength of their military machine. Those who now follow them will rise up against them, if the warriors are victorious against Agricola's forces: 'The [enslaved/allied] Britons will recognize our cause as their own; the Gauls will remember their lost liberty; the rest of the Germans will desert them' (Tacitus 1970: 32). Again in direct speech a now named leader refers to other elements of the Barbarian world as though he belongs to a wide sea of non-Roman peoples. Before battle commences Agricola addresses his troops, and challenges the claims of Calgacus. These are just robbers stealing forth in the night, runaways and cowards. All the courageous Britons have fought and lost, and these fight from fear; not for freedom. The battle goes as expected. These brave warriors fall to the ranks of the legionaries, and their allies, and Agricola is victorious once more: '[a]n awful silence reigned on every hand: the hills were deserted, houses smoking in the distance, and our scouts did not meet a soul' (Tacitus 1970: 38). This victory is absolute in the eyes of Tacitus, and Agricola's earlier plans of 'social betterment'; bath, temple, public squares, liberal arts, arcades and banquets can continue. The Britons believed this to be a form of civilization, but it was 'only a feature of their enslavement' (Tacitus 1970: 21). This is a study of freedom, power and in part reflecting upon the tyranny of Domitian. It is a study of freedom and virtue, seen through two interconnected worlds.

In his *commentarii*, Caesar writes of the Gauls and their way of life (see Haywood 2014: 62–72). He establishes the strong internal rivalry within tribes and families, and implies a rudimentary client relationship (e.g. 1982: 6.11). His arrival upset the balance of power, previously between the Aedui and Sequani, with the Sequani ascendant because of German allies. Beyond this political image,

---

[8] This speech by Calgacus can be compared to other speeches by barbarian leaders in Roman historiography. A good example is the speech by Mithridates in Trogus' work. See Smart (2020c).

Caesar writes that there are only two classes worth discussing: the druids and the knights. This simplified dichotomy no doubt conceals a much greater social complexity than is visible here; but both are important aspects of the Celtic world according to Caesar. The druids do not appear to oppose him in any great way, but instead perform the integral tasks of social life throughout the many tribes. They are religious leaders, judges, and what they decide has lasting impact throughout the Celtic world: '[a]ny individual or tribe failing to accept their award is banned from taking part in sacrifice – the heaviest punishment that can be inflicted upon a Gaul' (1982: 6.11). They are thus poisoned individuals, shunned by all, fearing that any conversation or interaction will spread the polluted miasma. It is the Druids that perform the human sacrifices. The Gauls have 'regular state sacrifices' and some groups 'have colossal images of wickerwork, the limbs of which they fill with living men; they are then set on fire, and the victims burnt to death' (1982: 6.16; see also Webster 1999). Caesar then places their pantheon of gods into the familiar Roman religious construct (Mercury, Mars, Jupiter, etc.), but notes that they believe themselves descended from Father Dis, a spirit of darkness, and therefore they ordered their lives by night and not day. The interaction of fathers and sons appears strict, as does the threat of capital and corporal punishment. The knights are aristocrats, suggesting perhaps a more nuanced and oligarchic network of power, and Crumley has observed that 'individual and collective wealth was distributed both extensively and intensively across the landscape, and individuals [...] could exercise considerable power in the absence of the control of the chief *oppidum*' (1995: 28).

In the main body of his narrative Caesar also gives us more information, noting the importance of *oppida*, fortified settlements that dominated the lived Celtic environment (see Dietler 1998). In one of his two forays to Britain, he remarks of the shared Celtic cultural traits. It has a significant population, with 'the ground thickly studded with homesteads, closely resembling those of Gaul, and the cattle very numerous' (1982: 5.12). The people live on milk and meat, and dress in animal skins. Every Celtic Briton, according to Caesar, dye their bodies blue, and the men leave only their upper lip unshaven (1982: 5.14 and 4.33). There is a grudging admiration for the enemy cavalry and charioteers, and the Britons appear similar to (if somewhat more exotic than) their counterparts across the water. Caesar also presents differences within Gaul: the Nervii appear moderate and determined, whereas the Helvetii are slippery and suspicious (1982: 2.17 and 1.1–3). Caesar develops the most comprehensive depiction of the Celtic world; but of course we must remember that this is his Roman, classically controlled image of the people he sees.

The Romanized Rigante

The world of the Rigante exists on two levels. The first, and most obvious, is in the romanticized realm of Celtic myth, explored by Sims in this volume (e.g. through the creation of complex characters and heroic individuals). The names, the magic and the focus on nature are deliberate echoes of an imagined Irish, Welsh and Scottish tradition. The otherworldly nature of spirits and deities, the sense of harmony and peace with the land and the enduring heroic culture can be found in nineteenth-century versions of the Irish *Táin Bó Cuailnge* and the Welsh *Mabinogion*. Dimitra Fimi has exposed how fragile the relationship can be between this romanticized image and the mediaeval manuscripts, and the Rigante can be certainly viewed through this lens (Fimi 2017: 7–8, 10–11). However, beyond this first level of world-creation, the Rigante rests on foundations formed not in medieval myth or nineteenth-century Romanticism but rather classical ethnography. This world is built from the ground up along the plans of Caesar and Tacitus. The Keltoi of *Sword in the Storm* and *Midnight Falcon* may appear deeply mythological, but are historical creations, drawn from ancient writings. They reflect not only classical perspectives on the ancient Celts, but also Roman and Greek attitudes towards barbarians.

First and foremost, the world of the Keltoi reflects the simplified dichotomy that existed within classical writings: the complexity of Rome and Greece in contrast to the homogeneous simplicity beyond its borders. Throughout *Sword in the Storm*, Gemmell paints an image of a barbarian world that is unified alongside cultural and ethnic similarities. This is a world of many tribes, but who all recognize a shared bond: '[l]ike all the Keltoi race, the Rigante were a passionate and volatile people, and there were often fights among them' (Gemmell 1999: 145). This becomes a recurring theme throughout the narrative. When Connavar wishes to provide a captive to the Stone general Jasaray, the Gath he is fighting alongside refuses, because the 'man is Keltoi' and although he is not of his tribe, there is a shared bond between them (Gemmell 1999: 276). Carac, the king of the Perdii, has aspirations for his people 'to be pre-eminent among the Keltoi' (Gemmell 1999: 285), still reinforcing that cultural and ethnic unity. Connavar upon his return to the lands of his people warns would-be robbers that he does not wish to 'spill more Keltoi blood' (Gemmell 1999: 308), while his stepfather Ruathain attempts to resolve a blood feud through the gift of cattle '[a] gesture of respect and in keeping with the traditions of the Keltoi' (Tacitus 1970: 21; Gemmell 1999: 300). When faced by the possibility of collusion between the Pannone and warriors from beyond the sea, Connavar maintains that they are still Keltoi, and may be in need of aid (Gemmell 1999: 451). This characterization of a shared Celtic tradition and identity is born not in Celtic mythology, history or archaeology; but rather the ancient writings of Caesar and Tacitus (Fimi 2017: 7–15).

The lived world of the Rigante, the settlements, the cultural traits, the way they dress and the way they fight come from classical interpreters. The small village of Three Streams, paying homage and loyalty to the Laird of Old Oaks, fits into the pattern of governance seen in both Caesar and Tacitus. Old Oakes is an *oppidum*, a hilltop fort that provides the sense of leadership in the Rigante world (Gemmell 1982: 7.16–20; 1999: 159–70). The Perdii paint themselves in red ochre before war; in Caesar the Britons paint themselves blue instead (1982: 5.15, 4.33). The feuding and the internal conflicts of the Fisher Laird, and Connavar's rivalry with Fiallach and Govannan, are built upon ancient perspectives of barbarian culture (1982: 6.11; Tacitus 1970: 21; Gemmell 1999: 300 and 323). Valanus laments Keltoi battle tactics: '[t]hey attack in vast numbers, expecting to overwhelm us. It is the only way they know how to fight. There is no real organization, no officers, no clearly defined command structure. Their battle plan is always the same: there is the enemy go charge them and see what happens' (Gemmell 1999: 273). Banouin, a former Stone general (once teacher to Jasaray), and now a travelling merchant, provides a similar image: '[l]ike all the tribespeople I have met, here and beyond the water, you fight largely without armour. You fall upon the enemy in great numbers and each battle breaks down into a thousand skirmishes between heroes' (Gemmell 1999: 141–2). In his *Agricola*, Tacitus tells us that the Roman soldiers

> obedient to orders, rode round from the front of the battle and fell upon the enemy in the rear. The open plain now presented a grim, awe-inspiring spectacle [...] On the British side, each man now behaved according to his character. Whole groups, though they had weapons in their hands, fled before inferior numbers; elsewhere unarmed men deliberately charged to face certain death.
> (Tacitus 1970: 13, see also *Germania*: 6)

The Perdii forces are an avalanche of human activity, the perfect example of the Celtic war machine in Roman eyes. Furthermore, king Carac fights from upon a chariot, as the classical writings tell us was the norm for the Celtic aristocracy (Tacitus 1970: 36; Caesar 1982: 4.24; Gemmell 1999: 285).

In questions of religion and law, the druids of the Rigante are the living embodiments of those found in Caesar. Although there is no human sacrifice here (instead that belongs to execution devoid of religious formula), it is the druid and the local lord that mete out punishment and justice. In one scene Brother Solstice questions a man accused of rape and murder. He does so through an ability to see the emotions and souls of those he talks to, and is the only figure who can ascertain the truth of the man's words (Gemmell 1999: 159–66; 327–8). This whole display reinforces Caesar's description of the druids as those who 'act as judges in practically all disputes' (1982: 6.13). In another example of legal practice, the guilty party's legs were bound together, hands tied, and he was cast into the bog: '[t]he murky waters had swiftly closed over his head, his body floating down to join the other murders in the silt below' (Gemmell 1999: 328). This of course provides an interpretation of archaeological finds (e.g. Cashel Man, Lindow Man, Old Croghan Man, etc.), but still places them within the parameters of classical ethnography: '[t]hey think the gods prefer the execution of men taken in the act of theft or brigandage, or guilty of some offence' (Caesar 1982: 6.16).

The empire of Stone and the world of the Keltoi are presented as opposites, reinforcing the ideas of classical ethnography. The Gath leader Ostaran is presented as the opposite of the imperial general Valanus in the bathhouse, unaccustomed to the luxuries of civilization (Gemmell 1999: 232–6). This is delivered through the perspective of the Stone general, and reflects Roman writings and concerns. Earlier, the Stone merchant and former general Banouin in a moment of introspection recognizes his strong feelings for the Keltoi: '[h]e loved these mountains with a passion he had not believed possible [...] He admired them and the shrewd simplicity of their lives. He thought of his own people, and it was if a chill wind blew across his skin' (Gemmell 1999: 52). Banouin is one of the more sympathetic interpreters of Keltoi culture, but he cannot see beyond those inherited prejudices of civilized and barbarian. While he may provide a bridge between these two worlds, he nonetheless remains a product of the ancient past. He is a mentor to Connavar and teaches him the language and ways of Stone. In one sense he is almost a Tacitus and Caesar figure himself, providing a classical ethnographic treatise upon the Rigante. At the Feast of Beltine, 'Banouin watched the scene with both affection and envy. The closeness of the Rigante, their easy tactility, their obvious enjoyment in each other's company was good to see, yet it was a joy he could not share', for he 'was a solitary man, not given to any form of tribalism' (Gemmell 1999: 171; see also 140–3). He remains the 'foreigner', and if war does reach the Rigante he tells Connavar that he will head west, to 'fabulous lands, rich and fertile' (Gemmell 1999: 142). He knows, just as Tacitus does, the terrible cost of defeat for those barbarians who fight against the legions: 'Across the water Banouin had witnessed the aftermath of a great battle, the bodies of thousands of young Keltoi tribesmen – men like Ruathain and Connavar – being dragged to a great burial pit. Thousands more had been captured and sold into slavery' (Tacitus 1970: 38; Gemmell 1999: 52; Tacitus 2008: 14.37). He provides a meeting point between Rigante and Stone; but is the embodiment of Republican virtue, an idealized Roman, like Tacitus' Agricola, whose 'mind was full of abstracts: honour, nobility, courage, conscience' (Gemmell 1999: 265; see also Balmaceda 2017).

This separation manifests in another way as well: the simplified idealization of a 'pure' barbarian world, a familiar tenet of the ancient writings. In a discussion between the laird and the druid, both turn to think on the nature of the Rigante, in contrast to those of Stone. The laird says that he had always believed his people special, and better than the foreigners, but he now questions that conviction. Brother Solstice's response is pure Tacitus: 'I have travelled as far as Stone. Everywhere there are criminals and outlaws, killers, rapists, and seducers. Everywhere. In the large cities crimes against people take place almost hourly […] we live in relative harmony with our neighbours' (Gemmell 1999: 328; see also Lavan 2011). When pressed further the druid responds again '[m]aggots will always enter some fruit – even on the finest tree' (Gemmell 1999: 329). After the defeat of the Perdii, Connavar finds himself empty, vengeance sated, 'thinking of the green hills of the Rigante, the towering snow peaks of Caer Druagh, and the gentle pace of life in Three Streams' (Gemmell 1999: 292). This also echoes the romanticized image of the nineteenth century where Fimi has shown 'Wales and Scotland in particular were admired for their wild landscapes and the wistful echoes of their "lost" cultures' (Fimi 2017: 11).

The character of Connavar is the guiding force of *Sword in the Storm*. In one sense he appears a mirror of Cú Chulainn, a great warrior without compare, fraught in love and life, but a hero like no other. There is a deliberate effort to match aspects of the narrative to the legends of Ireland's most famed mythic warrior. The battle against the bear, that so defines the young Connavar, finds sharp parallel with an episode in the life of Cú Chulainn (Gemmell 1999: 103–11). So too both suffer from terrible fits of rage of anger; Connavar after the death of his friend and mentor Banouin, and also after his infidelity and the death of his wife Tae, and Cú Chulainn outside Emain Macha and in the fight with his son (Gemmell 1999: 223–4, 429–32). Although this rage can be viewed as *ríastrad*, as Sims argues in this volume, it also can be seen as a representation of barbarian characters seen in the ancient writings. The relationship with the Morrígan although different is a crucial part of both characters' journeys. Likewise, both must take care lest they break their *gessi* (sing. *geis*) for Connavar the killing of a dog; for Cú Chulainn the eating of dog meat. Gemmell modifies the term slightly to '*geasa*' (pl. '*geasas*'), but the meaning is the same, that of a prohibited act (Charles-Edwards 1999; Williams 2016: 23). Williams explores this through *fír flathemon,* 'a just equilibrium in which the ruler's righteousness is reflected in the success of his reign' (Williams 2016: 23; see Gemmell 1999: 178).

In truth however, this is only one possible comparison, and just one part of the patchwork cloak that informs and shapes the Rigante leader. The character of Connavar, although no doubt inspired and guided by Cú Chulainn, very firmly belongs to the Roman concept of a virtuous barbarian leader. He is part Vercingetorix and part Calgacus (but more successful than either): a product of both Caesar and Tacitus. Vercingetorix's rebellion against Rome has entered the canon of French history, much as Boudicca's revolt has in Britain (Bianchini 1994; Gillespie 2018). The presentation by Caesar of this Gallic leader is deployed of course to demonstrate his own, and thus Rome's, superiority over the barbarians. However, he still creates a noble military figure. The leader of the Rigante owes much to Caesar's Vercingetorix: 'a very powerful young Arvernian' who challenged the people 'to take up arms for the freedom of Gaul' (1982: 7.4). Declared king soon after, Caesar tells us he 'secured the support of the Senones, Parisii, Cardurci, Turoni, Aulerci, Lemovices, Andes, Pictones, and all the other tribes of the west coast' (1982: 7.4). Vercingetorix focused on military preparedness, the manufacture of arms and weapons, and paid 'particular attention to the cavalry' (1982: 7.4). Facing defeat at Caesar's hand, Vercingetorix then urges a continuation of war by any means, attacking supply lines and destroying Gallic food stores to deny the enemy (1982: 7.14). He speaks with conviction and authority, and wins over the Gauls whenever his plans are opposed (e.g. 1982: 7.20). In some ways he appears to mirror Roman attitudes towards warfare, and his victories resemble Caesar's own, and speak to some degree of Romanization (Rawlings 1998). His rebellion fails, outmanoeuvred by Roman military skill, and an inability to command absolute respect from the patchwork quilt of alliances he assembles. Connavar too creates an uneasy set of alliances between different peoples, and makes determined effort to present cultural homogeneity between the 'Keltoi' people (thus reinforcing the Roman view of the Celtic world). Moreover, the tactics that he sets out to fight against Rome are taken from Vercingetorix: arms, cavalry and supply lines. In serving the army of Stone, the young Connavar on his quest for vengeance sees the strength of imperial armies, and their inherent weakness. In creating a professional army, the general Jasaray required maintenance of supply lines.[9] Moreover, upon his return to the lands of the Rigante, Connavar orders the smiths to begin work on iron shirts, asks his brother, Braefar, to solve the issue of saddle and stirrups, and finally creates through the introduction of new horse lines the Iron-Wolves, who will take the fight to the forces he knows will invade. At a base level then, Connavar is Vercingetorix, Caesar's great opponent. However, he is also Tacitus' Calgacus. In contrast to the greater characterization and military skill of Vercingetorix, the Calgacus of the *Agricola* is a shining light of barbarian virtue, who speaks only of freedom and liberty. He is rather one-dimensional, a leader we know little about, used by Tacitus to rethink Roman imperial governance, as well providing a useful counterpoint to the speech of Agricola that follows. Tacitus also makes clear that these Britons, in his description rather than the *oratio recta* of the Roman general, are likewise pure and bold: '[t]he Britons were, in fact, undaunted by the loss of the previous battle, and were ready either for revenge or enslavement' (Tacitus 1970: 29). Calgacus becomes then a physical representation of 30,000 Caledonian warriors fighting for freedom. Connavar in one sense embodies this as well. He is, as are all Gemmell's heroes, wonderfully realized and deeply flawed, but he is also more than anything the figure of resistance to Stone and any enemy of the Keltoi people. He is the voice of Calgacus amongst the Rigante, and his willingness to speak the truth as he sees it, allows Connavar to be regarded as the most noble and virtuous barbarian leader, as used by Tacitus.

The final historical character we should consider is not a Celt at all, but a German: Arminius, victor of the Teutoberg Forest, as Pagán notes, a 'Cheruscan freedom fighter' (2017: 82). This comparison echoes the lack of distinction seen in ancient Greek writings between the Celts and Germans, and the parallel between him and Connavar is perhaps the closest of the three (see Chapman 1992; Sims-Williams 1998). Arminius served the armies of Rome (as Connavar served Stone), and he learnt how to expose Roman military weakness in war.[10] A Roman citizen, a noble with equestrian rank, fluent in Latin and seemingly

---

[9] Sims has argued that the character of Jasaray is an interpretation of Julius Caesar (using Suetonius and Caesar's own writings). See Sims (2018). One aspect I had not considered was Gemmell's familiarity with Vegetius' much-lauded and long-lasting *De Re Militari*. Sims pinpoints the moment shortly before Connavar meets Jasaray (Gemmell 1999: 259) where a line is used as a teaching tool and plot device. I am grateful to Alistair J.P. Sims for sharing this with me. On the long historical importance of Vegetius, see Allmand (2011: 1–10).

[10] Goldsworthy (2016: 201–6) is a useful starting point. See also Wolters (2008), especially chapters four and five; Winkler (2015), in particular pp. 25–54 and the excellent comparison with Tolkien's work by Makins (2016: 199–240).

loyal to the Empire, Arminius led the armies of Varus into the forests and then destroyed them. So great was his victory that Goldsworthy surmises: 'the effort to conquer Germany was never renewed' (2016: 202). Tacitus writes of him in his *Annals* as a noble barbarian figure, but also one disturbingly close to, and part of, the Roman world: 'If you prefer your fatherland, your ancestors, your ancient ways to overlords and to new colonies, follow as your leader Arminius to glory and freedom rather than Segestes to ignominious slavery' (cited in Pagán 2017: 99). Tacitus writes a eulogy of the barbarian leader:

> Arminius, roused by the fact that the Romans were retreating and King Maroboduus was driven out, held sway heedless of popular liberty. He attacked with force of arms, fought with mixed success and fell by the treachery of his kinsmen. He was without a doubt the liberator of Germania and one who fought not against the emergence of the Roman people, as had other kings and generals, but against the empire at its greatest. In battle his fortunes may have varied, but in war he was never conquered. He lived 37 tears, for 12 he held power, and he is still commemorated in song among barbarian tribes. He is wholly unknown to Greek historians, who admire only their own, and not duly celebrated by Romans since we extol the past and are uninterested in recent times.
>
> (cited in Pagán 2017: 140–1)

The battle of the Teutoberg forest entered into the historical consciousness of Rome and became a principal example of the dangers facing the Empire. The Roman general Varus is mirrored strongly in Gemmell's Valanus. In the epilogue the Stone general makes the terrible mistake of responding to the Morrígan. Asked what he desires, he responds with 'fame', which of course can be both negative and positive (Gemmell 1999: 477–8). Fame he would have, but just as in Rome, where the loss of the three legions was known as the *clades Variana* (Varian disaster), so too would Valanus enter the lived memory of both Stone and the Rigante. In creating Valanus as an enemy of Connovar, we see Arminius too.

The character of Connavar reinforces the Romanized focus of Gemmell's Rigante world. He is undoubtedly a Cú Chulainn figure; but in the same breath he is also a noble barbarian opponent as understood by Roman writers and classical authors. His fight against Stone in one sense then is already lost; for in Gemmell's creation, Stone and Rome have already won. The opponent they face is the opponent that Rome always faced; a noble barbarian figure who epitomized virtues that they could admire from a distance. This is an imagined barbarian world, created by placing the Celts into a pre-existing framework of understanding, that stressed Roman superiority and dominance. There are then two Celtic worlds visible in *Sword in the Storm*, the medieval and the ancient.

Conclusion

The world of the Rigante, which owes so much to the Celtic past and Celtic peoples, in reality is a mirror not on the Celtic tribes themselves, but how the Romans saw them. This should not, in any way, belittle the excellent and compelling images that Gemmell creates throughout *Sword in the Storm*. Instead, he too is a victim of Rome, much like Connavar and his people are victims of Stone. The world he creates for them is not the Celtic past he was aiming for, but the image found in classical ethnography, most tellingly a hybrid of Caesar and Tacitus. The final thought must be that much like those ancient authors who were prisoners of their own ethnographic historical tradition, modern fantasy literature is still not fully able to break those bonds of classical learning.

References

Adler, Eric (2011), *Valorizing the Barbarians: Enemy Speeches in Roman Historiography*, Austin: University of Texas Press.

Allmand, Christopher (2011), *The De Re Militari of Vegetius, the Reception, Transmission and Legacy of a Roman Text in the Middle Ages*, Cambridge: Cambridge University Press.

Almagor, Eran, and Skinner, Joseph, eds (2013), *Ancient Ethnography: New Approaches*, London: Bloomsbury.

Balmaceda, Catalina (2017), *Virtus Romana: Politics and Morality in the Roman Historians*, Chapel Hill: University of North Carolina Press.

Bianchini, Marie-Claude, ed. (1994), *Vercingétorix et Alésia*, Paris: Editions de la Réunion des Musées Nationaux.

Bonfante, Larissa, ed. (2011), *The Barbarians of Ancient Europe: Realities and Interactions*, Cambridge: Cambridge University Press.

Burns, Thomas (2003), *Rome and the Barbarians, 100 B.C.– A.D. 400*, Baltimore: Johns Hopkins University Press.

Caesar (1982), *The Conquest of Gaul*, trans. S. A. Handford and intro. Jane Gardner, London: Penguin.

Chapman, Malcolm (1992), *The Celts, the Construction of a Myth*, London: Palgrave Macmillan.

Charles-Edwards, T. (1999), 'Geis, Prophecy, Omen, and Oath', *Celtica*, 23: 38–99.

Crumley, Carole (1995), 'Building an Historical Ecology of Gaulish Polities', in Bettina Arnold and D. Blar Gibson (eds), *Celtic Chiefdom, Celtic State: The Evolution of Complex Social Systems in Prehistoric Europe*, 26–33, Cambridge: Cambridge University Press.

Dench, Emma (2005), *Romulus' Asylum: Roman Identities from the Age of Alexander to the Age of Hadrian*, Oxford: Oxford University Press.

Derks, Ton and Roymans, Nico, eds (2009), *Ethnic Constructs in Antiquity: The Role of Power and Tradition*, Amsterdam: Amsterdam University Press.

Dewald, Carolyn and Marincola, John, eds (2006), *The Cambridge Companion to Herodotus*, Cambridge: Cambridge University Press.

Dietler, Michael (1998), 'A Tale of Three Sites: The Monumentalization of Celtic *oppida* and the Politics of Collective Memory and Identity', *World Archaeology*, 30(1): 72–89.

Dougherty, Carol (2001), *The Raft of Odysseus: The Ethnographic Imagination of Homer's Odyssey*, Oxford: Oxford University Press.

Fimi, Dimitra (2017), *Celtic Myth in Contemporary Children's Fantasy, Idealization, Identity, Ideology*, London: Palgrave Macmillan.

Ford, Randolph (2020), *Rome, China, and the Barbarians: Ethnographic Traditions and the Transformation of Empires*, Cambridge: Cambridge University Press.

Freeman, Phillip (2000), 'Classical Ethnography and the Celts: Can We Trust the Sources?' *Proceedings of the Harvard Celtic Colloquium*, 20 (21): 22–8.

Geary, Patrick (2002), *The Myth of Nations*, Princeton: Princeton University Press.

Gemmell, David (1999), *Sword in the Storm*, London: Corgi.

Gillespie, Caitlin (2018), *Boudica: Warrior Woman of Roman Britain*, Oxford: Oxford University Press.

Goldsworthy, Adrian (2016), *Pax Romana, War, Peace and Conquest in the Roman World*, New Haven and London: Yale University Press.

Hall, Edith (1989), *Inventing the Barbarian: Greek Self-Definition through Tragedy*, Oxford: Clarendon Press.

Hartog, François (1988), *The Mirror of Herodotus: The Representation of the Other in the Writing of History*, trans. Janet Lloyd, Berkeley: University of California Press.

Haywood, John (2014), *The Celts: Bronze Age to New Age*, London: Routledge.

Herodotus (1972), *The Histories*, trans. Aubrey De Sélincourt, revis. and intro. A. R. Burn, London: Penguin.

Isaac, Benjamin (2014), 'The Barbarian in Greek and Latin Literature', *Scripta Classica Israelica*, 34: 117–37.

Johnstone, Andrew (2017), 'Nostri and "The Other(s)"', in Luca Grillo and Christopher Krebs (eds), *The Cambridge Companion to the Writings of Julius Caesar*, 81–94, Cambridge: Cambridge University Press.

Krebs, Christopher (2017), 'More Than Words. The Commentarii in Their Propagandistic Context', in Luca Grillo and Christopher Krebs (eds), *The Cambridge Companion to the Writings of Julius Caesar*, 29–42, Cambridge: Cambridge University Press.

Lavan, Myles (2011), 'Slavishness in Britain and Rome in Tacitus' *Agricola*', *The Classical Quarterly*, 61 (1): 294–305.

Livy (1967), *The Early History of Rome*, trans. and intro. Aubrey De Sélincourt, London: Penguin.

Maas, Michael (2012), 'Barbarians in Late Antiquity: Problems and Approaches', in Scott Johnson (ed.), *The Oxford Handbook of Late Antiquity*, 60–91, Oxford: Oxford University Press.

Makins, Marian (2016), 'Memories of (Ancient Roman) War in Tolkien's Dead Marshes', *Thersites*, 4: 199–240.

Meier, Christian (1999), *Athens: A Portrait of the City in Its Golden Age*, trans. Robert Kimber and Rita Kimber, London: John Murray.

Pagán, Victoria (2017), *Tacitus*, London: I.B. Tauris.

Rawlings, Louis (1998), 'Caesar's Portrayal of Gauls as Warriors', in Kathryn Welch and Anton Powell (ed.), *Julius Caesar as Artful Reporter: The War Commentaries as Political Instruments*, 179–92, Swansea: The Classical Press of Wales.

Riggsby, Andrew (2006), *Caesar in Gaul and Rome: War in Words*, Austin: University of Texas Press.

Rood, Tim (2006), 'Herodotus and Foreign Lands', in Carolyn Dewald and John Marincola (eds), *The Cambridge Companion to Herodotus*, 290–305, Cambridge: Cambridge University Press.

Sallust (2010), *Catiline's Conspiracy, the Jugurthine War, Histories*, trans. William Batsone, Oxford: Oxford University Press.

Shuttleworth Kraus, Christina (2017), 'Caesar in Livy and Tacitus', in Luca Grillo and Christopher Krebs (eds), *The Cambridge Companion to the Writings of Julius Caesar*, 277–88, Cambridge: Cambridge University Press.

Sims, Alistair J.P. (2018), 'Celtic Obsession in Modern Fantasy Literature', in Raimund Karl and Katharina Möller (eds), *Proceedings of the 2nd European Symposium in Celtic Studies. Held at Prifysgol Bangor University from July 31st to August 3rd 2017*, 21–35, Hagen/Westf.: curach bhan.

Sims-Williams, Patrick (1998), 'Celtomania and Celtoscepticism', *Cambrian Medieval Celtic Studies*, 36: 1–35.

Skinner, Joseph (2012), *The Invention of Greek Ethnography: From Homer to Herodotus. Greeks Overseas*, Oxford: Oxford University Press.

Smart, Anthony (2019), 'Review of Julius Caesar. The War for Gaul: A New Translation', *Bryn Mawr Classical Review* (24 Nov. 2019), https://bmcr.brynmawr.edu/2019/2019.11.24/, accessed 22 Jul. 2021.

Smart, Anthony (2020a), 'Pericles of Athens: Democracy and Empire', in Martin Gutmann (ed.), *Historians on Leadership and Strategy: Case Studies from Antiquity to Modernity*, 255–67, Cham: Springer.

Smart, Anthony (2020b), 'Understanding Collapse: Ancient History and Modern Myths, Review Essay', *European Journal of Archaeology*, 23 (2): 314–7.

Smart, Anthony (2020c), 'Ripensare la storia universal Giustino e l'epitome delle Storie Filippiche di Pompeo Trogo', Review, *The Classical Journal Online* (05 Jul.): 1–5.

Suetonius (2000), *Lives of the Caesars*, trans. Catharine Edwards, Oxford: Oxford University Press.
Tacitus (1970), *The Agricola and the Germania*, trans. Mattingly and Handford, London: Penguin.
Tacitus (2008), *The Annals, the Reigns of Tiberius, Claudius, and Nero*, trans. J. C. Yardley and intro., Anthony Barrett, Oxford: Oxford University Press.
Thomas, Richard (2010), 'The Germania as Literary Text', in A. J. Woodman (ed.), *The Cambridge Companion to Tacitus*, 59–72, Cambridge: Cambridge University Press.
Thomas, Rosalind (2019), *Polis Histories, Collective Memories and the Greek World*, Cambridge: Cambridge University Press.
Thucydides (1972), *History of the Peloponnesian War*, trans. Rex Warner and intro. M. I. Finley, London: Penguin.
Tober, Daniel (2017), 'Greek Local Historiography and Its Audiences', *Classical Quarterly*, 67: 460–84.
Tsakmakis, Antonis and Rengakos, Antonios, eds (2006), *Brill's Companion to Thucydides*, Leiden: Brill.
Virgil (2008), *The Aeneid*, trans. Frederick Ahl, Oxford: Oxford University Press.
Vlassopoulos, Kostas (2013), *Greeks & Barbarians*, Cambridge: Cambridge University Press.
Webster, Jane (1999), 'At the End of the World: Druidic and Other Revitalization Movements in Post-Conquest Gaul and Britain', *Britannia*, 30: 1–20.
Williams, Mark (2016), *Ireland's Immortals: A History of the Gods of Irish Myth*, Princeton; Oxford: Princeton University Press.
Winkler, Martin (2015), *Arminius the Liberator: Myth and Ideology*, Oxford: Oxford University Press.
Wolters, Rinehard (2008), *Die Schlacht im Teutoburger Wald: Arminius, Varus und das roemische Germanien*, München: Verlag C.H. Beck.
Woolf, Greg (2011), *Tales of the Barbarians: Ethnography and Empire in the Roman West*, Chichester; Malden, MA: Wiley-Blackwell.

6

Celts in Spaaaaace!

Cheryl Morgan

In 453 CE Saint Brendan the Astrogator took the survivors of the Celtic peoples so far over the Western Sea that they ended up on the far side of the galaxy with their own star systems to settle. The Coranians, their enemies from the days of Atlantis, were already there, and other peoples followed them to the stars. A galactic civilization was founded. Slowly but surely Earth caught up in the technology stakes. The scene was set for a climactic re-union of cultures.

That's not the usual sort of scene setting we expect in a space opera, but it may be one of the most audacious. It is the premise of a series of books known as the *Keltiad*[1] in which Patricia Kennealy re-tells Celtic legends in among stories of her own devising, in which magic and technology are inextricably linked. This chapter will look primarily at the first two books in the series: *The Copper Crown* (1984) and *The Throne of Scone* (1986).[2] The first *Keltiad* trilogy also includes a prequel, *The Silver Branch* (1991). These books have been followed with a trilogy re-telling the Arthurian legend,[3] and several other books.[4]

Kennealy is perhaps best known as a rock music critic, and for her relationship with Jim Morrison, the front man of The Doors. According to her autobiography (Kennealy 1992), she and Morrison participated in a hand-fasting ceremony in June 1970. Although the ceremony has no legal standing, and Morrison may not have taken it all that seriously as he allegedly had several other relationships in the year leading up to his death in July 1971,[5] Kennealy changed her legal name

---

[1] Kennealy-Morrison always spells Kelt with a K. This provides a useful distinction with actual historic Celts, and one which I shall adopt.
[2] The book was originally published by Penguin in the USA in 1986, but page references here are from the 1987 UK edition.
[3] *The Hawk's Grey Feather* (1992), *The Oak Above the Kings* (1994) and *The Hedge of Mist* (1996).
[4] *Blackmantle* (1997), *The Deer's Cry* (1998), *Tales of the Spiral Castle: Stories of the Keltiad* (2014).
[5] See, for example, Davis 2004 who notes that several paternity suits were pending against Morrison at the time of his death.

to add his, reflecting their marriage. Although the name change did not take place until after the first *Keltiad* books were written, I will be using the author's current name from this point on. Book references use the author's name as it appears in print.

Her biography in *The Copper Crown* notes that Kennealy-Morrison is a member of the Society for Creative Anachronism (SCA). This organization, whose founders included the writers Diana Paxton and Poul Anderson (OAC n.d.; Martin 2001), is 'devoted to the research and re-creation of pre-seventeenth century skills, arts, combat, culture' (SCA 2020). While SCA members put a great deal of effort into recreating the lives, skills and practices of historical peoples, the very scope of their period, and their presence in the modern world, leads to an inevitable amount of anachronism. Sometimes this is done creatively and playfully. The *Keltiad* books may be one of the most obvious expressions of this playfulness.

In an interview with the website, *The Wild Hunt*, Kennealy-Morrison describes herself as a 'Celtic Pagan', and the article describes her as a High Priestess (ZB 2015). While the *Keltiad* books are not overtly Neo-Pagan, knowledge of Neo-Pagan and occult ideas appear to inform the books. The *Keltiad* is therefore not exactly Celts in Space,[6] but rather an American Neo-Pagan view of Celts in Space. Given the leap of imagination necessary to create a galactic civilization of Celtic refugees from Earth, it seems churlish to object too much to lack of authenticity.

One consequence of this reliance on a modern, popular view of Celtic culture rather than strict adherence to archaeological and anthropological evidence is a tendency towards pan-Celticism, the idea that the various Celtic nations are, and perhaps always have been, united by a common culture.[7] Kennealy-Morrison therefore picks material from a wide range of actual ancient Celtic traditions. It should also be noted that her understanding of Celtic culture will have been based on ideas current at the time of writing, not modern academic research. Kennealy-Morrison relied heavily on various well-known enthusiasts for Celtic culture, in particular Robert Graves whose book, *The White Goddess* (first published in 1948, revised in 1952 and 1961), features strongly as an influence.[8]

---

[6] In an interview for the University of Rochester's Camelot Project, Kennealy-Morrison says that 'Celts in Space' is how she refers to the *Keltiad* books herself, and makes reference to *The Muppet Show* (and presumably their recurring 'Pigs in Space' sketches). See Thompson (1991).
[7] See Transceltic (n.d.) for a modern example.
[8] See 'A Note on Sources' in *The Silver Branch* (Kennealy-Morrison 1991: 478), for a list of acknowledged influences that also includes Lady Gregory and W.B. Yeats.

The first use that Kennealy-Morrison finds for her Celtic influences is in worldbuilding. The books come with a short history of the galactic civilization of which Keltia, the home of our heroes, is a part. This history melds material from the Irish *Lebar Gabála Érenn* ('The Book of the Takings/Conquests of Ireland', usually known as 'The Book of Invasions') and occult secret history. The *Lebar Gabála Érenn* is an eleventh-century pseudo-history, bringing together Biblical material and mythological traditions, and detailing successive waves of migration to the country, culminating in the current inhabitants, the Milesians, supposedly the ancestors of the Gaels. Versions of the work were popular in the 1970s when Kennealy-Morrison was writing her books. As a rock critic she would almost certainly have been aware of the superb 1976 concept album, *The Book of Invasions*, produced by Irish rock band, Horslips. Jim Fitzpatrick's beautiful graphic novel, *The Book of Conquests*, appeared in 1978.

Kennealy-Morrison derives her Keltic race from the Tuatha Dé Danann, a group generally associated with the pre-Christian deities of Ireland (Carey 2006b: 1693). However, she also draws in occult sources, tracing their ancestry back to Atlantis and crediting them with the construction of Stonehenge, the Great Pyramids, the Nazca Lines and Machu Picchu. Along with them to the stars she takes the Fomorians (Carey 2006a: 762), an ancient Irish race fought by more than one wave of invaders. The name Bres, who in the *Lebar Gabála* is a half-Fomorian who at one point becomes king of the Tuatha Dé Danann before being deposed for un-kingly behaviour, is given to a major villain of *The Copper Crown*. As in the original Irish legends, the Fomorians are not intrinsically evil and, in *The Silver Branch*, Bres's son, Elathan, becomes a key ally for the Kelts.

For the primary villains of the story, Kennealy-Morrison invents an Atlantean race called the Telchines whose culture is based loosely on ancient Egypt, though their origins are more Greek (Smith 1873b). Having destroyed Atlantis from space, the Telchines fly away to the stars where they become a people known as the Coranians. This name is taken from a minor race of magically powered people who appear in the *Mabinogion* as enemies of King Ludd (Davies 2007: 112, 252). Kennealy-Morrison's Coranians rule the Cabiri Empire, a dominion whose name is taken once again from Greek mythology (Smith 1873a). The primary villain of the story, Jaun Akhera, is the ambitious heir to the Cabiri throne. Although the Coranians appear to be a large and powerful civilization, they do not rule over all the non-Keltic worlds. The Fomorians and several other peoples are members of a loose alliance known as the Phalanx. This includes the

Yamazai, a 'matriarchy of warrior women' (Kennealy 1984: 146). If that isn't clue enough, we are later told that their Queen is called Panthissera, a name which may be intended to echo Penthesilea, the Amazon leader from the *Iliad*.[9] We are told that she bears a crescent moon tattoo on her forehead, which is entirely in keeping with feminist Neo-Pagan goddess worship.[10] In *The Throne of Scone*, the Amazons come to the aid of the Kelts.

The mixing of Greek and Egyptian references alongside the Celtic legends may seem odd, but it is well within the tradition of the *Lebar Gabála*. Like Virgil's *Aeneid*, and Geoffrey of Monmouth's *History of the Kings of Britain*, the *Lebar Gabála* is in large part an invented history that seeks to connect its subjects to a more illustrious ancestry.[11] The Milesians of the *Lebar Gabála* are descendants of a Scythian warrior living in Spain, there are links to Greece and Egypt, and the book also connects Ireland all the way back to Noah. Atlantean histories are particularly popular with occultists. The folklorist, Lewis Spence, whom Kennealy-Morrison cites as a source, had a particular interest in Atlantis, believing it to be the home of a lost Bronze Age civilization.[12]

According to Kennealy-Morrison the Kelts and their neighbours fled Earth following persecution by the Milesians, and in particular by Saint Patrick. Quite how a race of people that commanded magic and could build starships could be bullied out of Ireland by a Romano-British ex-slave armed only with his Christian faith is never quite explained, but the exodus took place and the various refugee peoples have prospered among the stars ever since.

The Kingdom of Keltia is divided into six star systems, each derived from an Earthly equivalent. They are Erinna (Ireland), Kymry (Wales), Scota (Scotland), Kernow (Cornwall), Brytaned (Brittany) and Vannin (the Isle of Man). The whole assemblage is ruled over by an Ard-rían (High Queen) or Ard-rígh (High King) based on the planet Tara. This mirrors the medieval Irish political structure where the four provinces of Ulster, Munster, Leinster and Connaught were ruled by a High King whose capital was on the Hill of Tara in County Meath.[13] As Keltia's Tara is a planet, the capital is called Caerdroia,

---

[9] In this case the Amazons do not enter the war. The Kelts are led by a woman and they refuse to go against her.
[10] See also Elizabeth Hand's *Waking the Moon* (1994), which makes considerable use of Neo-Pagan ideas and crescent moon symbolism in particular.
[11] See Ní Lionáin (2012) for discussion of how such ideas have been used to confer political legitimacy up to modern times.
[12] See, for example, his *Occult Sciences in Atlantis* (1970).
[13] See Byrne (1973) for a discussion of the historical and mythological evidence for this system.

which Kennealy-Morrison translates as The Spiral Castle.[14] This is a Welsh word meaning a turf maze or labyrinth.[15]

While smaller and less powerful than the Cabiri Empire, the worlds of Keltia have prospered thanks to the protection of the Curtain Wall, a magical barrier that hides them from the rest of the galaxy. The Coranians are prevented from invading because their fleets simply cannot find Keltia. The Curtain Wall is a creation of the great sorceress, Morgan Magistra, who was sister to the legendary Keltic king, Arthur. We'll be hearing more of him in due course.

While most of the action in the story is centred around characters who are Kelts, the two books are also a First Contact story. In the thirty-sixth century, a ship of the Terran Federacy makes contact with a Keltic ship outside of the Curtain Wall. The Kelts decide that they have hidden from their Earthly relatives for long enough, and decide to open negotiations. This gives us the opportunity to see Keltic civilization through other eyes. The Terran ship, the *Sword*, is crewed by a typical *Star Trek* style multinational crew. The captain, Theo Haruko, is described as 'Japanasian'. Of the rest of the crew, Sarah O'Reilly, the communications officer, will find a home in Keltia thanks to her Irish ancestry, while the science officer with the unmistakably English name of Hugh Tindal will betray our heroes to the Coranians. Here Kennealy-Morrison is clearly playing into modern British regional nationalism in which the ethnically Celtic nations of Ireland, Wales and Scotland are seen as in conflict with an oppressive and colonising England, which is seen as ethnically Saxon. Arthurian legend often plays a key part in underpinning such political ideas.

This is how Captain Haruko reacts to his first encounter with the Keltic flagship, the *Firedrake*:

> the central ship, the one they escorted – that was something else entirely. It looked like a golden dragon. An enormous sculptured head with jaws open, outstretched claws on stylized forelegs, swept-back wings and a curved forked tail; and it had to be ten miles long at the very least ... It was a statement of arrogant and ostentatious power, on a scale that Haruko could not quite grasp yet. *A military vessel like a work of art*, he thought numbly.
>
> (Kennealy 1984: 35)

---

[14] Chapter six of Graves's *The White Goddess* is titled 'A Visit to Spiral Castle'.
[15] A few of these ancient structures still exist. They are called 'Troy Town' in English and 'Trojeborg' in Swedish. The Welsh translates as 'Castle Troy'. There is an alternative etymology of 'Castle of Turns', and the labyrinths do have a spiral nature, but given the Troy names used elsewhere the Spiral Castle translation may be a modern invention. The name 'Troy Town' appears to be associated with the Lusus Troiae, an intricate cavalry drill which Vergil compares to the complexity of the Cretan Labyrinth. The name may link the custom back to Troy, but may also be derived from the verb *truare* which means a weaving or stirring motion, which takes us back to spirals. See Reed Doob (2019) for discussion.

While this is not quite our first view of the Kelts, it is a wonderfully dramatic way to introduce them to the story. And the idea that military equipment should also be works of art is very much in tune with the popular view of Celtic culture.[16] A similar technique is used when the Terran crew first set eyes on the Keltic royal palace:

> Leaving the groundcar at the sheltered entrance, they found themselves in a hall that would have graced and Imperial domicile. All around them was marble and silk and silver wrought in intricate knotwork patterns.[17] They peered shyly around, then looked at each other half in wonder, half in fear, feeling like children in an old story, creeping into the palace of the elf-king.
>
> (Kennealy 1984: 94)

The world of Keltia is described in very utopian terms, including a Golden Age which featured the advent of democracy and 'complete equality' (Kennealy 1984: 408). While they go through some fairly rough times politically after that, the Kelts of the time of *The Copper Crown* still have a very good life. Captain Haruko is astonished to learn, from the Keltic Taoiseach (Prime Minister), Morwen Douglas, that there are no poor in her worlds. She explains:

> All Kelts, from the highest rank to the lowest, have their basic needs assured by law: food, shelter, employment and the like. Of course, there is no law forcing anyone to take advantage of this – though I for one have met very few who wished to be hungry or homeless or idle – but in Keltia, the fear of these things at least is non-existent. That is the reality of the clann[18] system.
>
> (Kennealy 1984: 175)

Adam Roberts, in his book, *Silk and Potatoes: Contemporary Arthurian Fantasy*, describes the *Keltiad* as an 'Irish-American wish-fulfilment fantasy' of 'a noble, magical and technologically advanced Utopia'. He adds 'such compensatory fantasies on behalf of a people who have suffered more than their fair share of oppression in the last few hundred years are perhaps psychologically understandable' (1998: 76–7).

Roberts has a point here, but the Irish-Americans are not the only people of Celtic extraction who regard themselves as historically oppressed. This in

---

[16] There is some archaeological support for this idea. See Megaw and Megaw (1986).
[17] The 'Celtic' style of interlaced knotwork that is so famous today did not appear in Ireland until the late sixth century, by which time there had been significant contact with Anglo-Saxon culture in which such forms are common. See Morrison (2004/5).
[18] Kennealy-Morrison uses the spelling 'clann' in the books and I will use it here to distinguish it from real world social structures of Celtic-speaking peoples.

turn can give rise to political differences and at least a desire to make a better world. The economic system of Keltia has something in common with the idea of Universal Basic Income currently championed by various left-wing politicians around the world. Many Celtic-identified people on this side of the Atlantic share similar utopian ideals. Wales consistently returns a majority of Labour MPs to the Westminster Parliament, and all First Minister of the Senedd have been Labour. Scotland has largely abandoned Labour for the arguably more left-wing Scottish Nationalist Party.

A particular feature of the *Keltiad* books is the total gender equality of Keltic society. While this too might be put down to wish-fulfilment by a woman author, Kennealy may have felt that she had some historical justification for this stance. In 1972 a French writer known as Jean Markale published a book called *Women of the Celts* (1975). In it he claimed to show that Celtic society was one that exhibited great equality between the sexes. While Markale's work is now viewed as entirely too creative to be serious history, his work gained some popularity at the time and may have influenced Kennealy-Morrison. In an interview with Raymond H. Thompson of the University of Rochester, Kennealy-Morrison says:

> historically, women enjoyed a much more important place in Celtic society than they do now. They could own property, they could outrank their husbands, and, at least until the seventh century when the Church decreed otherwise, they were liable for military service.
>
> (Thompson 1991)

Roberts is also somewhat critical of the idealized characters of the women in the *Keltiad* (1998: 77). In particular, the lead character, Ard-rían Aeron Aoibhell, is impossibly beautiful, charming, skilled in all sorts of different areas, and beloved by her people. As any popularly perceived Celtic queen should, she has a mass of flaming red hair.[19] Another major character is the Taoiseach, Morwen Douglas. She and Aeron were childhood friends, but she is blonde where the Queen is a redhead. Morwen is neither a sorceress nor a warrior, but she is smart, cautious and practical, making an excellent companion for her more impulsive monarch. In her biography Kennealy-Morrison's SCA persona is given

---

[19] A Google image search for 'Celtic Queen' will illustrate the strength of this idea, although of course human genetics make the likelihood of most Celtic queens being redheads extremely small. The idea may be traceable back to the Roman historian Cassius Dio, who described Boudica's hair as *xanthotatē*, the superlative form of xanthos ('blonde'). The idea that Boudica was a redhead is probably traceable to Dudey and Webster's *The Rebellion of Boudica* (1962), where *xanthotatē* is translated as 'red'. See also Freeman and John Koch (2006), and Koch (2006).

as Lassarina Douglas. Lassarina is one of Aeron's given names, while Douglas is Morwen's clann name. A more obvious confession of a Mary-Sue would be hard to find, but Kennealy-Morrison is aware of this and happy to make a joke at her own expense. She understands the pronunciation of the Gaelic words she uses, providing a guide for the reader in the books. The Queen's clann name, Aoibhell, is pronounced 'evil'.

The other lead character is Gwydion ap Arawn, Aeron's love interest and Pendragon (war leader). While Aeron is from Errina and Morwen from Scota, Gwydion is Kymric. This is something of a relief for Welsh readers, as all the major Keltic traitors in the books, including Gwydion's twin sister, Arianeira, are Kymric. Kennealy-Morrison's commitment to pan-Celticism seems to wear slightly thin when it comes to the Welsh.

The main plot of the books centres around the arrival of the *Sword*, Aeron's decision to reach out in friendship to the Terrans, and how this is used by Jaun Akhera as an excuse to mount a pre-emptive invasion of Keltia. He uses fear of a Keltic-Terran alliance as justification for this. Arianeira, jealous of losing her twin brother to Aeron, is persuaded to use her magical skills to breach the Curtain Wall and allow the Coranian fleets access to Keltia. This plot provides plenty of excuse for military action, political intrigue and heroic adventure. From the point of view of this essay, however, the main interest is how Kennealy-Morrison uses Celtic folklore to shape the plot.

By the end of *The Copper Crown*, Jaun Ahkera and his forces have conquered Keltia. Gwydion, whom Aeron has formally married, stays behind as a prisoner to inspire resistance, while Aeron and Morwen escape into space in search of help. In Keltia's hour of need, there is only one person to call upon: Arthur. Much of the story of *The Throne of Scone* details Aeron and Morwen's attempts to follow the path of the historical (Keltic) Arthur[20] in his final days and find his resting place. While they don't expect to find him alive, they do hope to find the four Treasures of Keltia, artefacts that will aid them in the fight against the Coranians. Arthur's trail is revealed through the poem, *The Spoils of Annwn*, written by his bard, Taliesin, who was one of the seven survivors of his final expedition.

Of course, the *Preideu Annwfyn* ('Spoils of the Otherworld') is an actual Welsh poem detailing the Arthur's expedition to Annwn, an Otherworld that Kennealy-Morrison's sources, in particular Graves, typically interpret as the land of the dead. The poem is found in the *Book of Taliesin*, a surviving

---

[20] The Keltic Arthur lived in our twentieth century. There is no explanation in the books as to how his life story so closely dovetails that of the Terran legend.

version of which is dated to the fourteenth century. Kennealy-Morrison's adaptation of the text to describe a deep-space expedition is ingenious. This is perhaps not surprising as Graves too was given to creative interpretation of poems from the *Book of Taliesin*, in particular the *Cad Goddau* ('The Battle of the Trees').

In the *Preideu Annwfyn*, Arthur and his companions set sail in a ship called *Prydwen*, which Kennealy-Morrison makes a spacecraft. The place of the Celtic Otherworld, Annwn, is taken by a region of space called the Morimaruse. It is described thus:

> Ahead of them lay their first certain destination: the Morimaruse, the giant electromagnetic maelstrom that was the terror of this sector. There were others like it scattered throughout the galaxy, though none so vast or so violent, and the Morimaruse has a reputation that its fellows likewise did not share. It was a galactic graveyard for unwary or unlucky starships, and for their crews also; a slow rolling mass of dustclouds laced with flashes of sullen incandescence, a score of light-years edge to edge, its eddies of swirling dust and planet fragments troubled incessantly by soundless stellar concussions, like the summer lightning that is seen but not heard.
>
> (Kennealy 1987: 109)

The *Spoils of Annwn* (though not the *Preideu Annwfyn*) also makes reference to four great Treasures, all of which can be connected back to the *Lebar Gabála* and the 'four treasures' of the Tuatha Dé Danann. The sword of light is not a Jedi lightsabre, but rather the sword of Nuada Silver-Arm; the lance of battle is the spear of Lugh, one of the few figures who may come close to a pre-Christian Irish deity (see Williams 2016: 16–27); the Cup of the King of the Dead is the cauldron of the Dagda, which supposedly had the power to produce food continuously; and Fál's eye is the Lia Fáil, the coronation stone at Tara on which Irish kings were crowned. The scholarly consensus is that the 'four treasures' are part of later medieval Irish pseudo-historical invention, but these symbolic objects became very important during the Celtic Revival and were often imbued with mystical qualities (see Williams 2016: 148–53; 394–7). Because Kennealy-Morrison needs these treasures to be weapons she plays slightly fast and loose with their origins. In particular she conflates the Lia Fáil with the Eye of Balor, named after a one-eyed Fomorian king whose eye, if opened, could destroy whole armies (Simmons 2006: 164). The Eye comes from an entirely different literary source to the four treasures, *Cath Maige Tuired* ('The [Second] Battle of Mag Tuired').

Connections to Celtic lore continue in the shape of the allies that our heroes find in their struggle. The Kelts did not venture into space alone. Mythological creatures from Earth came with them: selkies, merrows and so on.[21] In escaping from captivity on Tara early in *The Throne of Scone*, Gwydion is aided by the merrows:

> Of middle height, the merrow was in shape like a human, though slimmer and shorter and lighter of build; but that was where the resemblance ceased. Its skin glowed red as a ruby even in the faint light of the Criosanna,[22] and the coarse, stiff, mane-like hair was the green of sea foam over sand, or the green of the great kelp-fans that sway like fans in the tidal swings. And the eyes – the eyes like the inside of an oyster-shell iridescent as nacre, filled with all the mystery of the wild waters.
>
> (Kennealy 1987: 124)

As it turns out, however, the merrows too have made good use of their centuries in space and have developed their own technology. As Gwydion dives into the water to avoid pursuit, a merrow fastens a red cowl over his face.

> To Gwydion's astonishment, he found that, deep under the cold black sea, he was not drowned; the red cowl-like thing appeared to be a sort of artificial gill, a selectively permeable membrane that enabled him to breathe and see and hear as a marine creature.
>
> (Kennealy 1987: 126)

In *The Throne of Scone*, Gwydion and Sarah O'Reilly are aided in an escape by selkies:

> The bobbing heads were very near now; one of them raised up out of the waves and turned to look at them. It was sleek, round, dark-furred, with long delicate whiskers; big dark eyes regarded them critically, and with an alarming degree of intelligence. Then the creature spoke, and O'Reilly jumped.
>
> (Kennealy 1987: 310)

Occasionally, however, Kennealy-Morrison cannot find what she needs in the mythological sources and appears to make things up. The planet of the Fomorians is also home to small, tree-dwelling creatures called Dûhín who aid Morwen when she becomes lost in their forest home. The Isle of Avalon turns out not to

---

[21] Although selkies and merrows are primarily found in folk tales from Celtic countries, they are not found in ancient Celtic sources and were therefore not necessarily known to pre-Christian Celtic people.

[22] The 'woven belts', Tara is a ringed planet like Saturn.

be Glastonbury, but rather the terrifying volcano planet of Afallinn, inhabited by the reptilian Salamandri. However, this unique geography does allow Aeron to find Arthur and his knights in a cave under a hill (well, mountain).[23]

The most obvious element of Celticity, however, is that fact that the entire plot of the books hinges on a classic geis, usually a taboo or prohibition in medieval Irish texts, the violation of which can lead a hero to his doom. One of the minor villains is Arianeira's servant, Kynon ap Accolon. Betrayed by his mistress when he is no longer of any use, he falls into the clutches of Aeron's forces and is brought before her for questioning. Aeron has her Archdruid bring in a Cremave, or swearing stone.[24] When Kynon tries to lie, the stone burns him and he loses his hand. In revenge he curses Aeron.

> 'I set this doom upon you, Aeron Aoibhell', he said, his voice deadly soft. 'The stars' wandering between you and the brother of the one who betrayed me. Your crown from your head, your lord from your bed, and may the Shining Ones themselves ride forth to war before you return again as Queen to Caerdroia.
>
> (Kennealy 1984: 252)

Of course the story must unfold according to the geis. Aeron herself chooses to relinquish the Copper Crown of Keltia, hiding it away where Jaun Akhera and his forces cannot find it. The needs of the resistance force her and Gwydion to take separate paths for most of the rest of the story. As for the Shining Ones, surely they are but a myth. And yet O'Reilly, being of Celtic blood herself and therefore more in tune with Keltia than the other Terrans, has seen something:

> I was out riding the other day, over Miremoss with Eiluned and Kieran and a few other people, and we met a woman walking with her child. Naturally we all stopped to talk, and the oddest thing happened. It was like – like walking light, or ribbons of air, all silvery and glowing with iridescent colors. It came down the face of the hill like a sailboat. You'll probably think I'm crazy [...] but it seemed to *bow* to us.
>
> (Kennealy 1984: 192)

Aeron and Gwydion know better. Like the selkies and merrows, the Sidhe, or 'the Shining Ones', have accompanied Kelts into space. It is the King under the Hill to whom they entrust the Copper Crown for safekeeping. Gwydion himself,

---

[23] In Thompson (1991), Kennealy-Morrison claims that this was an unconscious borrowing.
[24] Kennealy-Morrison probably got the story of the cremave from Lady Francesca Wilde's *Ancient Legends, Mystic Charms, and Superstitions of Ireland* (1919), which she cites as a source work.

as the most powerful sorcerer among Aeron's inner circle, is entrusted with the mission, for he alone is likely to be able to resist faerie enchantment.

> The vibration boomed and died away, and then with no sound at all the hillside opened, light pouring out to lap like a silver streamlet at Gwydion's boots. Music – a dancing tune, harmonious and rhythmic, utterly enchanting – came from the depths of the hill, and he knew that the palace of the Sidhe stood open for him, that he was bidden to enter. He set his foot on the broad smooth stair that now was where no stair had been a moment ago, and went in at the huge green doors.
>
> (Kennealy 1984: 336)

Gwydion drives an iron dagger into the doorpost to anchor him to the human world before entering. He resists the temptations of the Sidhe, and completes his mission. In doing so he feels some kinship with Captain Haruko, being as much in awe of the faerie king, Gwyn,[25] as Haruko was of Aeron on first meeting her.

It is Gwyn who advises Gwydion and Aeron to search for the lost Treasures on board the *Prydwen*. Echoing the witches of *Macbeth*, he promises that 'the very trees' will come to Gwydion's aid. He also presents Gwydion with a gift.

> Gwydion looked down at it with wonder: a small horn all of dull gold, wrought with great skill, coelbren letters[26] carved upon its worn grip and a faded green silk baldric threaded through rings at mouthpiece and bell. He turned the horn one way and another, until the letters caught the light and blazed so that his eyes were dazzled. But for all his learning and lore, he could not read the writing on the horn.
>
> (Kennealy 1984: 341)

The use of trees in battle is not original to Shakespeare. In the *Cad Goddau* ('The Battle of the Trees') a magician called Gwydion ap Dôn animates the trees of the forest to fight for him. In the *Keltiad* Kennealy-Morrison makes Dôn Gwydion's family name; so although he is Gwydion ap Arawn (son of Arawn), he is also Gwydion of Dôn.

As we know must happen, Aeron and Morwen retrieve the Treasures from the wreck of Arthur's ship, consigning the legendary king and his companions to a proper burial at last. They are then re-united with Gwydion and can return

---

[25] Based on Gwyn ap Nudd, the otherworldly King who features in the Welsh Arthurian tale, *Culhwch and Olwen*.
[26] Coelbren y Beirdd, the bardic alphabet invented by the eighteenth-century Welsh literary forger, Iolo Morganwg. See Morgan (1983).

to Tara to wrest their kingdom back from Jaun Akhera and his Coranian army. Naturally the faerie horn must be blown:

> Gwydion, who sat on his horse midway down the valley floor, was thunder struck to see moving before him like a black wall the forest trees themselves. The words were written upon his mind in letters of flame, burning in the air before his eyes, and he rose in his irons and began to chant.
>
> (Kennealy 1987: 388)

Thus the Faerie King's prophecy is fulfilled, and Kennealy-Morrison gets an opportunity to use the *Cad Goddau* in her story. Unlike Graves, she takes it very literally.[27] There are, of course, also echoes of the attack of the Ents on Isengard in Tolkien's *The Two Towers*.

Meanwhile Aeron summons the faerie army. She does this using the Bratach Bán, a white flag that Kennealy-Morrison has taken from Scottish legend. In Dunvegan Castle on the Isle of Skye, there is a white flag that the leader of Clan Macleod is supposed to be able to use to call the faerie folk in time of dire need (Dunvegan Castle & Gardens n.d.). Of course faerie aid is always dangerous. Etain, the Faerie Queen, tries to steal Gwydion away. It takes all of Aeron's strength of will and magical knowledge to keep her man. Others were not so lucky. The Cŵn Annwn, the magical hounds owned by Gwyn ap Nudd, hunt down and kill Powell of Dyved, a Keltic lord who collaborated with Jaun Akhera during the occupation.

Much of the final narrative hinges upon the proper and improper use of magic. Way back in *The Copper Crown*, Aeron refuses to use her magic to defend Tara. Magic is powerful, but using it in battle is somehow cheating. He who succumbs to temptation and uses it first is fated to lose. Jaun Akhera, whose ambition overcomes his wisdom, uses magic to break the siege of Caerdroia. From then on, he is doomed. Even the Coranian high priest understands this, as he tells Jaun Akhera's mother:

> If he loses, he shall lose a good deal more than a war, or even his life.
> Helior was silent for a while. Then: 'Because of Aeron's sorcery?'
> 'Because of his own'.
>
> (Kennealy 1987: 301)

---

[27] Graves believed that the Battle of the Trees was a veiled reference to a contest for supremacy between two Druidic alphabets, arising from a clash of matriarchal and patriarchal cultures in ancient times. For an overview, see Fimi (2017: 204).

Aeron, however, must be careful not to lose the advantage by inappropriate magic use of her own. The Treasures, in particular the Eye of Balor, prove very useful in the final conflict. However, when the battle comes down to ritual combat between herself and Jaun Akhera, she eschews use of the sword of light and relies instead on her own abilities.

The combat takes the form of a magical duel of the sort that Taliesin might have sung about. Both rulers summon magical creatures to aid them. One of Aeron's spells calls up a Púca[28]:

> The between them on the duelling-ground stood a giant black dog. Enormous and terrible, its smooth coat gleaming over rippling muscles and its powerful tail, thick at the base, tapering to a narrow tip, it crouched protectively in front of Aeron, and its eyes as it looked at Jaun Akhera were blazing red.
>
> (Kennealy 1987: 422)

The battle continues furiously. The two armies halt, awaiting the outcome, and the families of the two combatants look on helplessly, unable to intervene in the magical duel. Eventually Aeron, moved to desperation, calls upon the spirit of the planet itself for help. The battle is being fought beside a river called the Avon Dia (the River of the Gods) and at Aeron's call she rises up. The force of the river washes away, not just Jaun Akhera, but most of his retinue and army as well. Keltia has at last been cleansed of invaders.

The Copper Crown was a finalist for the 1985 Compton Cook Award, which is a fan-run award for first novels. Aside from that the *Keltiad* books have not attracted much critical attention. Kennealy-Morrison was probably unlucky with her timing, arriving on the scene just as the field was becoming obsessed with dystopian cyberpunk novels. It is probable that the cod-mediaeval language will irritate some readers. However, anyone interested in Celtic mythology and space opera will probably enjoy spotting all of the references to ancient legends in the books, and the way in which Kennealy-Morrison has adapted those legends to her purposes. Fans of Robert Graves will doubtless appreciate her ingenuity in adapting the medieval and more recent Irish and Welsh mythological and folkloric material to a science-fictional setting, while lovers of modern-day Celticity will warm to her vision of a Celtic future in space. Academic experts on Celtic history and mythology may be less impressed, but they should take into account how our understanding of ancient Celtic culture has changed in the decades since the *Keltiad* was first conceived.

---

[28] As with selkies and merrows, Púca are not attested in ancient Celtic myth, though they are common in more modern folk tales. Kennealy-Morrison's pan-Celtic approach to collection of sources extends through time as well as geographically.

In the interview with the University of Rochester, Kennealy-Morrison says that her motivation in writing the stories was 'pure self-indulgence'. She goes on:

> I like spaceships and I like Druids; I wanted to write a book in which I could deal with both of them together. It appealed enormously to me to be able to take the fabric of the past, enriched over the ages by so many talents and gifts, and to fashion from it a story set in the future.
>
> (Thompson 1991)

Later on she notes, 'Religion is really a subtext in all my books, nothing more'. The interviewer, Raymond H. Thompson, presses her on this, asking what sort of religion she means. Her response is:

> For the Kelts, it's their own; for me it's self-discovered. It draws upon Druidism, Gnostic paganism, polytheistic Catharism, and other traditions. I practice it myself actually. In Keltia, it's not a state religion in the formal sense, though it is tied up with the land, with the way the Kelts perceive their environment and themselves: all one and interdependent. Perhaps it's what the historical Celtic religions might have evolved into had not Christianity intervened. It's non-hierarchical, for the most part. Everyone is to some extent a priest or a priestess, capable of interceding directly with the gods, or with the One Supreme Being. Annointed Druids and annointed Ban-draoi (female Druids or sorceresses) are important as preservers of the faith, but in the end it's the Kelts themselves who make the religion live. They relate to the gods as only the next step up in spiritual evolution; the gods are required to have faith in humanity, not just humanity have faith in the gods. The search for the divine in the human is what the quest is all about.
>
> (Thompson 1991)

Whether these ideas bear any relation to historical Celtic religion, if indeed there can be said to be such a thing, they do form an ideal of neo-pagan Celticity drawing on the likes of Morganwg and Graves, all the way through to the Hippy culture of the 1960s. Kennealy-Morrison was a significant part of that culture, and for her at least the dream of a long-lost, spiritual Celticity is every bit as important as the dream of a lost England was for Tolkien.

References

Byrne, Francis (1973), *Irish Kings and High Kings*, London: HarperCollins.
Carey, John (2006a), 'Fomoiri', in John T. Koch (ed.), *Celtic Culture: A Historical Encyclopedia*, 762, Santa Barbara, CA: ABC-CLIO.

Carey, John (2006b), 'Tuath Dé', in John T. Koch (ed.), *Celtic Culture: A Historical Encyclopedia*, 1693–6, Santa Barbara, CA: ABC-CLIO.

Davies, Sioned, trans. (2007), *The Mabinogion*, Oxford: Oxford University Press.

Davis, Stephen (2004), *Jim Morrison: Life, Death, Legend*, London: Ebury Press.

Dudey, Donald R., and Webster, Grahame (1962), *The Rebellion of Boudica*, London: Routledge & Kegan Paul.

Dunvegan Castle & Gardens, 'Fairy Flag', https://www.dunvegancastle.com/castle/fairy-flag/, accessed 11 Jun. 2021.

Fitzpatrick, Jim (1978), *The Book of Conquests*, Cheltenham: Paper Tiger.

Freeman, Philip and Koch, John (2006), 'Tacitus', in John T. Koch (ed.), *Celtic Culture: A Historical Encyclopedia*, 1645, Santa Barbara, CA: ABC-CLIO.

Graves, Robert (1991), *The White Goddess*, London: Faber & Faber.

Guest Contributor (2015), 'Conversations with Patricia Kennealy-Morrison (side A)', *The Wild Hunt: Pagan News and Perspectives* (6 Dec.), https://wildhunt.org/2015/12/guest-post-conversations-with-patricia-kennealy-morrison-side-a.html, accessed 11 Jun. 2021.

Hand, Elizabeth (1994), *Waking the Moon*, New York: HarperCollins.

Horslips (1976), *The Book of Invasions: A Celtic Symphony*, London: DJM Records.

Kennealy, Patricia (1984), *The Cooper Crown*, New York: Signet.

Kennealy, Patricia (1987), *The Throne of Scone*, London: Grafton.

Kennealy, Patricia (1992), *Strange Days: My Life with and without Jim Morrison*, New York: Dutton/Penguin.

Kennealy-Morrison, Patricia (1991), *The Silver Branch*, London: Grafton.

Kennealy-Morrison, Patricia (1992), *The Hawk's Grey Feather*, London: Grafton.

Kennealy-Morrison, Patricia (1996), *The Oak Above the Kings*, London: HarperCollins.

Kennealy-Morrison, Patricia (1996), *The Hedge of Mist*, London: HarperCollins.

Kennealy-Morrison, Patricia (1997), *Blackmantle*, New York: HarperPrism.

Kennealy-Morrison, Patricia (1998), *The Deer's Cry*, New York: HarperPrism.

Kennealy-Morrison, Patricia (2014), *Tales of the Spiral Castle: Stories of the Keltiad*, New York: Lizard Queen Press.

Koch, John T. (2006), 'Boudīca', in John T. Koch (ed.), *Celtic Culture: A Historical Encyclopedia*, 235, Santa Barbara, CA: ABC-CLIO.

Markale, Jean (1975), *Women of the Celts*, Rochester, VT: Inner Traditions.

Martin, Douglas (2001), 'Poul Anderson, Science Fiction Novelist, Dies at 74', *The New York Times* (3 Aug.), https://www.nytimes.com/2001/08/03/books/poul-anderson-science-fiction-novelist-dies-at-74.html, accessed 11 Jun. 2021.

Megaw, Ruth, and Megaw, J. V. S (1986), *Early Celtic Art in Britain and Ireland*, London: Shire Publications.

Morgan, Prys (1983), 'From a Death to a View: The Hunt for the Welsh Past in the Romantic Period', in Eric Hobsbawm and Terence Ranger (eds), *The Invention of Tradition*, 43–100, Cambridge: Cambridge University Press.

Morrison, Tessa (2004/5), 'Behind the Patterns and Designs that Cross Cultural Boundaries: Towards a Holistic Approach', *International Journal of the Humanities*, 2 (1): 119–27.

Ní Lionáin, Clíodhna (2012), '*Lebor Gabála Érenn*: The Use and Appropriation of an Irish Origin Legend in Identity Construction at Home and Abroad', *Archaeological Review from Cambridge*, 7 (2): 33–50.

Online Archive of California, 'Collection of Society for Creative Anachronism, Inc. materials', https://oac.cdlib.org/findaid/ark:/13030/c8kh0tq9/, accessed 11 Jun. 2021.

Roberts, Adam (1998), *Silk and Potatoes: Contemporary Arthurian Fantasy*, Amsterdam: Rodopi.

Reed Doob, Penelope (2019), *The Idea of the Labyrinth from Classical Antiquity through the Middle Ages*, New York: Cornell University Press.

Simmons, Victoria (2006), 'Balor', in John T. Koch (ed.), *Celtic Culture: A Historical Encyclopedia*, 164, Santa Barbara, CA: ABC-CLIO.

Smith, William (1873a), 'Cabeiri', in *A Dictionary of Greek and Roman Biography and Mythology*, London: John Murray, Perseus Digital Library, http://www.perseus.tufts.edu/hopper/text?doc=Perseus%3Atext%3A1999.04.0104%3Aalphabetic±letter%3DC%3Aentry±group%3D1%3Aentry%3Dcabeiri-bio-1, accessed 11 Jun. 2021.

Smith, William (1873b), 'Telchi'nes', in *A Dictionary of Greek and Roman Biography and Mythology*, London: John Murray, Perseus Digital Library, http://www.perseus.tufts.edu/hopper/text?doc=Perseus%3Atext%3A1999.04.0104%3Aalphabetic±letter%3DT%3Aentry±group%3D3%3Aentry%3Dtelchines-bio-1, accessed 11 Jun. 2021.

Society for Creative Anachronism, 'About', https://www.sca.org/about/, accessed 11 Jun. 2021.

Spence, Lewis (1970), *Occult Sciences in Atlantis*, London: HarperCollins.

Thompson, Raymond H. (1991), 'Interview with Patricia Kennealy', *The Camelot Project*, University of Rochester (9 Aug.), https://d.lib.rochester.edu/camelot/text/interview-with-patricia-kennealy, accessed 11 Jun. 2021.

Transceltic, 'Home Page', https://www.transceltic.com/, accessed 11 Jun. 2021.

Wilde, Lady (1887), *Ancient Legends, Mystic Charms, and Superstitions of Ireland*, Boston: Ticknor and Co.

Williams, Mark (2016), *Ireland's Immortals: A History of the Gods of Irish Myth*, Princeton, NJ: Princeton University Press.

Part Three

Celtic fantasy beyond the anglophone

7

From *Vertigen* to *Frontier*: The fate of the Sidhe in Léa Silhol's fiction

Viviane Bergue

Léa Silhol is certainly one of the most original voices of French fantasy fiction. Her first works were published in the early 2000s and rapidly gained critical acclaim. With the publication of *La Glace et la Nuit: Opus un. Nigredo* (2007) and *Avant l'Hiver: Architectonique des Clartés* (2008a), it has become clear that all her stories are related to each other, in a much larger narrative that she refers to as the Weave *(la Trame*[1]*)*, the two main sequences of which, *Vertigen* and *Frontier*, reinvent Faërie and create a parallel history of the Sidhe.[2] Here Faërie is definitely 'Celtic', that is mainly rooted in Gaelic and Welsh folklore, hence the name of the human-sized fairies, Sidhe, which explicitly refers to the *Daoine Sidhe* from Irish tradition. These Sidhe are not simply fairies, they are the gods of old in new shape, struggling to survive in a world where they are no longer worshipped. They are indeed threatened by the One God of Christianity, and they will find a way to come back as Fays among humans in contemporary times.

---

[1] Léa Silhol often uses the term in her interviews, blogs and social media posts, to refer to her whole set of stories. However more recently, she has revealed the name of the complete meta-series to be *Transmeare*, from the Latin verb meaning 'to go across, to cross, to travel across', which emphasizes the notions of crossing and threshold *(seuil* in French), though still generally using the term *la Trame*. In this essay, I have purposefully chosen to stick to this usage.

[2] Currently, *Vertigen* is mainly composed of two novels, *La Sève et le Givre* (2002) and *La Glace et la Nuit* (vol. 1 *Opus un. Nigredo*, 2007; vol. 2 *Opus deux. Albedo*, 2020), a yet incomplete story which according to Léa Silhol's professional blog, Winterdaze, will also include two other volumes (Silhol n.d.), and the collection *Avant l'Hiver: Architectonique des Clartés* (2008a). Opus 3, *Cauda Pavonis*, was published in 2001, after this essay was written. The name *Vertigen* refers to the thrilling (vertiginous) sensation one experiences when crossing from the mortal world to the land of Faërie. The *Frontier* sequence is for now composed of the collection *Musiques de la Frontière* (2004a, recently reprinted at Nitchevo Factory) and the novel *Possession Point* (2016a), the novella 'À travers la fumée' (in *Sacra, Parfums d'Isenne et d'ailleurs, Opus un: Aucun cœur inhumain*, 2016b), the novella 'Le Maître de Kôdô' and the short story 'The Passenger' (in *Sacra, Parfums d'Isenne et d'ailleurs, Opus deux: Nulle âme invincible*, 2016c). Besides, since 2018, Léa Silhol has added to these two main sequences the *Seppenko Monogatari* sequence which mostly takes place in Japan and South Korea and is both related to *Frontier* and *Vertigen*.

Slowly but surely, Léa Silhol builds a secret history of our world told from the point of view of the Sidhe (and their godly cousins from other mythologies), which explores the perpetual reinvention of myth through the fate of her Sidhe people. From the medieval setting of *Vertigen* to the alternative present of *Frontier* where they face discrimination, the Sidhe cross the ages, changing, reinventing themselves and crossing the paths of humankind.

This chapter examines how Léa Silhol transforms 'Celtic' folklore to produce a fantasy strongly rooted in myth and fairy tale. First of all, it will be observed that Léa Silhol's fiction relies both on a Romantic vision of 'Celtic' folklore and a common association, fixed in the nineteenth century, of 'Celtic' with magic and fabulous characters and settings. Secondly, it will be argued that Léa Silhol's fiction is at once mythopoeic and postmodern in its construction and its use of 'Celtic' figures and motives, along with characters and motives from other mythologies.

Romantic vision and the identification of fairies as 'Celtic'

As already noted, the name of the human-sized fairies of *Vertigen*, Sidhe, is a direct reference to the *Daoine Sidhe* from Irish tales. This is however not the first time that a fantasy work associates fairies with magical people from Gaelic folklore. Actually, more often than not, fantasy fairies are generally perceived as definitely 'Celtic', whether they are explicitly linked to the *Daoine Sidhe* and other traditional Gaelic – mainly Irish – creatures such as the Leprechauns, or whether they do speak a Celtic language, when they are not linked to Merlin and the 'Celtic' roots of the Arthurian legend (see, for example, the chapter by Cox in this volume). In Susanna Clarke's *Jonathan Strange and Mr Norrell*, fairies speak some kind of Gaelic, and places associated with them also have a Gaelic name (see chapter by Laity in this volume), even though the whole narrative mainly takes place in England. Seanan McGuire's *October Daye* series (2009–ongoing) has its fairies obviously identified with the *Daoine Sidhe*, just like those of Emma Bull's *War for the Oaks* (1987), though both stories are set in the USA.[3] Besides, many High Fantasy series build their xeno-encyclopaedia[4] on 'Celtic' folklore

---

[3] It can be argued that here the presence of *Daoine Sidhe* in Northern America is related to Irish diaspora, which is, however, beyond the scope of this essay.

[4] According to Richard Saint-Gelais, Science Fiction replaces the shared cultural encyclopaedia of realistic fiction, as defined by Umberto Ecco (i.e. bits of knowledge that point at implicit rules of the world as we know it), by a xeno-encyclopaedia, that is a set of imaginary beings, plants, places, data,

and mythology, ranging from the numerous rewritings of the Arthurian legend to stories where any elusive magical being seems reminiscent of 'Celtic' folkloric creatures, something that is often supported through the use of names that ring either Welsh or Gaelic, as is shown in many chapters of this volume.

It is then not surprising that in Léa Silhol's novel *Possession Point*, from the *Frontier* sequence, Ireland is the only country where the Fays (i.e. the reborn Sidhe) are not discriminated and persecuted but much welcome, because of a 'Celtic cultural exception' ('*exception culturelle celtique*') (Silhol 2016a: 291). Indeed for Finnegan O'Riordan, leader of the Sidh Feinn (a party obviously named after the nationalist Sinn Féinn), Fays are the resurgent *Daoine Sidhe* from Irish folklore and therefore are to be seen as a cultural Irish treasure and oddity. Consequently, Ireland becomes a refuge for many Fays before Shade, the Fay leader from Seattle, (re)discovers Frontier, the Fay city set in the West, beyond World's End, at the exact same location as *Seuil*, the Perilous Court that Angharad and Finstern are looking for in *La Glace et la Nuit* (*Vertigen* sequence).[5]

Although Léa Silhol is a French writer, the connection she establishes between fairies and 'Celtic' folklore, and more specifically with Gaelic lore, follows the steps of previous fantasy works by British and American authors. This can be explained by the relatively recent development of French fantasy fiction,[6] which has been deeply influenced by its British and American counterparts, namely Tolkien's works, thus borrowing their themes and tropes. Obviously French fantasy acknowledges the association of magic, fairies and 'Celtic' folklore because of the vivid persistence of such an association in British and American fantasy but also because fantasy has long been perceived in Romance-speaking Europe as a fiction infused with and deeply rooted in legends from Britain and Ireland.

Such a perception is mostly due to the reception of Tolkien's works, in which motifs from 'Celtic' folklore are as prominent as those from Norse mythology and

---

that may have its own rules, which conjures up an unreal, yet consistent, world. The same concept can be applied to Fantasy fiction. See Saint-Gelais (1999). See also Wolf (2012), especially chapter three, which discusses secondary world infrastructures. According to Wolf, imaginary worlds are 'dynamic entities' (3) made of different infrastructures: maps, timelines, genealogies, nature, culture, language, mythology, philosophy and narrative.

[5] For Seuil's connections with the 'Celtic' Otherworld, see *infra*. Angharad and Finstern are the two main characters of the *Vertigen* sequence. Note that Angharad is a distinctively Welsh name, still in use today.

[6] Though André Lichtenberger's *Les Centaures* (1904) is now considered as the first fantasy novel to have been written in French – it was originally seen as a prose poem – French Fantasy truly started to develop in the 1980s, that is more than twenty years after the first publication of *The Lord of the Rings*, and became more popular from the 1990s on.

sagas (see Burns 2005; Fimi 2006 and 2007; Ferré 2007), and to the still popular subgenre of Arthurian Fantasy in both English- and French-speaking areas. It can even be argued that the popularity of the Arthurian legend operates as a link between 'Celtic' folklore and common notions of the marvellous, since on both sides of the Channel, King Arthur is considered as a Briton king who reigned on the Celtic peoples of Britain, in a time of magic and impossible feats (see chapter by Cox in this volume). But it can also be related to the origins of fantasy fiction, as a genre born in Victorian Britain (see Besson 2007), the Anglo-Irish revival of the nineteenth century that claimed (in a context of growing nationalism) that the Irish fairies were more genuine and rooted in tradition,[7] and the perenniality of Romantic stereotypes which define the Celt type as visionary and elusive.

In the anthology *Emblèmes hors-série 2: Les Fées* (2004b)[8] that she edited, Léa Silhol provides an annotated bibliography of essays, treatises, art books and collections of tales dealing with fairies, in which works focusing on either Irish, Scottish, Welsh or British folklore feature prominently. These include William Butler Yeats's *The Book of Fairy and Folk Tales of Ireland*, which compiles *Fairy and Folk Tales of the Irish Peasantry* (1888) and *Irish Fairy Tales* (1892), and *The Celtic Twilight* (1893), which all did feed the notion of a privileged, if not intrinsic, connection between fairies and Irish lore. The same bibliography also mentions Jack Zipes's *Victorian Fairy Tales: The Revolt of the Fairies and Elves* (1987).[9] Besides, the bibliography is preceded by an article by Marie-Laure Nouhaud, 'Les Fées celtes, ces invisibles voisins', the first paragraph of which equates British and 'Celtic' Faërie, and excerpts from Thomas Keightley's *Fairy Mythology* (1880), and is followed by another annotated bibliography providing a list of fantasy works in which fairies are mostly from 'Celtic' sources.

These bibliographies, and their accompanying texts, clearly support the idea that, for French authors such as Léa Silhol, fairies have definitely something to do with 'Celtic' folklore, and confirm that this idea is heavily influenced by British and American works.[10] They also show Léa Silhol's knowledge of

---

[7] According to Diane Purkiss, revivalists such as William Butler Yeats connected fairies and fairy lore to Irishness. See Purkiss (2000: 294).

[8] This is the second anthology on the theme of fairies that Léa Silhol edited. The other one, *Il Était Une Fée* (literally 'Once Upon a Fairy'), was published in 2000.

[9] The annotated bibliography also mentions Laurence Harf-Lancner's works, *Les Fées au Moyen Âge: Morgane et Mélusine* (1984) and *Le Monde* (2003). Laurence Harf-Lancner argues that medieval French fairies are a confluence of the Parcae and the 'Celtic' mother goddesses, something that might have influenced Léa Silhol in her tendency to connect the various mythologies of the world (see second part of this chapter).

[10] The composition of the anthology also favours stories which rely on either 'Celtic' or British folklore: this includes seven out of the thirteen collected stories.

Victorian and early twentieth-century developments of Faërie, something that is also evidenced by her quoting Walter Scott and Walter de la Mare in both *La Sève et le Givre* and *La Glace et la Nuit*. There is thus little doubt that her fiction has been induced by Victorian visions of Faërie and Celticity, and that her Sidhe are partly moulded by her reception of works from that era.

Yet Victorian Britain's conception of fairies was twofold: on the one hand the popular genre of fairy painting shaped visual representations of fairies as tiny and winged creatures such as Tinkerbell in *Peter Pan*,[11] whereas on the other hand the human-sized medieval enchantresses were rediscovered through Victorian transpositions of the Arthurian legend in pre-Raphaelite works and Tennyson's poetry.[12] Léa Silhol's Sidhe obviously resemble more the latter than the first, since they are human-sized, a feature that they share with fairy characters from medieval romances, such as Marie de France's twelfth-century *Lais*, and with the *Daoine Sidhe* as they are traditionally portrayed, just like Tolkien's Elves.

However, the entry 'Sidhe' in the glossary of *La Sève et le Givre* implies that the Sidhe are not the only sort of fairies but that the name refers to the fairies who are closer in appearance to mortals, that is relatively tall and wingless (*'de taille moyenne à grande, dépourvues d'ailes'*, 2002: 366). This alludes to the Victorian winged fairies and to the diversity of size and look of folkloric creatures, even though the narrative and the subsequent *Vertigen* stories do not feature such beings. The Sidhe remain the main protagonists, most of them being identified with well-known figures from Gaelic and Welsh folklore such as the Túatha Dé Danann, Nicnevin (the Fairy queen in the folklore of Scottish lowlands), or Arawn, the king of Annwn, the Welsh Otherworld. But unlike characters of folklore, their speech and manners are more solemn and theatrical, something which make them closer to the Romantic reinterpretation of medieval figures in nineteenth-century literature and to Tolkien's High Elves, despite a sense of playfulness and cruelty.

There is indeed a wild, dangerous aspect attached to these Sidhe, who are certainly not harmless, and Léa Silhol does not hide the fact that they can play with and take mortal lives, though they are not evil by nature. They are simply 'other'. For instance, the parents of Angharad, one of the main protagonists of the *Vertigen* sequence, steal the life of a young man to conceive their child, since

---

[11] Though *Peter Pan* is an Edwardian work, it still demonstrates typical Victorian attitudes regarding childhood and Faërie.

[12] Nicola Bown provides a thorough study of the use of fairies in visual art and literature of the time in *Fairies in Nineteenth Century Art and Literature* (2001).

immortals cannot normally give birth to a new being. Likewise, both *Vertigen* and *Frontier* evoke the concept of changelings, but *Frontier* reverses the view: its so-called changelings,[13] born among humans and not swapped with human babies, point at the changeling affairs that were still occurring in nineteenth-century Ireland, such as the Bridget Cleary case in 1895, where people were falsely accused of being fairies and even killed for that (see Bourke 1999). Hence many parents in the *Frontier* sequence give the name Rowan to their child in the hope that they will not turn out to be a Fay. In Britain, rowan was believed to be a protection against fairies.[14] The fact that many parents turn back to this old superstition and despise Fay children as changelings is part of the dystopic construction of the alternative present depicted in *Frontier*, in which the radical otherness of the Fays and their rejection by humans serve as an exploration of the process of dehumanization at the core of any racism phenomena.

Unmistakably Léa Silhol's Sidhe are as much modelled by folklore and nineteenth-century beliefs and representations of fairies as by previous fantasy fairies. Their depiction is consistent with the author's ambition to carry the legacy of storytellers of old, evidenced in the narrative framework of *La Sève et le Givre* and *La Glace et la Nuit*. Both novels are introduced by fictitious tellers: the mythical bard Oisin/Ossian in *La Sève et le Givre*, who leaves his place to an anonymous Fili[15] in the prelude of *La Glace et la Nuit*, who in turn is replaced by an equally anonymous scribe. Indeed, for Léa Silhol who has been called 'tribe teller' ('*conteuse de la tribu*'), a term she originally applied to Tanith Lee, fantasy fiction is the heir of myth and fairy tale, and it is therefore necessary to root it in mythology and folklore.[16] To create this sense of continuity, she has her Sidhe people being the main protagonists of her meta-series,[17] emphasizing the change they go through from the ancient times when they were gods to the alternative present where they are reborn as Fays. In doing so, she follows a Romantic

---

[13] In the *Frontier* sequence, Fays are first identified as changelings.
[14] See Keightley (1882: 354–5), and Vickery (2019: 824). According to Vickery, 'throughout the British Isles, but especially in Ireland and the Highlands and Islands of Scotland, rowan was valued for its protective powers' (p. 824). He provides several examples of such beliefs, which consider rowans as wards against witches and bad fairies.
[15] The *filid* were a cast of poets and learned professionals in medieval Ireland. They are often considered as guardians of the pre-Christian tradition, though this view is debatable. See Williams (2016: 46). In Léa Silhol's fiction, the Sidhe Filidh are presented as tellers, guardians of the tradition and prophets.
[16] See Silhol (2005), in which she expresses her belief that fantasy is the heir of myth and fairy tales, and considers fairies as the linking point between myth and fairy tale. I have discussed her views on this matter in Bergue (2016).
[17] Anne Besson (2004) uses the term meta-series ('*méta-cycle*') to refer to a set of narratives that is composed of several series or cycles.

vision, that remains very common in fantasy fiction, of seeing 'Celtic' folklore as something ancient, mysterious and deeply connected with nature.

As Dimitra Fimi observes, 'Romanticism's fascination with nature and the exotic quickly configured the "Celtic" countries and cultures as "Other", perceived positively as ancient, mysterious, and wildly exciting' (2017: 11). This characterization particularly fits Léa Silhol's Sidhe who are very ancient ageless beings, connected with nature – their Courts are associated with seasons, Cailleach and Bride respectively embody winter and spring, and they have a special link with trees and elements – and though they have dealings with human beings from time to time, their Courts only exist on another level of reality and are thus hardly accessible to mortals. When they are reborn as Fays, their special connection with nature still remains one of the characteristics that set them apart from humans. Interestingly, the *Frontier* stories emphasize the tribal aspects of the Fay culture (such as ritual tattoos), linking it to shamanism: there is the idea that the Fays return to a more authentic and more significant way of life, than the modern technological one.

The Romantic vision attached to 'Celtic' folklore also serves Léa Silhol's project of building a fantasy that can support the claim of being the direct heir of myth and fairy tale, since it provides a sense of antiquity to her stories, all of which use actual mythological and folkloric sources to fuse them in a multi-layered vast narrative that embraces both mythological and historical times from the beginning of the world to its very end.[18] The Sidhe are at once agents and witnesses of the evolution of the world, and their history turns out to be a secret history of the world, in which the Sidhe's glamour keeps the reader fascinated.

A postmodern mythopoeic fiction

However, in order to embrace both mythological and historical times in a global frame, Léa Silhol does not only rely on 'Celtic' mythology and folklore. She also makes use of other mythologies, namely the Greek one, building surprising bridges between the different stories of her rather fragmented fiction. As a result, the meta-series of *la Trame* appears as a vast puzzle, in which the Sidhe/Fays are a constant that gives the overall sense of consistency and continuity to a fiction that is both postmodern and mythopoeic.

---

[18] Léa Silhol has actually already written the end of her vast set of narratives in the triptych 'Mille ans de servitude', 'Tous des anges' and 'La Faille céleste', which tells the end of the world and a new creation. See Silhol (2008b: 227–80).

Fragmentation, rewriting and borrowing are indeed key features of postmodern fiction that also define Léa Silhol's set of narratives. Unlike typical High Fantasy series, in which calendars and genealogies abound along with an explicit chronological order of the different volumes that compose them, the different sequences and stories of *la Trame* are neither published nor given in a smooth chronological order. Chronology and the overlapping of the stories are to be reconstructed by the reader, like the pieces of a giant puzzle, in which every element can have retrospectively a special significance for the whole fiction. This is the reason why the entanglement of the *Vertigen* and the *Frontier* sequences is not immediately obvious until one reads *La Glace et la Nuit: Opus un. Nigredo*, in which *Seuil* – the future Frontier – is evoked. Narratives from *Avant l'Hiver* (2008a) and *Sacra* (2016b, 2016c; see especially the novella 'Le Maître de Kôdô' in the latter) confirm that the Fays of *Frontier* are the reborn Sidhe whose stories are told in *Vertigen*, whereas *Possession Point* hints at that reality through references that might be obscure to a new reader.

Léa Silhol's fiction also appears as fragmented because of its predilection for short stories, rather than novels, even though the author has regularly claimed in interviews that she prefers writing longer stories (e.g. Brosse 2016). In this regard, the composition of *Avant l'Hiver* is particularly interesting: the stories are first introduced as the contents of mysterious journals discovered at the end of the twentieth century, by Élisabeth Massal, who lives in Bantry, Ireland.[19] This fictitious editor is then replaced by the narrative voice of Kelis Ombrecœur (his name literally means 'Shadowheart') a character from *La Glace et la Nuit*, who acts as compiler and commentator of the stories, which all appear as fragments of an ancient time that no longer exists. Besides the collection is presented as a 'tattered novel' ('*roman en lambeaux*') on the title page, whereas *Vertigen* is said to be a 'series in fractals and chunks' ('*cycle en fractales et morceaux*').

This fragmentation mirrors the fragmentation of 'Celtic' mythology sources which, for a large part, are medieval manuscripts written long after the Christianization of the Celtic-speaking countries, as well as oral material collected and published much later, in the nineteenth century, often brought together through the idea that fairy tales are remnants of pagan mythologies. Such perceptions are consistent with the composite construction of Léa Silhol's reinvention of Faërie, which connects the different mythologies of the world.

---

[19] The location is, of course, not accidental for a book which gathers stories about the Sidhe's secret history. This also feeds a common idea that, unlike other Celtic-speaking countries, Ireland is somehow the 'keeper of a very ancient culture'. See Williams (2016: 46ff) and his discussion of nativist views regarding Ireland as guardian of the tradition.

Thus in *La Sève et le Givre*, the first novel of *Vertigen*, the Sidhe have dealings with the Parcae, the female personifications of destiny from classical mythology, and Angharad's mother is both a seelie Sidhe and a dryad – a forest nymph in Greek mythology. Later, in *La Glace et la Nuit*, the reader learns that Angharad, as an impossible being who is both a spring and a winter Sidhe[20] and who has taken charge of the Cailleach Bheur and Bride, reflects in 'Celtic' lands the Greek Persephone whose presence or absence from the surface of the Earth presides over the change of seasons, just like Angharad's lover Finstern is a reflection of Hades (see Silhol 2007: 167–81). Similarly, in the alternative present of *Frontier*, the novella 'Le Maître de Kôdô' in *Sacra, Parfums d'Isenne et d'ailleurs: Opus deux: Nulle âme invincible* introduces the Fays to Japanese folklore and the figure of the Yuki Onna, connecting Eastern Asia and the Western lore.[21]

The comparison between the couples formed by Angharad and Finstern and by Persephone and Hades, and the presence of the Parcae, who play a major role in *La Sève et le Givre*, also signal the original divine nature of the Sidhe. Here Léa Silhol supports the idea that fairies are former pagan gods that have become diminished beings in folklore. Hence the Túatha Dé Danann, the gods of Irish mythology, are Monarchs of some of the Kingdom Courts ('Kingdom' is the term referring to Faërie in *Vertigen*). In *La Glace et la Nuit*, it is stated that the Sidhe and the other gods of old, such as Persephone and Hades, are threatened to disappear because of the growing belief in the One God of Christianity,[22] a situation which might explain why the Sidhe are receding from the mortal world and are no longer seen as divine beings.

At the same time, the novel reveals that Finstern is a former angel, another evidence of Léa Silhol's composite postmodern construction. The angelic origins of Finstern hint at another belief from folklore according to which fairies are actually fallen angels who did not choose a side when Lucifer rebelled. An instance of this belief is to be found in the episode of the Paradise of Birds in Benedeit's *Le Voyage de Saint Brendan* (twelfth century): while he is looking for the earthly paradise, Brendan arrives on an island that is only populated by

---

[20] In *Vertigen*, intermarriages between seelie Sidhe (associated with spring and summer) and unseelie Sidhe (associated with either winter or autumn) are forbidden, so the conception and birth of Angharad breaks the rules and sets her apart.

[21] Léa Silhol develops further her exploration of Eastern Asian folklore in the *Seppenko Monogatari* sequence which revolves around the story of the Izôkage family, a lineage cursed by a Yuki Onna and connected to the Sidhe of *Vertigen* through one of his members who married the unseelie queen Nicnevin.

[22] The One God is explicitly presented as the enemy in the novel, although he remains hidden and does not seem to intervene in the course of action.

birds. One of them tells him that they were once angels and that Lucifer brought them down with his fall (2006: 78–83).[23] Unlike the birds encountered by saint Brendan, Finstern purposefully left Heaven, and this makes him logically an adversary of God. However Léa Silhol does not identify all her Sidhe with angels, since Finstern and his Nishven are an afterthought of the Kingdom. But, in the *Frontier* sequence, the Fay called Fallen, whose birth name is Ange, reminds nonetheless of this angelic origin.

The fate of the Sidhe is then linked to the fate of other mythological beings, but unlike Persephone and Hades who do not seem ready to break the ancient rules represented in the *Vertigen* sequence by figures such as the Parcae or Titania,[24] and therefore change so as to maintain an actual connection with the mortal world, the Sidhe try to act against destiny. In this context, Léa Silhol's reinterpretation of Gaelic and Welsh mythology and folklore informs the tension in Faërie between a need for transformation and a desire to avoid any change and thus freeze the Sidhe society.

In *Vertigen*, Faërie appears as a Kingdom that is a confederation of Courts, not dissimilar to ancient Ireland in its structure. Each Court is associated with a Clarity: there are Seven Courts of Light, Nine Courts of Shadow and Three Courts of Twilight; and in each of them a Monarch reigns, but all are under the dominion of the High Queen Titania. The different Clarities are linked with the nature of the Sidhe who inhabit the Courts. Hence the Courts of Light are homes to the seelie Sidhe whereas the Courts of Shadow are those of the unseelie ones, and although the Courts of Twilight represent an in-between, their inhabitants are also unseelie. Léa Silhol borrows this distinction between seelie and unseelie Sidhe from Scottish folklore, but removes its moral aspect: whereas in Scottish folklore, seelie Sidhe are seen as good and unseelie Sidhe as bad (see Briggs 1976), in *Vertigen*, the distinction is only in degrees of wilderness and connection with specific seasons. The narratives mostly favour unseelie Sidhe, and characters who are associated to unseelie Sidhe such as Finstern, as their main protagonists. In *La Sève et le Givre*, Léa Silhol also introduces an important rule: seelie and unseelie Sidhe cannot marry each other, at the sole exception of the High Queen and High King for political purposes. This rule is one among

---

[23] The much earlier Latin version of the text, *Navigatio sancti Brendani abbatis*, also has the Paradise of Birds scene. Ian Short and Brian Merrilees observe that similar episodes exist in three Irish *imramma*, *Immram curaig Máele Dúin*, *Immram curaig Ua Corra* and *Immram Snédgusa ocus Maic Riagla*, and that the representation of souls as birds is part of medieval traditions.

[24] Shakespeare's *A Midsummer Night's Dream* is also an important intertext in fantasy fiction, and it is therefore not surprising that the High Queen of the Kingdom is called Titania.

many which constrain the Sidhe and prevent their society from evolving. The invention of Angharad, a completely fictive character whose very existence breaks the law, initiates a series of transformations, as she embodies freedom and the rejection of the old rules. Her bond with Finstern, another invented character who represents Chaos – he is the ruler of the Ninth Court of Shadow[25] and his name literally means *dark*, from the German adjective *finster*[26] – creates the possibility of change in a crumbling Kingdom that is prisoner of its own rules. Their quest for Seuil, the Perilous Court, will destroy the current order so as to re-establish Faërie and set the path for the rebirth of the Sidhe as Fays in the alternative present of *Frontier*.

The quest is mediated by another quest, the completion of which is necessary to find Seuil. Indeed Angharad and Finstern need to have the Treasures of the Túatha Dé Danann – the Hallows[27] – to open the doors of Seuil, since that mythical place was once the home of the Túatha Dé Danann, Tréaga.[28] Seuil is a particularly interesting place, in regard to the use of 'Celtic' folklore in the *Vertigen* sequence: its ancient name, Tréaga, means 'Three Times' or 'The Triple', and alludes to the mysterious Three Islands which the Túatha Dé Danann are supposed to come from in the *Lebar Gabála Érenn* ('The Book of the Takings of Ireland', often called 'The Book of Invasions') which chronicles the different invasions of Ireland by semi-divine mythical peoples. Likewise the other name of Seuil, Tairseach the Perilous, or the Perilous Court, recalls both of the phrase 'the Perilous Realm' sometimes used to refer to Faërie (as, for example, in

---

[25] Obviously an allusion to his former angelic nature and his link with Lucifer. Finstern is also called Finstern the Dark (*Finstern le Noir*) and Dealra or Dealra-ciardhubh (which literally means 'dark sparkle' in Gaelic) and one of his titles is Shadow of the Síd (*Ombre du Síd*).

[26] Although it could be tempting to see in the name Finstern a reference to the Gaelic *finn*, which means 'white, bright', joined with the German *Stern*, 'star', thus implying that the name could be translated as 'bright star' (as a reminder of Lucifer as light bearer) such an interpretation is very unlikely, given the clear connection between the character and darkness throughout Léa Silhol's narratives. If Finstern is indeed associated with Lucifer, he is not to be confused with him, since Lucifer appears in some of the narratives of *Sacra*. Besides, in *La Glace et la Nuit: Opus deux. Albedo* (Silhol 2020: 27), Finstern clearly states that his name is of Germanic origin.

[27] Following the Irish mythological tradition, Léa Silhol mentions four Hallows: Lugh's Spear, the Dagda's Cauldron, the Stone of Sovereignty and the sword Fragarach the Answerer. The Four Treasures of the Túatha Dé Danann are mentioned in the *Lebar Gabála Érenn* ('The Book of the Takings/Conquests of Ireland', usually known as 'The Book of Invasions'). Mark Williams (2016: 148ff) examines in detail the concept of the Four Treasures and the four cities they came from (see next endnote) and notes that later writers, such as William Butler Yeats, 'were forcibly struck by the apparent symbolism here, which seemed to evoke the four elements of natural philosophy and esoteric doctrine' (149; see also the chapter by Wood in this volume). Léa Silhol's fiction follows the same path, since the subtitles of the two first volumes of *La Glace et la Nuit*, *Nigredo* and *Albedo*, which recount the quest of the Hallows, refer to alchemical stages.

[28] As in the Irish pseudohistory, the Túatha Dé Danann and their treasures came from four cities: Falias, Goirias, Muirias and Findias (Williams 2016: 149).

Tolkien's 'On Fairy-stories'), and of the Perilous Chair on which no one can sit down unless he is the knight who will complete the quest for the Holy Grail in the Arthurian legend. This signals that not anyone can reach Seuil, you have to be worth of it. Besides Seuil is located in the West, beyond World's End, just like some representations of the Otherworld in Gaelic and Welsh folklore.

Consequently, this mythical place that Angharad and Finstern are looking for and where the Fays will find refuge and build their city of Frontier combines different features that link it to 'Celtic' folklore, while being at the same time an elusive ideal and a promised land,[29] the usual name of which – Seuil (literally 'Threshold') – simply emphasizes the notion of passage – from one world to another, or from one condition to another. This land differs from Tír-na-nÓg, i.e. Titania's Court, where an everlasting spring reigns as a result of a deadly wish to freeze time.[30] Though they are traditional Otherworld locations in the Irish and Welsh material respectively, both Tír-na-nÓg and the Welsh Annwn[31] are part of the Kingdom that needs to be destroyed and re-established in Seuil.

In this perspective, the Túatha Dé Danann represent the bridge between the ancient times preceding the foundation of the Kingdom,[32] the medieval times of *La Glace et la Nuit* and the future times of the refoundation of Faërie. Not only Angharad and Finstern need their Treasures to find Seuil, they also need the Túatha Dé Danann to leave the roles that have been appointed to them in the Kingdom, to break the rules too and become agents of change. So Lugh has to become an ally and give freely his Spear, Gaé Assail, to Angharad and Finstern. Similarly, Mabb,[33] who is also Mebd Lethderg, guardian of the Nameless Court and the Stone of Sovereignty at Tara,[34] ends up helping the two lovers, whereas the Dagda recognizes Angharad's right to hold the Cup – the Dagda's Cauldron – after she won it in a game.[35]

---

[29] The future name of Seuil, Frontier and its location in the West, beyond World's End, also allude to the American myth of the Frontier, and the fact that the Fay city appears as merely utopian compared to the dystopian alternative USA depicted in the *Frontier* sequence equally evokes the conception of America as a promised land that remains to be discovered.

[30] For more details on this aspect of Titania's Court in the *Vertigen* sequence, see Bergue (2015: 190–3).

[31] Annwn is the second Court of Shadow.

[32] These are the times of Aana, the Mother, as the reader is told in 'De l'or dont on fait les Âges (la Reine en son privé)', in *Avant l'Hiver*. Although Aana's name brings to mind Dana/Danu, the hypothetical mother goddess of the Túatha Dé Danann, they are too different characters in the *Vertigen* sequence.

[33] Though Mebd is not one of the Túatha Dé Danann, she is somehow associated with them in *La Glace et la Nuit* because she is the guardian of the Stone.

[34] The location of the Stone in Tara links myth and history, since Tara was the seat of the high kings of Ireland (*ard ríg na hÉrenn*) (see Bhreathnach 2006).

[35] Incidentally, the Cup will be later identified with the Grail in the Urban Fantasy short story 'Désaccordé (Tune in Dagdad)', thus fusing Irish mythology with the Arthurian legend (see Silhol 2008c). The events of this short story are to be considered as contemporary to those of the *Frontier* sequence.

This urge to choose Seuil and freedom against Titania's law seems justified since, retrospectively, the period of the Kingdom appears as a time of false pretence, where everyone plays a role, hence the borrowing of Titania's and Mabb's names from Shakespeare, the later being a bastardization of the Irish figure of Medb, often considered as a personification of sovereignty in Irish tradition.[36] The Kingdom reflects a certain vision of Faërie where nothing is really what it seems to be, and where fairies are amoral and cruel, eager to play with the life of others, whether they are mortal or immortal. *La Sève et le Givre* illustrates this aspect, showing the reader a world infused with preciosity, in which appearance seems to prevail over truth and integrity, and where everyone has to play games obeying cruel rules. In the novel, the Kingdom is reminiscent of Versailles and its intrigues but a fantastic Versailles where the Parcae work in the shadows to trap Finstern in a romance that might destroy him simply because they want to punish him for not falling in love with any of them.

Both *La Glace et la Nuit* and *Avant l'Hiver* reject this order: when Angharad tries and convinces Lugh to become her ally in her quest for Seuil, she presents the future society they will build there as one which values fraternity[37] – something that hardly exists in the Kingdom. Similarly, in *Avant l'Hiver*, Kelis is proud to have been part of the revolution that ended the time of the Kingdom and Titania's reign. Consequently, it can be inferred that in helping Angharad and Finstern in their quest, the Túatha Dé Danann can expect to have their former grandeur renewed and become free again.

Indeed when Lugh replies to Angharad that he could refuse to follow her, she tells him:

> Then we will fail. And all will lose. You will be able to use your remaining time peacefully to say goodbye. To the life you have enjoyed, to what you achieved long ago, and to all you made of yourself. And contemplate the future Lugh: a pretty idle warrior, cherishing his aborted dreams under unchanged skies, lying at Titania's feet among the other dogs of her pack. You will do well, then, yes, to get used to the endless taste of defeat.
>
> (Silhol 2007: 336)[38]

---

[36] And indeed, in *Vertigen*, Mabb was once the High Queen of Faërie before her unseelie nature was treacherously changed into a seelie one. Only in Tara she connects to her old grandeur.

[37] '*La terre où nul, jamais, n'est laissé derrière*' ('The land where no one is ever left behind') (Silhol 2007: 338).

[38] '*Alors nous échouerons. Et tous perdront. Tu pourras user paisiblement du temps qu'il te reste à faire tes adieux. À la vie que tu as aimée, à ce que tu accomplis jadis, et à ce que tu fis de toi-même. Et contempler le Lugh à venir: un joli guerrier oisif, berçant ses rêves avortés sous des cieux inchangés, couché aux pieds de Titania parmi les autres chiens de sa meute. Tu feras bien, alors, oui, de t'habituer au goût interminable de la défaite*'.

The possible outcome that Angharad describes to Lugh is one of volunteer slavery in a Faërie which would be definitely cut off from mortality and time. Therefore it is not a future to wish for, as it would mean that the Sidhe would have completely receded from the lands of mortality and would have left them to the total dominion of the One God while they would linger in a very small Kingdom. But if Lugh agrees to follow her, then he will have the possibility to 'remain the one that nothing restrains, and who refuses to define himself' (*rester celui que rien ne limite, et qui refuse de se définir*) (Silhol 2007: 337). In other words, he will remain free and still able to change and reinvent himself, and, as the reader can assume, achieve new deeds.

Here Léa Silhol connects freedom and change: in a frozen world where rules are immutable and everyone has to stick to a specific role, freedom is an intellectual concept. Likewise, the Sidhe, as mythical beings who refuse to disappear, have to accept change if they want to survive and not become entirely diminished and at the mercy of the One God. They need to become an embodiment of the perpetual reinvention of myth, ever changing, ever taking new forms, through the passage of time.

The return of the Sidhe as Fays in the alternative present of *Frontier* fulfils this necessary transformation. However, in the current state of publication of the author's works, it is impossible to say how this transformation is achieved: *La Glace et la Nuit* is still incomplete, and neither *Musiques de la Frontière* nor *Possession Point* – the two main books of the *Frontier* sequence – gives any clue. Most Fays, like Anis, the narrator of *Possession Point*, do not know what and who they really are. They are simply conscious that they are the resurgence of something ancient in a time when technology prevails. The recent *Seppenko Monogatari* sequence (Silhol 2018a, 2018b, 2019a, 2019b, 2019c) goes further by clearly stating that the Fays are the reborn Sidhe[39] but so far its narratives do not provide any explanation on how this rebirth has become possible.

But the novel *Sous le lierre* (Silhol 2016d), loosely connected to the *Vertigen* sequence through the figure of Herne the Hunter,[40] whose spirit haunts the woods surrounding Savernake and who is the object of a strange cult surviving at the very beginning of the twentieth century, might provide a possible clue. As the main character and narrator, Ivy finds out, in each generation, the villagers pair a boy and a girl to re-enact the union of Herne with a mortal. The boy

---

[39] Hence we learn that Crescent is the reborn Nicnevin.
[40] Herne is another example of the syncretism of Léa Silhol's fiction: indeed he is not a genuine figure of folklore but much probably an original creation by Shakespeare. See Hutton (2019).

who has been possessed by Herne's spirit is then sent away, to America, and the child who is conceived through this union is doomed to play the same role as either his/her father or mother in the next generation. One can assume that the offspring of these ritual unions, being all children of Herne, a minor character of the *Vertigen* sequence, carry a Sidhe heredity which will be primordial to allow the Sidhe to get reincarnated as Fays among humans.

In any case, the return of the Sidhe as Fays literalizes the survival of magic and myth in the twenty-first century, and highlights the idea that myth constantly evolves and is subjected to new interpretations. Therefore, Léa Silhol's fiction appears not only as postmodern but also as mythopoeic, in the sense given by the Mythopoeic Society:

> We define [mythopoeic fiction] as literature that creates a new and transformative mythology, or incorporates and transforms existing mythological material. Transformation is the key – mere static reference to mythological elements, invented or pre-existing, is not enough. The mythological elements must be of sufficient importance in the work to influence the spiritual, moral, and/or creative lives of the characters, and must reflect and support the author's underlying themes. This type of work, at its best, should also inspire the reader to examine the importance of mythology in his or her own spiritual, moral, and creative development.
>
> (Mythopoeic Society n.d.)

Reworking and transforming existing mythological material is truly at the heart of Léa Silhol's fiction as a close look at its use of 'Celtic' folklore and other mythologies demonstrates. The fate of her Sidhe people also comments on the place of myth in our modern society: a symbolic irrational discourse that is far from having disappeared completely in our highly scientific and technological reality and that has the potentiality to resurge through new unpredictable forms (see also Attebery 2014 on this wider argument).

Conclusion

Summing up, from *Vertigen* to *Frontier*, Léa Silhol indulges us in a postmodern mythopoeic fiction which mainly focuses on the fate of the Sidhe/Fays to explore the many transformations of myth and highlights the fact that change cannot be avoided. Hence the Sidhe are and are not the fairies from 'Celtic' folklore, they have been more and they will take new shapes as Fays, just like myth does not stop changing over time. As a composite postmodern construct, they still bear features from nineteenth-century fairies and Romantic vision of 'Celticity' but these are combined with new reinterpretations so as to make them the true cousins of the Greek gods and other divine or semi-divine beings. As a result, Faërie appears as even more fascinating, being both threatened and sometimes threatening, perilous and welcoming.

The fate of the Sidhe might still be uncertain but there is no doubt that their story will keep mirroring the pervasiveness of myth and our modern time fascination with 'Celtic' folklore.

References

Attebery, Brian (2014), *Stories about Stories: Fantasy and the Remaking of Myth*, Oxford: Oxford University Press.
Benedeit (2006), *Le Voyage de saint Brendan*, ed. and annot. Ian Short and Brian Merrilees, Paris: Champion.
Bergue, Viviane (2015), *La Fantasy: Mythopoétique De La Quête*, CreateSpace.
Bergue, Viviane (2016), 'Léa Silhol ou La Féerie au Prisme du Mythe', *M@gm@*, 14 (3): http://www.analisiqualitativa.com/magma/1403/articolo_04.htm, accessed 22 Jun. 2021.
Besson, Anne (2004), *D'Asimov à Tolkien: Cycles et Series en Literature de Genre*, Paris: CNRS éditions.
Besson, Anne (2007), *La Fantasy*, Paris: Klincksieck.
Bhreathnach, Edel (2006), 'Teamhair (Tara)', in John T. Koch (ed.), *Celtic Culture: A Historical Encyclopedia*, 1663–4, Santa Barbara, CA: ABC-CLIO.
Bourke, Angela (1999), *The Burning of Bridget Cleary: A True Story*, London: Pimlico.
Bown, Nicola (2001), *Fairies in Nineteenth Century Art and Literature*, Cambridge: Cambridge University Press.
Briggs, Katharine (1976), *An Encyclopaedia of Fairies: Hobgoblins, Brownies, Bogies, and Other Supernatural Creatures*, New York: Pantheon.
Brosse, Luigi (2016), 'Un Entretien Fleuve avec Léa Silhol', *Elbakin.net: La Fantasy au quotidien* (30 May 2016), http://www.elbakin.net/interview/exclusive/Un-entretien-fleuve-avec-Lea-Silhol, accessed 23 Jun. 2021.
Burns, Marjorie (2005), *Perilous Realms: Celtic and Norse in Tolkien's Middle-earth*, Toronto: Toronto University Press.
Ferré, Vincent (2007), 'De Tristan à Tolkien: Beren, Túrin et Aragorn: I – Fonder la comparaison; II – L'amour fatal', in Anne Besson and Myriam White-Le Goff (eds), *Fantasy: Le Merveilleux Médiéval Aujourd'hui*, 17–30, Paris: Bragelonne.
Fimi, Dimitra (2006), '"Mad" Elves and "Elusive Beauty": Some Celtic Strands of Tolkien Mythology', *Folklore*, 117: 156–70.
Fimi, Dimitra (2007), 'Tolkien's "Celtic type of legends": Merging Traditions', *Tolkien Studies*, 4: 51–71.

Fimi, Dimitra (2017), *Celtic Myth in Contemporary Children's Fantasy: Idealization, Identity, Ideology*, London: Palgrave Macmillan.
Hutton, Ronald (2019), 'The Wild Hunt in the Modern British Imagination', *Folklore*, 130 (2): 175–91.
Keightley, Thomas (1828), *The Fairy Mythology*, London: George Bell & Sons.
Lichtenberger, André (1904), *Les Centaures*, Paris: Calmann-Lévy.
Mythopoeic Society, 'About the Society', http://www.mythsoc.org/about.htm, accessed 23 Jun. 2021.
Purkiss, Diane (2004), *Troublesome Things: A History of Fairies and Fairy Stories*, London: Penguin.
Saint-Gelais, Richard (1999), *L'Empire du Pseudo: Modernités de la Science-Fiction*, Québec: Nota Bene.
Silhol, Léa, ed. (2000), *Il Etait Une Fée: 15 Contes entre Clair et Obscur*, Montpellier: L'Oxymore.
Silhol, Léa (2002), *La Sève et le Givre*, Montpellier: L'Oxymore.
Silhol, Léa (2004a), *Musiques de la Frontière*, Montpellier: L'Oxymore.
Silhol, Léa, ed. (2004b), *Emblèmes Hors-Série 2: Les Fées*, Montpellier: L'Oxymore.
Silhol, Léa (2005), 'Fées et Fantasy: Un Mariage Heureux?', in Léa Silhol et Estelle Valls de Gomis (eds), *Fantastique, Fantasy, Science-fiction: Mondes Imaginaires, Etranges Réalités*, 30–43, coll. «Mutations» no. 239, Paris: Autrement.
Silhol, Léa (2007), *La Glace et la Nuit: Opus un. Nigredo*, Lyon: Les Moutons Electriques.
Silhol, Léa (2008a), *Avant l'Hiver: Architectonique des Clartés*, Lyon: Les Moutons Electriques.
Silhol, Léa (2008b), *Fo/véa: Leçons de gravité dans un Palais des Glaces*, Auch: Le Calepin Jaune.
Silhol, Léa (2008c), 'Désaccordé (Tuned in Dagdag)', in Lucie Chenu (ed.), *De Brocéliande en Avalon*, 175–96, Dinard: Terre de Brume.
Silhol, Léa (2016a), *Possession Point*, Montpellier: Nitchevo Factory.
Silhol, Léa (2016b), *Sacra, Parfums d'Isenne et d'ailleurs Opus un: Aucun cœur inhumain*, Montpellier: Nichevo Factory.
Silhol, Léa (2016c), *Sacra, Parfums d'Isenne et d'ailleurs, Opus deux: Nulle âme invincible*, Montpellier: Nitchevo Factory.
Silhol, Léa (2016d), *Sous le Lierre*, Montpellier: Nitchevo Factory.
Silhol, Léa (2018a), *Hanami Sonata*, Montpellier: Nitchevo Factory
Silhol, Léa (2018b), *Romaji Horizon*, Gridlock Coda vol.1, Montpellier: Nitchevo Factory.
Silhol, Léa (2019a), *Masshiro Ni*, Montpellier: Nitchevo Factory.
Silhol, Léa (2019b), *Hangul Express: Première partie*, Gridlock Coda vol. 2, Montpellier: Nitchevo Factory.
Silhol, Léa (2019c), *Hangul Express: Deuxième partie*, Gridlock Coda vol. 2, Montpellier: Nitchevo Factory.

Silhol, Léa (2020), *La Glace et la Nuit: Opus deux. Albedo*, Montpellier: Nitchevo Factory.
Silhol, Léa, 'Winterdaze', https://winterdaze.wordpress.com/blog-flux/, accessed 22 Jun. 2021.
Silhol, Léa (2021), *La Glace et la Nuit opus trois. Cauda Pavonis*, Montpellier: Nitchevo Factory.
Vickery, Roy (2019), *Vickery's Folk Flora*, London: Weidenfeld & Nicolson.
Williams, Mark (2016), *Ireland's Immortals: A History of the Gods of Irish Myth*, Princeton, NJ: Princeton University Press.
Wolf, Mark J. P. (2012), *Building Imaginary Worlds: The Theory and History of Subcreation*, New York: Routledge.

8

'Chaidh e nas doimhne agus nas doimhne ann an seann theacsaichean': Gaelic history and legend in *An Sgoil Dhubh* by Iain F. MacLeòid

Duncan Sneddon

When we think of Celtic elements within fantasy literature, we are usually thinking of the use of elements of Celtic-language literary, legendary and folk tradition or retellings of medieval Celtic-language narratives in English-language writings. This chapter will look instead at one recent novel in Gaelic, *An Sgoil Dhubh* ('The Black School') by Iain F. MacLeòid (2014).[1] *An Sgoil Dhubh* is set in a fictional world (or, rather, in several connected fictional worlds), but is also very clearly rooted within Gaelic historical and legendary traditions. In many respects it resembles mainstream modern fantasy, with such common genre tropes as the return of an ancient dark lord and a young man from apparently humble origins finding his destiny as a saviour figure. However, while many fantasy books share a generally Western European-style setting and frames of reference, MacLeòid makes use of personal and group names, creatures, weapons and concepts from a range of Gaelic sources, from folk tales to Old Irish sagas, creating an unmistakably Gaelic setting for his work.

This chapter will attempt to situate *An Sgoil Dhubh* within the contexts of Gaelic tradition and modern fantasy literature, while also considering how MacLeòid uses elements of Norse traditions to create his fictional world. It will investigate how he blends a range of historical and folkloric elements familiar to a Gaelic-speaking audience with others drawn from the medieval Irish literary tradition into a fictional present in a fantasy version of Gaelic culture in a fantasy

---

[1] All translations of quotations from the novel are mine, and I take full responsibility for any errors in them.

world. This also includes drawing aspects of Norse history and literature into that narrative present, in part due to the influence of the Norse settlement on the real-world history and culture of Gaelic Scotland. *An Sgoil Dhubh* is thus a novel that fits very comfortably into the conventions of fantasy literature, and which is also deeply and distinctly *Gàidhealach*.

Literature in Gaelic is often ignored in assessments of Scottish literature, including of Scottish fantasy literature. For instance, Colin Manlove's classic critical anthology of Scottish fantasy literature includes short stories and folktales in Scots and English, but none at all in Gaelic, apparently on the grounds that 'these tales are closer to Irish and Gaelic than to a peculiarly Scottish tradition' (Manlove 1996: 19). That book does contain extracts from Macpherson's *Ossian* and the Celtic Twilight writer William Sharp, alias Fiona MacLeod, meaning that there is room made for appropriations or imitations of Gaelic literary traditions in English, which we must therefore assume is sufficiently peculiarly Scottish, but none for actual work in Gaelic. What this means in practice is that understandings and critical assessments of 'Scottish' literature are constructed that exclude any Gaelic perspectives, so that 'Scottish' effectively comes to mean 'English- and Scots-speaking Scotland'.[2] This chapter cannot hope to correct this imbalance, but it does aim to demonstrate that fantasy literature in Gaelic is worth engaging with critically. If more critics do so going forward, a more comprehensive understanding of Scottish literature can be built, including fantasy literature, that does not exclude Gaelic perspectives, nor fill in the Gaelic-shaped gaps with dubious Romantic appropriations in English.

There is another impetus for this study. The corpus of fantasy and science fiction in Gaelic, while still small, has seen marked growth in recent years, and as Gaelic fiction continues to grow and diversify, it is likely that more fantasy and science fiction will be produced in the language in the coming years. As such, critical approaches to Gaelic fantasy and science fiction that assess these works within their wider genre contexts will become an increasingly worthwhile endeavour, as we come to see these works as not simply Gaelic novels, but Gaelic novels which participate in international genre currents.

While there is a rich store of heroic ballads, folk tales and legendary material in the Gaelic literary tradition, the corpus of modern fantasy literature, a form

---

[2] This exclusion of Gaelic materials is a widespread issue, and arises from the fact that few Scottish literary and cultural critics are able to understand Gaelic. So an otherwise excellent study such as Julian D'Arcy's *Scottish Skalds and Sagamen: Old Norse Influence on Modern Scottish Literature* (2012) does not include much relevant material in Gaelic. Donald E. Meek (2018) has recently critiqued this conflation of (mostly urban) Lowland perspectives with 'Scottish' perspectives as a whole, in the context of modern understandings of the 'Scottish' Enlightenment.

of literature that often builds on or makes use of such traditional narrative material, is very small. There are some low fantasy works, such as the short novel *A' Choille Fhiadhaich* ('The Wild Wood') by Coinneach Lindsay, a young adult novel aimed at Gaelic learners (2017). There are also two notable low fantasy short stories, 'An Dùdach' ('The Horn') by Anna Fhriseal (1962) and 'Oisein ann an Tìr nan Òg' ('Oisein in the Land of Youth') by Màrtainn Mac an t-Saoir (2003), which are in some respects similar to *An Sgoil Dhubh* in that they adapt traditional Gaelic narratives, both being about the 'return' of long-dormant heroes of Gaelic legend to the modern world. Inasmuch as there is a tradition of modern fantasy literature in Gaelic, therefore, we can note that one of its marked features is the use of characters and themes from Gaelic tradition, something which as we shall see is very much the case in *An Sgoil Dhubh*.

An Sgoil Dhubh is a high fantasy novel, set across a number of connected worlds. The worlds are shut off from each other, and only a select few individuals are able to pass between them. One such individual is Sgàire, the novel's main character. While he is introduced as, and believes himself to be, an ordinary young man of humble origins, it is soon clear that he is in fact destined for greater things, and finds himself embroiled in a struggle against the Draoidhean, a caste of wizards who have usurped the throne of his world, Erda, and assassinated its king. Assisting the king's daughter, Eimhir, and trying first to escape and then to defeat Am Maighstir ('The Master'), a returning dark lord seemingly defeated long ago, Sgàire passes between the worlds, on the way making common cause with their peoples and assembling a cast of allies who in the end take on and defeat Am Maighstir and his forces. The worlds in question are Erda (*uaine agus bàigheil*, 'green and friendly'), Fairge (which means 'ocean', an ocean planet), Arhell (a desert planet) and Is (an ice planet). These worlds share access to a fifth planet, Saoghal nam Marbh ('World of the Dead'), to which their dead go to a gloomy afterlife, and in which Am Maighstir has long bided his time.

The novel is 190 pages long and written in the third person. Extra information is occasionally supplied by extracts from in-world historical and mythological texts, printed in italics. Some of these texts also play a role in the plot of the novel, and are read by characters within it. While not explicitly marketed as a young adult novel, it certainly shares some common features with that genre, including adolescent protagonists and issues around first romantic relationships. *An Sgoil Dhubh*, in keeping with MacLeòid's other work, is fast-paced and entertaining, with well-written, vividly realized action sequences, but the characters are rather two-dimensional, and the story is at times too rushed (Watson 2011: 160–4). It is a flawed novel, but nevertheless an interesting one in the ways in which MacLeòid situates the world of his novel within the contexts of fantasy literature and Gaelic tradition.

The novel is written entirely in Gaelic (unlike MacLeòid's earlier historical fiction novel *Am Bounty* (MacLeòid 2008), which featured considerable stretches of dialogue in English), and consistently uses forms from MacLeòid's own Lewis dialect. On the lexical level, for instance, he uses *bùrn* and not *uisge* for 'water', *man* and not *mar* for 'like' or 'as' and *feagal* and not *eagal* for 'fear'. There are also instances in which, conforming to common usage in Lewis and some other places, homorganic consonants do not block lenition as they do in other dialects, as for instance in *ann an seann theacsaichean* ('in old texts'), and not *ann an seann teacsaichean* (MacLeòid 2014: 88).[3] It should be noted that these features are used consistently by characters from across the range of worlds in the novel, and in the authorial voice. They are not markers of the dialect or origin of any particular character or community within the text, they are simply part of the language in which the novel is written.

An Sgoil Dhubh connects to the wider web of fantasy in several ways, including in the use of common fantasy tropes which can be found in some of the most popular and most influential writings in the genre. While MacLeòid is not primarily a fantasy writer (this is the only one of his six novels to be a fantasy novel, though he has also written one science fiction novel, *An Taistealach* (MacLeòid 2017)), a familiarity with certain foundational fantasy and science fiction texts can probably be assumed, whether as books or in some cases in cinematic adaptations. The works of J.R.R. Tolkien, Frank Herbert and Ursula K. Le Guin would fall under this category. Similarities to certain works by other writers such as Gene Wolfe and Steven Erikson can also be detected, as will be discussed below. This does not necessarily mean that individual instances of similarities between *An Sgoil Dhubh* and other works are all the result of direct borrowing or influence from certain texts, but rather that MacLeòid's work exists within the wider context of fantasy literature, and that the more familiar readers are with that wider context, the more points of contact they will find between *An Sgoil Dhubh* and other writings they know, whether intended by MacLeòid or not. Some of these points of contact are to do with the construction of the novel, such as supplementing the narrative with quotations from in-world historical documents to provide exposition; or with its plot, such as the unsurprising revelation that the protagonist Sgàire, while initially appearing to be an ordinary young man of humble origins, in fact has a great destiny to fulfil. Others involve

---

[3] I am grateful to Joan NicDhòmhnaill and Liam Alastair Crouse for advice on this matter.

the use by MacLeòid of certain physical objects and settings within the novel. Some of those points of contact will be discussed here, helping us to situate the novel within the wider tradition of modern fantasy literature, before we go on to situate it in its specifically Gaelic context. There are many such instances in *An Sgoil Dhubh*, of which the following few will suffice to demonstrate the use of established fantasy tropes.[4]

One common trope within fantasy literature is the presence of an ancient weapon, usually a sword, which is presented to or discovered by a character who will wield it while fulfilling some grand destiny. The most famous example in fantasy literature, as with many such tropes, is probably that in J.R.R. Tolkien's *The Lord of the Rings*, in which the sword Narsil/Andúril has such a function for Aragorn, marking him out as the heir of Isildur. David Gemmell's *The Sword in the Storm*, discussed in this volume by Anthony Smart and Alistair J.P. Sims provides another example (Gemmell 2001). This is now so well established as a fantasy trope that it can be considered a cliché, and is parodied as such in Terry Pratchett's comical fantasy novel *Guards! Guards!*, in the battered, unimpressive-looking sword of the six-foot tall (adopted) dwarf Carrot Ironfoundersson (Pratchett 1989). MacLeòid furnishes Sgàire with such a sword, *an Claidheamh Gorm* (the Blue Sword), introduced in a prophecy in a passage from 'Leabhar Stairsich', '*Agus aithnichidh daoine e [.i. fear ... a dh'fhosglas na Dorsan]oir bidh an Claidheamh Gorm aige agus bheir e beatha gu tè a bha marbh*' ('And people will know him [i.e. a man ... who opens the Doors], for he will have the Blue Sword and he will give life to one who was dead') (MacLeòid 2014: 84) both of which prophecies are indeed fulfilled. As we shall see later, Sgàire also wields another sword, which roots him in the Gaelic folklore tradition as clearly as *an Claidheamh Gorm* roots him in the fantasy tradition.

Another point of contact with Pratchett's Discworld books comes at the very end of the novel, in which Sgàire and Am Maighstir have their final confrontation in a vast hall of books, with each book containing a full record of an individual's life: *Air a sgrìobhadh ann, ann an litrichean beaga, bìodach, bha beatha cuideigin – gach mionaid a bha iad air an t-saoghal air innse gu grinn agus gu mionaideach* ('Written in it, in tiny little letters, was somebody's life – every minute that they

---

[4] Raghnall MacilleDhuibh, in his positive review of the novel in *The Scotsman* (2016), admitted that he has very little familiarity with fantasy literature at all, and did not attempt to assess it in the context of fantasy literature as such. While critical assessments of *An Sgoil Dhubh* certainly must engage with its use of Gaelic tradition, as well as MacLeòid's writing style, pacing, etc. as MacilleDhuibh does, a more comprehensive assessment of the novel should also try to set it in its genre context, which is what is attempted here.

were in the world, told elegantly and in minute detail') (MacLeòid 2014: 186). In Pratchett's *Mort*, similar books are to be found in the library in Death's house, writing themselves in accordance with the lives of the people whose biographies they are (Pratchett 1987: 58-9).

In chapter fourteen of *An Sgoil Dhubh* Am Maighstir, wearing the body of the dead Rìgh nan Draoidh, is able to access the latter's memories. This functions to fill in some backstory about Rìgh nan Draoidh, and how he fell under Am Maighstir's influence, but it also connects *An Sgoil Dhubh* to the wider context of fantasy literature. The living being able to take on the memories and consciousnesses of the dead is not unknown in fantasy. A good example is the person of the dead Chatelaine Thecla, and later the persons of all previous Autarchs living in and being accessible to Severian, in Gene Wolfe's science fantasy series *The Book of the New Sun* (2000a, 2000b). Similarly, the arcs of the mage Quick Ben and of Toc the Younger/Anaster/Toc Anaster in Steven Erikson's *Malazan Book of the Fallen* (1999-2011) series illustrates the same basic idea, if on a much larger and more ambitious scale.

When Sgàire travels to the ocean world Fairge, he finds that the people there live on giant ships called *birlinnean*. *Birlinn* is of course simply the ordinary Gaelic word for a galley, such as were commonly used in the western Highlands in the late medieval period, but in *An Sgoil Dhubh* the *birlinnean* are of a much greater order of magnitude, being essentially floating towns. While by no means a very common fantasy trope, similar floating communities can be found in at least two very popular classics of the genre, in the island boats of the lake dwellers in Gene Wolfe's *Sword of the Lictor*, in his *The Book of the New Sun* series (Wolfe 2000a, 2000b), and perhaps in a more closely analogous form in the great rafts of the Children of the Open Sea in Ursula K Le Guin's *The Farthest Shore* (see Le Guin 2012).

The final example is of a somewhat different kind, in that it is not a trope but a demonstration of MacLeòid's connection to the wider fantasy tradition. Additionally, our previous examples have all been taken from fantasy literature, but it should be recognized that a contemporary writer of fantasy is not sealed off from fantasy in other media, but rather inhabits a culture in which fantasy is present in films, television, visual art and games of various kinds (note that Stephen Erikson and Ian Cameron Esslemont originally developed the world of the vast *Malazan* series through role-playing games). All of these may influence a fantasy writer, and certainly form part of the wider web of understandings and expectations about fantasy worlds which readers bring with them to new texts. In at least one instance a direct line of influence from a fantasy film on *An Sgoil*

Dhubh can be posited, where MacLeòid writes, '*Ach cha robh Am Maighstir a' roinn a chumhachd le duine eile, ge bith cò iad*' ('But The Master did not share his power with anyone, whoever they were') (MacLeòid 2014: 91). This bears a striking resemblance to a line spoken by Gandalf to Saruman in Peter Jackson's film adaptation of *The Fellowship of the Ring*, but not found in Tolkien's book: 'There is only one Lord of the Ring, only one who can bend it to his will. And he does not share power!' This should remind us that when contemporary fantasy writers create their works that non-literary fantasy media are often among their influences, and form part of the wider context in which their work should be interpreted.

If the tropes discussed above mean that *An Sgoil Dhubh* can be situated fairly comfortably within the genre conventions of modern fantasy, it is also a text deeply rooted in Gaelic tradition. MacLeòid creates a web of allusions to Gaelic oral tradition, history and medieval literature to create a very *Gàidhealach* setting for his novel, a text that is not merely written in Gaelic, but is built on recognisably Gaelic foundations. In the discussion above, it was observed that the greater degree of familiarity a reader has with fantasy literature as a genre, the more they will see connections between *An Sgoil Dhubh* and other texts, and be able to assess it in relation to them. The same is true of the use of Gaelic tradition in the novel: the more familiar a reader is with Gaelic folklore, history and literature, the more they will recognize in the creation of a new, fictional world, seeing the use in a new setting of materials familiar to them. The titular black school itself is an example of this: *sgoil dhubh Shàtain* ('Satan's black school') was where certain individuals learnt magic from the Devil (Campbell 2005: 157–8).

We can see this in MacLeòid's use of personal names. For instance, the princess of Erda who escapes the assassination at the start of the novel, and who becomes Sgàire's companion, is named Eimhir, a modernized spelling of Emer, the wife of Cú Chulainn in the early medieval Irish literary tradition. MacLeòid is of course not the first modern Gaelic writer to repurpose Emer – Sorley MacLean also did so in his poem-cycle *Dàin do Eimhir* ('Poems to Eimhir') of 1943. Such is the reputation and prominence of MacLean's cycle in Gaelic literature that any reader encountering the name (which is not a common one in Scotland) would surely be reminded of *Dàin do Eimhir*. MacLeòid thus makes a double reference in using this name, to both medieval and modern Gaelic literary traditions. MacLeòid uses the name from medieval literature, but he does not use the medieval character: Eimhir is not Emer dropped into his novel.

The same is true of Maedhbh. Medb, another prominent character in early medieval Irish literature, has her name repurposed in *An Sgoil Dhubh* as the leader of one of the great *Birlinnean* of the sea-planet Fairge. Unlike Medb, Maedhbh is not a queen, and again we should note that she is not simply the medieval literary character transposed into the novel, though her temperament is certainly reminiscent of Medb's: *Dh'fhairich Sgàire gur e boireannach cunnartach a bh' innte agus gu robh i cleachdte ri faighinn na bu mhiann leatha* ('Sgàire felt that she was a dangerous woman and that she was used to getting what she wanted') (MacLeòid 2014: 44).

Sgàire's mother is named Gormshuil, which is also the name of a Lochaber witch known in oral tradition well into the twentieth century (Calum MacLean Project 2017). MacLeòid may have taken the name from this witch, though Gormshuil in the novel is not herself a witch. The name may also have been prompted by Dùn Ghormshùil, an Iron Age broch in Carnish, Uig in the Isle of Lewis. Another possible source of inspiration is the novel *Gormshuil an Rìgh*, written by Fionnlagh MacLeòid, the uncle of Iain F. MacLeòid, which also incorporates folkloric and Norse elements (MacLeòid 2010a).

These are major characters in the novel, but there are also very minor characters whose names are clearly derived from medieval literary traditions or Gaelic oral tradition. For instance, Gormshuil's charioteer is named Laog, presumably based on Cú Chulainn's charioteer, Lóeg. Moving away from proper names and from the Old Irish literary tradition, we can see the use of more recent Gaelic tradition in the nickname of one of the characters, Torcuil nan Cath ('Torcuil of the Battles'). The nickname form 'X nan Cath' is well-attested in Gaelic tradition, and in using it MacLeòid works in a network of allusions that most readers will recognize. Most famously, the nickname is applied to Eachann nan Cath (known in English as Hector MacDonald), a very distinguished soldier of the Victorian era, and also Eachann Ruadh nan Cath, a MacLean chief killed at the Battle of Harlaw in 1411, and subject of the *ceòl mòr* tune 'Cumha Eachann Ruadh nan Cath'. MacLeòid draws upon the assumed knowledge of his readers, who will recognize the allusions to significant figures in Gaelic history.

Different aspects of the martial history of Gaelic Scotland are also woven into *An Sgoil Dhubh*. For instance, the group of mercenaries who attack Sgàire's village in chapter 10 are called the *Gall-òglaigh*, after the actual historical mercenaries of late medieval Gaelic Scotland, many of whom found violent employment in Ireland (McDonald 1997: 154–6). More recent martial traditions are referenced in the presentation of the Fàidhean in *An Sgoil Dhubh*, who function as a royal bodyguard. Their battle cry is *Cuidich an Rìgh!* ('Aid the King!'), which is also the motto of the Seaforth Highlanders, a historical Highland infantry regiment now part of the Royal Regiment of Scotland (see Am Baile n.d.). In this instance, as in many of the others discussed here, this reference would not survive a hypothetical translation of the novel into English. The cry 'Aid the King!' would make sense in the immediate context as a fairly obvious battle cry for the royal guard, but the reference to a regiment of historic importance in Gaelic Scotland would be lost, an example of the very specifically *Gàidhealach* worldbuilding of the novel.

Other references are to places and objects from the medieval Irish literary tradition, primarily (as with the personal names mentioned above) drawn from the Old Irish saga *Táin Bó Cuailnge* ('The Cattle Raid of Cooley'). For instance, during the aforementioned battle with the Gall-òglaigh, *[T]hog [Gormshuil] Gae-bolg, an gath uabhasach sin a dh'fhosgladh brù duine le ceud gath beag eile na bhroinn.* ('[Gormshuil] lifted the Gae-bolg, that terrible dart that opens a man's belly with a hundred other small darts inside it') (MacLeòid 2014: 60). The Gae-bolg is, of course, the fearsome weapon with which Cú Chulainn kills his foster-brother Fer Diad in *Táin Bó Cuailnge* (O'Rahilly 1976: 94, 207).

Cú Chulainn and Fer Diad had of course been trained as warriors by Scáthach. In *An Sgoil Dhubh*, there is also an elite warrior school run by a woman, but it is called *Sgoil Cogaidh Aoife* ('Aoife's School of War'). Why the role of Scáthach in the Old Irish tradition should have been transferred to Aoife (Old Irish *Aífe*) is unclear – the two are certainly not interchangeable in the source material. Aside from her name, Aoife in the novel has nothing in particular in common with Aífe in the medieval tradition: indeed, we could say that her character is basically that of Scáthach but named after Aífe. Another minor change from the Old Irish source material can be seen in one of MacLeòid's place names. The open space in front of the castle in the Prìomh Chathair ('Main City') of Erda is called *Emain Machra*, clearly derived from Emain Macha, the court of Conchobar in *Táin Bó Cuailnge* and other sagas (O' Rahilly 1976: 12–17, 136–9). MacLeòid does not 'update' the spelling here, as he does with Aífe > Aoife and Emer > Eimhir, leaving the lenition of the *m*s unmarked. This may be because Aoife and Eimhir are both well-established contemporary spellings of those names, whereas Emain Macha is usually known only in its older spelling. There seems to be no particular reason for the addition of the *r* in *Machra*, and it may simply be a spelling error.

Also drawn from *Táin Bó Cuailnge*, though apparently via English translation, is MacLeòid's *solas a' ghaisgich* ('hero's light'). From the context, *Chitheadh iad solas a' ghaisgich os cionn Ghormshuil agus Dia nan Cath còmhla rithe agus chuir i uabhas air na fir air a' bhàta* ('They saw the hero's light above Gormshuil, and the God of Battles together with her, and she terrified the men on the boat')

(MacLeòid 2014: 63), it seems clear that this is based on descriptions of the *lúan láith* in *Táin Bó Cuailnge*, which O'Rahilly in her edition of the first recension translates as 'the champion's light' (O' Rahilly 1976: 14, 137) and Ciaran Carson in his popular translation renders 'hero's light' (Carson 2007: 38).

Cú Chulainn provides another model for MacLeòid in the aftermath of the battle: *An dèidh a' chatha bha an solas-gaisgeil cho làidir os cionn Gormshuil gu robh aca ri bogadh ann an tocasaid uisge fuar, agus thàinig ceò bhon uisge sin agus bhlàthaich e, gus bho dheireadh thall ghabh Gormshuil riochd boireannaich a-rithist* ('After the battle the heroic light over Gormshuil was so strong that they had to immerse her in a barrel of cold water, and steam came from that water and it was warmed, until eventually Gormshuil regained her womanly form again') (MacLeòid 2014: 64). This is clearly derived from the account of the young Cú Chulainn needing to be immersed in water to cool him down after his first expedition in the *macgnímrada* section of *Táin Bó Cuailnge* (O' Rahilly 1976: 25, 147–8).

As Raghnall MacilleDhuibh notes in his review of the novel, *An Sgoil Dhubh* contains *iomadh mac-talla ann bho bheul-aithris na Gàidhlig* ('many echoes of Gaelic oral tradition'), of which a few will now be considered (MacilleDhuibh 2016). For instance, when MacLeòid writes of *na Sìth* and *eich uisge*, he writes of creatures well known to anyone with the faintest passing knowledge of Gaelic folklore, commonly translated as 'fairies' and 'water horses' or 'kelpies', respectively (Campbell 2005: 1–27, 106–17). MacLeòid uses them to create dangerous antagonists for Sgàire and his companions, building from the associations he can assume his readers will have with these creatures, while presenting them in new and original contexts, including an extensive original backstory for the Sìth.

The backstory concerns an ancient feud between two brothers named Torcuil and Tormod, which are both ordinary Gaelic names of Norse origin. Their descendants are known as Sìol Thorcuil and Sìol Thormoid ('the seed of Torcuil' and 'the seed of Tormod'), which are also the usual names in Gaelic for the MacLeods of Lewis and Harris and the MacLeods of Skye, respectively. Sìol Thormoid here are the Sìth, and their progenitor Tormod becomes one of the antagonists, Sìol Thorcuil are the true royal line, to which Sgàire himself belongs.[5]

---

[5] Since Iain F. MacLeòid is himself a MacLeod from Lewis, and therefore of the (real world) Sìol Thorcuil, it is perhaps not surprising that he makes his fictional family-namesakes the 'good guys' here!

We can also observe that at some points the fantasy tropes in the novel overlap with the use of Gaelic traditional materials, which is perhaps to be expected given that much fantasy literature builds on folkloric and medieval literary traditions. For instance, Sgàire's sword (before he is given *An Claidheamh Gorm*, discussed above) glows brightly in the dark: *Thug e a-mach a chlaidheamh agus chitheadh e gu robh e air atharrachadh. Far an robh e air a bhith dorch, bha e a-nis cho soilleir ri daoimean le faobhar air nach gabhadh srucadh.* ('He took out his sword and he saw that it had changed. Where it had been dark, it was now as clear as a diamond, with an edge that could not be scuffed') (MacLeòid 2014: 67). Later, in the dark hall of the many books, he uses the light from his sword as a torch. Glow-in-the-dark swords are of course not unknown in fantasy literature (a good example is Bilbo's sword Sting, from *The Hobbit*, later given to Frodo in *The Lord of the Rings*), but *An Claidheamh Sholuis* ('The Sword of Light'), which often appears in Gaelic folk tales, sometimes as an object of quests, may be the reference here (Campbell 1994: 91–109, 206–17). A double-facing reference, looking both to Gaelic tradition and to fantasy tradition, this helps to create a fictional world that fits comfortably in both.

This is also true of the description of Sgàire's native island, which is both fictional and fantastic (having portals to other worlds) and also easily recognizable to anyone familiar with the Western Isles: *Fada gu siar air a' phrìomh chathair agus gàrraidhean brèagha a' Chaisteil Dheirg, bha sreath de dh'eileannan a bha coltach ri seudan nan laighe air a' mhuir* ('Far to the west of the main city and the beautiful gardens of the Red Castle was a series of islands like jewels lying on the sea') (MacLeòid 2014: 16); *'S e eilean beag rèidh bhon tàinig Sgàire, gun mòran chraobhan air ...* ('Sgàire came from a small, flat island without many trees ...') (MacLeòid 2014: 48). When Sgàire returns from Sgoil Cogaidh Aoife, he spends some time on his own: *Bha e a' fuireach air eilean beag ann an seann teampall far an robh iad ag ràdh a bhiodh daoine cràbhaidh aig aon àm. Bha na teampaill sin a-nis nan tobhtaichean le feur a' fàs orra.* ('He was staying on a small island in an old temple where they said that devout people used to be at one time. Those temples were ruins now, with grass growing on them'.) (MacLeòid 2014: 123). This could easily be imagined as any one of dozens of old chapel sites in the Western Isles, about which MacLeòid's uncle, Fionnlagh MacLeòid, has written a book (F. MacLeòid 1997). The setting is one that Iain F. MacLeòid clearly finds intriguing, and one rooted in, and symbolic of, the histories of particular locations, as in another of his novels, *Ìmpireachd* ('Empire'), he has his protagonist sit in the ruins of an old chapel and contemplate the long history of the place and his own and his community's fleeting part in it (MacLeòid 2010b: 129). In setting, then, as with the use of Gaelic historical, folkloric and medieval literary materials, MacLeòid can be seen to be building a very *Gàidhealach* fictional world, one which is in many respects recognizable to Gaelic readers, but also new and set within a literary genre that most of its readers will know only or mainly in English.

The novel also makes use of elements of Norse history and literature, some of which also overlap in interesting ways with aspects of Gaelic tradition. Personal names provide one strand of the Norse element in *An Sgoil Dhubh*. Some of these are straightforward Norse names, such as Fenrir. Fenrir in the novel is the king of the great wolves who live on the island where Aoife keeps her warrior school. He is clearly inspired by the wolf of that name in medieval Norse literature but, as with Eimhir and Maedhbh, is not simply the existing medieval character drafted into the novel, he is a new character who happens to bear a familiar name.

Gormshuil's mother in the novel is named Astridr. This is interesting for two reasons. Firstly, even if a reader does not recognize this as a Norse name, the fact that it violates the *caol ri caol agus leathan ri leathan* Gaelic spelling rule means that it would strike them immediately as 'foreign'. Secondly, the fact that Gormshuil (who bears, as we have seen above, a name known in Gaelic folklore traditions) has a mother with a Norse name is an indication of the blending of these two cultures in the novel, the bringing together of Norse and Gaelic traditions to create the fictional culture of the people of Erda.

Other examples include personal names that are Norse in origin, but which have become common in Gaelic, and which readers may or may not know come from Norse.

These are presented in their ordinary Gaelic spellings, which at one level conceal their Norse origin (in contrast to 'Astridr'), but on another epitomize the historical blending of Gaelic and Norse cultures in the real world in parallel with the blending of the 'Gaelic' and 'Norse' elements to make the fictional culture of Erda.

Examples in the novel are Tormod, Torcuil, Ìomhair, Amhlaidh and Sgàire. Sgàire (sometimes Anglicized as the Biblical name 'Zachary', though it has no etymological connection with that name) is the least common of these names today, though many Gaelic readers will know it from the song 'Òran Chaluim Sgàire', and there is a ruined chapel in the cemetery of Bragar in Lewis called Cill Sgàire, the Norse derivation of which is noted by Fionnlagh MacLeòid (F. MacLeòid 1997: 19).

Norse elements are also used in place names in the novel. Sgàire's home island is called Flodeiy, which is explained as meaning *eilean ìosal* ('low island'). Again, even if a reader would not recognize this as Norse, they would see it as markedly non-Gaelic, both because it violates the *caol ri caol agus leathan ri leathan* spelling rule, and because it contains the letter *y*, which is not used in Gaelic. Likewise, the parliament of Erda is called *Tingvalr nan Daoine*, a mixed Norse-Gaelic form. 'Tingvalr' is of course derived from Norse *Þingvöllr* ('Assembly field'), whence such place names as Dingwall in the Highlands and Tingwall in Shetland. A reader with an interest in place names would be likely to recognize *Tingvalr* as a Norse element here, but again even if they did not the presence of the letter *v* and the violation of the *caol ri caol agus leathan ri leathan* rule marks it as clearly non-Gaelic.

Another Norse-derived place name is Brisingr, the island where Aoife keeps her warrior school. This is a curious example because it is derived from Old Norse *Brísingr*, which is not a place name at all but rather a family or people, best known in the compound phrase *men Brísinga* (i.e. Freyia's necklace). It was also used as the title of a bestselling young adult fantasy novel by Christopher Paolini, *Brisingr*, and in Alan Garner's older *The Weirdstone of Brisingamen*, discussed in this volume by Gwendolen Grant, so it may be that here again we have references to both medieval literary traditions and contemporary fantasy books, with *An Sgoil Dhubh* facing in both directions (Paolini 2008; Garner 2010). Again, whether or not this was MacLeòid's intention, readers familiar with either the medieval source material or modern fantasy or both will bring their own associations to the text when they encounter the word *Brisingr* in the novel.

The people of Flodeiy have several features of their material culture which are clearly derived from very well-known elements of medieval Norse material culture. For instance, Sgàire and his family live in a *taigh-fhada* ('longhouse') (MacLeòid 2014: 60), and they sail in what is quite recognizably a Norse longship: *Bha i [.i. long cogadh muinntir Flodeiy] iargalt, le dràgan fiodha na toiseach agus targaiden suas na cliathaichean*. ('It [i.e. the warship of the people of Flodeiy] was forbidding, with a wooden dragon at its prow and shields along the sides') (MacLeòid 2014: 25). Less well known, but certainly grounded in medieval Norse literary tradition, is the following, describing the settlement of Flodeiy: *Ma bha cuideigin airson talamh fhaighinn dha fhèin bhiodh iad a' seòladh air falbh bho tìr agus a' sadail cabair taighe thar na cliathaich. Far am bualadh e tìr, 's ann an sin a bhiodh iad a' dèanamh an dachaigh, agus sin a rinn Gormshuil agus Aonghas*. ('If someone wanted to get some land for themselves they would said out from the land and throw the house post over the side. Where it came ashore, that is where they would make their home, and that is what Gormshuil and Aonghas did'.) (MacLeòid 2014: 16). This can be compared to *Laxdæla Saga*, in which Bjorn Ketilsson makes his settlement in Iceland where his high-seat posts washed ashore at what was thereafter called Bjarnarhaven. In their translation of that saga, Magnus Magnusson and Hermann Pálsson note 'settlers would often put them overboard within sight of land and build their new homes at the spot where they were washed ashore' (Magnusson and Pálsson 1975: 39). As a point of interest, there is also a place called Lacasdal (Eng., Laxdale) in Lewis.

We can see therefore that the Gaelic and the Norse elements in *An Sgoil Dhubh* are similar in some respects, for instance in that both repurpose personal names from the medieval literary traditions. However, this is much richer, and much more detailed on the Gaelic side, requiring of the reader a more detailed knowledge of Gaelic tradition and history, while most of the Norse references would be understood by anyone with a basic familiarity with any Viking-themed film, television show, computer games or art, even if they had not read much or any medieval Norse literature themselves. The real detail is in the use of the Gaelic material; the Norse material is simpler, but still creates a network of references that give a Norse 'flavour' to the novel. However, the nature of these Norse elements, and the manner in which they blend with some of the Gaelic ones, suggests that MacLeòid is trying to give the fictional *Gàidhealach* culture of his novel a counterpart to the real-world historical influence of the Norse on Gaelic Scotland. The family lineages, in which characters have parents and grandparents with markedly Norse or Gaelic names, the use of common Gaelic personal names of Norse origin and the use of the Norse form of a well-known town in the Highlands as a place name in the novel, all work to fold Norse culture into the *Gàidhealach* culture of the novel. While the blending of Gaelic literary, historical and folkloric materials from different periods into a fictional narrative present creates a fantasy-world version of Gaelic culture, the way in which MacLeòid works Norse elements into that culture brings the period of the Norse settlement of and hegemony over the western seaboard of Scotland into that fictional present, in the same way as he included the Norse settlement as part of the long history of his community in *Ìmpireachd* (MacLeòid 2010b: 129). This was a crucial period in the development of Gaelic Scotland, and especially of the Western Isles, in which iconic elements of the culture of the Western Isles, such as the birlinns and the Lewis Chessmen, to say nothing of the many Norse-derived place-names, especially in Lewis, were created, as described in 'Na Lochlannaich a' tighinn air tìr an Nis' ('The Norsemen coming ashore at Ness') by the Lewis poet Ruaraidh MacThòmais (MacThòmais 1970: 40). More generally, the medieval-style elements of the novel (swords, spears, castles and so on) work to make the novel fit in with both the evocations of the prestigious medieval literary tradition and with the conventions of most high fantasy literature.

MacLeòid also makes references to names and concepts from other literatures and traditions. These include Old English (there is one mention of Grendel, though here the monster is female, not male as in *Beowulf*) and Buddhist thought (a single reference to a character having attained *nirbhana*), but these are not as prominent, and since they are only passing references they are not as fully integrated into the fabric of the text as the Gaelic and Norse elements discussed above.

Iain F. MacLeòid has written a very *Gàidhealach* fantasy novel, which integrates a range of different references from Gaelic history and folklore as well as Old Irish literature to create a fictional world which is culturally recognizable to Gaelic readers. It also works in, albeit in less detail, elements of Norse history and literature. This is a culture less familiar to Gaelic readers, but the history of Norse settlement, especially in the Western Isles, as well as its prominent influence in modern fantasy literature, films and games make it appropriate for elements of it to be worked into this *Gàidhealach* fantasy. And that fantasy is specifically a Gaelic one, not a more generalized 'Celtic' one. Of course, being set in a fictional world to a great extent removes *An Sgoil Dhubh* from issues of real-world debates about 'Celticity', or about the supposed unities and continuities of Celtic-speaking cultures. However, the use of literary and historical materials from a range of periods being brought into a fictional narrative present creates an interesting alternative version of Gaelic culture, one in which early medieval literary elements, late medieval history and modern folklore are all equally present and equally real, a synthesis of different aspects of Gaelic culture into a richly-textured fictional world. It is a fantasy world of warriors and wizards that nevertheless feels recognizable to Gaelic readers in the twenty-first century. For all its flaws in pacing and characterization, this is a very interesting and ambitious novel (indeed, the first high fantasy novel in the language), and one that repays critical attention.

References

Am Baile: Highland History and Culture, 'Colours of the 6th (Morayshire) Battalion, Seaforth Highlanders', http://www.ambaile.org.uk/detail/en/23140/1/EN23140-colours-of-the-6th-morayshire.htm, accessed 9 Jul. 2021.

Calum MacLean Project (2017), 'The Most Powerful Witch of All', https://calumimaclean.blogspot.com/2017/03/the-most-powerful-witch-of-all-great.html, accessed 18 Jun. 2021.
Campbell, John Francis, ed. and trans. (1994), *Popular Tales of the West Highlands: Volume I*, Edinburgh: Birlinn.
Campbell, John Gregorson (2005), *The Gaelic Otherworld*, Edinburgh: Birlinn.
Carson, Ciaran, trans. (2007), *The Táin*, London: Penguin.
D'Arcy, Julian (2012), *Scottish Skalds and Sagamen: Old Norse Influence on Modern Scottish Literature*, East Linton: The Tuckwell Press.
Erikson, Steven (1999–2011), *The Malazan Book of the Fallen* (series), London: Bantam Books.
Fhriseal, Anna (1962), 'An Dudach', *Gairm*, 10: 366–9.
Garner, Alan (2010), *The Weirdstone of Brisingamen*, London: HarperCollins.
Gemmell, David (2001), *The Sword in the Storm*, London: Del Rey Books.
Le Guin, Ursula K. (2012), *Earthsea: The First Four Books*, London: Penguin.
Lindsay, Coinneach (2017), *A' Choille Fhiadhaich*, Dingwall: Sandstone Press.
Mac An T-saoir, Màrtainn (2003), 'Oisein ann an Tìr nan Òg', *Gath*, 2: 10–15.
McDonald, R. Andrew (1997), *The Kingdom of the Isles: Scotland's Western Seaboard, c. 1100–c. 1336*, East Linton: Tuckwell Press.
MacilleDhuibh, Raghnall (2016), 'A' bualadh a' chòrr ás an uisge', *The Scotsman* (2 Jan.), https://www.scotsman.com/lifestyle/a-bualadh-a-chorr-as-an-uisge-1-3989679, accessed 18 Jun. 2018.
MacGill-Eain, Somhairle, Whyte, Christopher, and Dymock, Emma, eds (2011), *Caoir Gheal Leumraich/ White Leaping Flame: Collected Poems*, Edinburgh: Polygon.
MacLeòid, Fionnlagh (1997), *Na Teampaill anns na h-Eileanan an Iar*, Stornoway: Acair.
MacLeòid, Fionnlagh (2010a), *Gormshuil an Rìgh*, Inverness: Clàr.
MacLeòid, Iain F. (2008), *Am Bounty*, Inverness: Clàr.
MacLeòid, Iain F. (2010b), *Ìmpireachd*, Inverness: Clàr.
MacLeòid, Iain F. (2014), *An Sgoil Dhubh*, Stornoway: Acair.
MacLeòid, Iain F. (2017), *An Taistealach*, Dingwall: Sandstone Press.
MacThòmais, Ruaraidh (1970), *An Rathad Cian*, Glasgow: Gairm.
Magnusson, Magnus, and Pálsson, Hermann, trans. (1975), *Laxdæla Saga*, London: The Folio Society.
Manlove, Colin, ed. (1996), *An Anthology of Scottish Fantasy Literature*, Edinburgh: Polygon.
Meek, Donald E. (2018), 'O'Donnell Lecture, 2018: The Gaelic Literary Enlightenment: The Making of the Scottish Gaelic New Testament and Associated Books, 1760–1820', https://www.youtube.com/watch?v=zo4R_EgAbJU, accessed 16 Jun. 2021.
O' Rahilly, Cecile, ed. and trans. (1976), *Táin Bó Cúailnge: Recension I*, Dublin: Dublin Institute for Advanced Studies.
Paolini, Christopher (2008), *Brisingr*, New York: Alfred A. Knopf.
Pratchett, Terry (1987), *Mort*, London: Gollancz.

Pratchett, Terry (1989), *Guards! Guards!*, London: Gollancz.
Tolkien, J.R.R. (1937), *The Hobbit*, London: Allen and Unwin.
Tolkien, J.R.R. (1954–55), *The Lord of the Rings*, London: Allen and Unwin.
Watson, Moray (2011), *An Introduction to Gaelic Fiction*, Edinburgh: Edinburgh University Press.
Wolfe, Gene (2000a), *The Book of the New Sun Volume 1: Shadow and Claw*, London: Gollancz.
Wolfe, Gene (2000b), *The Book of the New Sun Volume 2: Sword and Citadel*, London: Gollancz.

Part Four

Fantastic perceptions of Celticity

9

The Celtic Tarot in speculative fiction

Juliette Wood

In 1909, the occult publishing firm Rider and Co. issued a pack of Tarot cards created by two members of The Hermetic Order of the Golden Dawn, the artist Pamela Colman Smith and the esoteric writer Arthur Edward Waite.[1] Instructions for this new Tarot included a divinatory 'spread' of cards called the 'Celtic Cross' (Waite 1910; Waite 1911; Wood 2008: 102). This created an imaginative, although unhistorical, link between current ideas about Celtic myth and a divination device that dated back only to the eighteenth century. As the most available Tarot in the twentieth century, the Rider pack has provided an enduring set of images and meanings for Tarot mythology. The writings of A.E. Waite and W.B. Yeats, Jessie Weston's interpretation of the grail quest and Eliot's use of the cards in *The Waste Land* fixed the image of a Celtic Tarot as the embodiment of an esoteric quest, while Pamela Colman Smith's drawings have influenced the imagery of subsequent packs. The belief that Tarot reflects a cultural ritual that originated as Celtic myth is fundamental to modern practice. It continues to influence speculative fiction and to create new interactive storytelling memes through Tarot readings.

The seventy-eight cards in the deck consist of twenty-one numbered trump cards, an unnumbered 'Fool' (The Major Arcana), plus four 'suits', each with ten pips and four court cards (The Minor Arcana). The earliest elaborately painted decks date to the fifteenth century, but cheaper printed versions appeared as tarot games became popularized (Farley 2009: 33–44). In the late eighteenth century, French esoteric writers introduced the idea that Tarot concealed ancient hidden wisdom with a hint of Celtic influence even at this early stage (Farley 2009: 102 n.4, 106–11, 117–21, 126–30). The most significant development for the subsequent

---

[1] This influential Tarot published in 1909 and again in 1910 is called the Rider pack, the Rider-Waite, or the Rider Smith pack. This article uses the term Rider pack.

importance of a 'Celtic' Tarot in speculative fiction occurred once the focus of the occult revival shifted to Britain. Tarot was re-interpreted not merely as an ancient survival, but as a living esoteric tradition with the potential for multiple meanings and the power to transform individual lives. Central to this were the Celts, their literature and their traditions. Speculation about a mythic Fisher King and a questing hero that could be accessed through these cards suggested that an important cultural truth existed beneath the romantic liminality of the Celtic world (Wood 2008: 85–105). Tarot imagery now appears in fantasy and science fiction novels, urban gothic and noir fiction, films, internet games, blogs and related commercial spin-offs. Professional organizations offer courses and certification in Tarot reading, and the application of Jungian psychology has further expanded the range of possible meanings (ATA n.d.; Nichols 1980; Auger 2004). This chapter argues that the use of Tarot in speculative fiction and modern card reading, even when the Celts are not mentioned specifically, depends ultimately on assumptions about a hidden quest at the heart of Celtic tradition. The Celtic Tarot is now a self-sustaining fantasy which has become a vehicle for trans-media storytelling through fiction, cartomancy and the internet. In addition to adopting images and meanings inherent in the idea of a Celtic Tarot, contemporary speculative fiction and Tarot practice frequently reference their own history, creating continuity between early references, later literature and card reading practices introduced in the 1980s.

The Tarot as Celtic myth

Celtic origins were popular among folklorists, literary scholars and occultists at the end of the nineteenth century. In the context of esoteric speculation, this became fused with the idea that secret wisdom in Celtic myth had been transmitted through medieval grail romances, and, crucially, that this mystic experience was available to all (Wood 1998, 2000). Earlier theories linked the Tarot to lost wisdom, but the grail quest, realized as a Celtic myth about a Fisher King, was deemed to be a living tradition that unified ancient Celtic magic, timeless mystic experience and medieval romance. An exact timeline for the emergence of the Celtic Tarot is difficult given the interactions between members of the Golden Dawn and their associates. W.B. Yeats, A.E. Waite, Pamela Colman Smith and G.R.S. Mead were all members at some time, while the Arthurian scholar, Jessie Weston, belonged to Mead's Quest Society. Whatever the specific history through which the literary grail theme became a transformative esoteric search, a personal quest in the form of a journey remains a fundamental assumption whether the Tarot is used for divination, as a fantasy trope or for psychological meditation, and the Celts are indispensable to this process.

At the end of the nineteenth century, scholarly interest in the grail favoured a myth about a pagan talisman associated with abundance for which medieval Irish and Welsh texts, together with a rich, oral folk heritage in Celtic countries, came to be regarded as an ultimate source (Wood 2008: 85–95). In his study of the Celtic origin of the grail myth, Alfred Trübner Nutt identified talismanic vessels and questing heroes as key elements. His suggestion that such a myth existed in early Celtic culture echoed assumptions about the antiquity of Celtic tradition and the role of Christianity in preserving and transforming pagan myth.[2] As scholar and publisher, Nutt actively encouraged collecting in areas where Celtic languages were spoken, and the wealth of material uncovered contributed to the notion of a unique, ancient, but still living, heritage.[3] Celts epitomized the belief that human intellect, while progressive, never left the past entirely behind. Their 'pagan' imagination was fashionable thanks to such writers as Matthew Arnold, and it was about to become more so under the spur of romantic 'revivals' of Celtic culture.

The Celtic Tarot as an esoteric quest

A number of factors contributed to the role of the Celts in the emergence of Tarot as a living 'secret tradition'. The noted French scholar, Theodore de la Villemarqué, proposed a tentative link between the grail and a magic cauldron in a medieval Welsh poem (Villemarqué 1842: 192–4). Ernest Renan suggested that *peir dadeni* (the cauldron of rebirth) in the *Mabinogion* was both a pagan source for the grail and an initiation rite for 'a kind of freemasonry'. By the time Renan's essay appeared in English, elements of myth and secret initiation rites, intertwined with the perceived nature of Celtic tradition, were established as a viable, if speculative, approach to their history (Renan 1859). For Sabine Baring-Gould, similarities between Celtic magic objects and beliefs among the Templars suggested that grail romance preserved 'a mysterious relic of a past heathen rite'

---

[2] A significant portion Nutt's output discusses Celtic tradition. See Nutt (1888, 1899, 1902), notes and appendix in Arnold (1910), and notes in Guest (1902).
[3] Nutt's introduction to Hyde (1890) stresses the importance of collecting.

(Wood 2008: 43, 201 n. 22–4). The grail quest as hidden ritual provided a critical link between Tarot and Celtic myth and strengthened the assumption that the Celts preserved imaginative and moral faculties which, although lost, could be recovered by the modern Tarot seeker (Wood 2002; 2008: 99–111). As a result, the Celts, perceived as culturally liminal in European society, were central to recapturing the ideology of a lost world.

These ideas found their most imaginative synthesis in the writings of Arthur Edward Waite. His eclectic intellect embraced a range of occult-related subjects that included the medieval grail romances. His conviction that a secret tradition could regenerate the human race seems naïve and quaint now, but his writings reflect a commitment to the belief in the importance of Celtic tradition as a means of channelling fundamental mystical truths (Waite 1909a; Wood 2008: 96–105). For Waite, the Tarot as a path to higher consciousness and union with the divine was available to all. This departed somewhat from the notion of Tarot as elite ancient wisdom, but made sense in the context of the newly re-configured Celtic quest romance which encouraged individuals, through dialogue with the cards, to fulfil the role of 'questing' knight and relive the mythic endeavour of healing the land and its 'King'. Waite's 'rectified' Tarot drew inspiration from French occultists, from historical Tarot decks, and from modern designs created by the Swiss occultist Oswald Wirth (Dummett 1980: 76, 114–20; Farley 2009: 117–18). Another esoteric writer, Howard Bayley, suggested that early watermarks symbolized a hidden grail, and illustrations on the Ace and Queen of Cups in the Rider pack resemble examples printed by him (Bayley 1909: 65–78, 232, 262–3; Waite 1911: 10–11; Wood 2008: 101). The illustrations produced by Pamela Colman Smith for this new pack have become visually iconic. She was a member of the Golden Dawn who employed synaesthesia as an artistic technique (Raine 1972: 59; Coldwell 1977: 32–3). As a long-time friend of Yeats and his family, she may also have adapted material from Yeats's personal Golden Dawn ritual books. Waite acknowledged her contribution in an article for the *Occult Review* about the forthcoming publication of his Tarot deck (Waite 1909b),[4] and her images have recently received greater attention (see Kaplan 2009).

Although Tarot cards had been associated with fortune telling and esoteric investigation since the eighteenth century, they became irrevocably linked with an esoteric, pseudo-academic legend about the grail quest as living secret tradition in the context of an occult revival in Britain from the 1880s to the 1930s

---

[4] This article cited another Rider publication, Papus's *Tarot of the Bohemians* with Smith's illustration for The Wheel Trump on the cover.

(Dummett 1980: 10-19; Wood 2008: 96-105). Crucially this led the seeker not to by-gone Egyptian wisdom, but to an accessible world of Celtic peoples still living in Western Europe. This shift in perception informs the somewhat eccentric theories of Jessie Laidley Weston (Grayson 1992; Weston 1993: 186-7). Before publishing her thoughts, she consulted 'a mystic of experience' who assured her that the grail romances concealed 'the story of an Initiation'. The mystic was probably G.R.S. Mead, founder of the Quest Society of which Weston was a member. Mead had invited Waite to lecture on the esoteric links between Tarot and Arthurian literature (Waite 1909c), and his own book, *Fragments of a Faith Forgotten*, used symbolism in a similar way to reconstruct, not an ancient lost original, but a living esoteric tradition (Mead 1906; Wood 2008: 96, 102).

The exact motivation for the new pack is complex. Waite's ideas about the universal availability of mystical experience were at odds with the elitism which lay at the heart of many occult theories, especially in continental esotericism which he had begun to distrust (Waite 1896). The Celts were already influential in British occultism. Golden Dawn members William Wynn Westcott and MacGregor Mathers stressed their Celtic affiliations (Farley 2009: 128-9), and Waite had collaborated with his friend, the Anglo-Welsh writer Arthur Machen, on a 'mystery play' about the grail (Waite 1906: 140; Gilbert 1983).[5] Romantic writers increasingly identified the mystical and melancholy 'Celtic temperament' as part of Britishness, which made their traditions all the more attractive. Comparisons between supernatural objects described as the 'Grail Hallows' of the Túatha Dé Danann and the grail procession in medieval romances offered a 'Celtic' interpretation for Waite's revised Tarot. The suit of cups was equated with the grail; the suit of wands with the sacred lance, swords was linked with the broken sword of grail romance, and pentacles with the golden platter. Although this glossed over fundamental textual problems, it provided a link between Celtic mythology, medieval romance and the mysticism of the Tarot cards (Waite 1909a: 600-14; Waite 1933: 572-460; Wood 2000; Wood 2008: 102). The 'Four Grail Hollows' (cup, sword, spear and platter)

---

[5] R.A. Gilbert's *A.E. Waite: A Bibliography* (1983) addresses some of the challenges of Waite's bibliography. Waite published extensively and wrote articles for journals as diverse as *The Quest*, *The Unknown World*, *The Occult Review* and *Horlicks Magazine*. Reprints of his work are significant for the revival of Tarot in the second half of the twentieth century, but titles vary. His study of the grail seems to appear as: *The hidden church of the Holy Graal: its legends and symbolism considered in their affinity with certain mysteries of initiation and other traces of a secret tradition in Christian times* (London: Rebman, 1909 – see Waite (1909a) in the list of references), *The Holy Grail, its legends and symbolism: an explanatory survey of their embodiment in romance literature and a critical study of the interpretations placed thereon* (1933) and an American edition, *The Holy Grail: The Galahad Quest in the Arthurian Literature* (1961).

that appear on the Magician Trump card present the clearest Celtic reference in the Rider pack. However, the knight laid on a tomb (Four of Swords), the disembodied hand offering a cup to a seated figure (Four of Cups) and the hand holding an elaborate chalice (Ace of Cups) hint at 'ritual' links with grail romances. A.E. Waite's explanations for his new 'rectified' Tarot appeared in a short exegetical booklet and a longer volume which illustrated the cards. As part of this exegesis, Waite described a divinatory 'spread' of cards laid out as a cross and a column which, he claimed, was 'used privately in England, Scotland and Ireland', and this soon became the 'Celtic Cross' spread. While the reason for the name is unclear, the 'Celtic Cross' remains the most widely used template in divination readings. Significantly, for current use, Waite's explanations valourized Tarot as a way of developing intuitive and clairvoyant faculties (Wood 2008: 102; Mountfort 2014: 191).

These esoteric developments culminated in Jessie Weston's speculations about a Fisher King myth in her book, *From Ritual to Romance*. Her reputation as an Arthurian scholar, and the fact that her prose is more readable than Waite's, was, no doubt, contributing factors to the book's popularity. Weston adapted a myth concerning a vegetation god who died with the passing of the growing season and was reborn each spring. This myth was central to James G. Frazer's anthropological theories in which the sacrificial death of a divine king to ensure fertility as reflected in primitive agricultural rituals gave way to the quaint 'survivals' of popular folklore belief and custom (Frazer 1993). The esoteric grail myth effectively inverted Frazer's model. The quaint survivals became evidence for the continued existence of a secret initiation tradition, a mystery cult driven underground by a rival belief system, namely Christianity. Weston equated the Fisher King of medieval romance with Frazer's dying god, and the fertility of his wasteland kingdom could only be renewed by a suitably initiated young hero who restored the 'grail hallows' and symbolically replaced the wounded Fisher King. Although she acknowledged the lack of clear textual and cultural connections between treasures, grail, tarot cards and ritual, Weston nevertheless found 'evidence' for them in folk customs. In a telling footnote, she compared the pentacle symbol from Waite's Tarot pack with a sword-dance figure and with the image on Gawain's shield in a medieval poem (Weston 1993: 80, 94). Having demonstrated, to her own satisfaction, that tarot suits, grail objects and folk customs were derived from ancient fertility rituals, Weston re-interpreted medieval grail romances as an esoteric initiation ritual. In effect, this created a hidden Celtic myth about the Fisher King by altering the symbolism in the desired direction and citing the alterations as proof. Although her work was certainly a tour de force, there is no evidence for such a myth in Celtic texts, and no evidence that the original Tarot was ever used as anything other than a card game (Wood 2017).

Speculative literature and the Tarot

Although fantasy tropes and mythic traditions share a number of structural and aesthetic concerns such as primordial or pre-modern settings, heroic and supernatural characters, and motifs of quest and apotheosis, it is important to keep in mind that the Celtic Tarot is a construct of modern revivals (Auger 2004: 53–88).[6] British esoteric writers popularized the idea that Tarot cards were conduits for the transmission of mystical experience and that the Celts were central in preserving this phenomenon. In speculative fiction, the Tarot appears as a plot device foreshadowing events, reveals the personality and fate of a character or provides a metaphor for an actual or an interior journey. The interplay between the Rider pack, speculative fiction and modern Tarot praxis offers a space to model alternate meanings for the world. In the ever-growing number of Tarot decks and the proliferation of Tarot readings on the internet, it becomes a metaphor of a quest that transforms the reader (or querent) into an active participant in a journey of self-discovery.

The Fisher King myth and the questing knight are key themes in Eliot's *The Waste Land* (1922), one of the most influential literary appearances of Tarot. The poem's 'wicked pack of cards' – the drowned Phoenician Sailor, Belladonna, 'the man with three staves', the Wheel, the one-eyed merchant, a 'blank' card and The Hanged Man – draws on the Rider pack. The Wheel and The Hanged Man are named major arcana cards. The Three of Wands ('man with three staves') shows a figure standing next to flowering wooden stakes, and Belladonna, 'the Lady of the Rocks', may suggest the Queen of Pentacles who sits in a rocky landscape. Critics have argued about Eliot's familiarity with the esoteric Tarot (Gibbons 1972; Waitinas 2014), nevertheless, his identification of a tarot card with the Fisher King established the theories of British occultists as a viable theme for subsequent speculative literature.

The *Stories of Red Hanrahan* by the poet and occultist W.B. Yeats is another, less noted, contribution to creating a modern myth about sacred talismans,

---

[6] For examples of fiction featuring Tarot, see: https://www.goodreads.com/list/show/5230.Stories_Where_Tarot_Reading_Plays_A_Role.

Tarot and Celtic traditions. The *Stories* first appeared in 1897 and were later revised to create a more folktale-like quality (Yeats 1913; Williams 2016: 148–52, 284–5, 312–30, 332–41). At Samhain, the poet Red Hanrahan follows a pack of cards, which have been transformed into the Wild Hunt, to an Otherworld dwelling where a beautiful queen and four old women offer him a cauldron, a stone, a spear and a sword (objects which became known as 'The Grail Hallows'). Hanrahan, like the knight in the grail romances, fails to ask the proper questions and falls asleep. When he wakes, he experiences the sense of loss that accompanies a failed quest. The character, based on an historical Gaelic poet, reflects Yeats's personal relation to Irish mythological tradition, and the line, 'And I Myself Created Hanrahan' from 'The Tower' (1928), expresses the poet's own yearnings and awareness of loss (Hirsch 1981: 882–7). Critics differ as to the pervasiveness of Tarot imagery in Yeats's work (Raine 1972: 17–22), but the stories of Red Hanrahan established early literary links to Celtic tradition, an esoteric quest, the Tarot and an otherworld female, eventually called 'the sovereignty goddess', who embodies and controls the talismans.

There is always a danger in overemphasizing Celtic explanations. For Aleister Crowley's 'Book of Thoth' Tarot, illustrated by the artist Frieda Harris, arcane Egyptian lore remained the ultimate source. Crowley's Tarot was never as influential as the Rider pack, but the 'gypsy' (i.e. Egyptian) outsider who understands the power of Tarot remains an important character in speculative fiction. A Roma family seek the original Tarot in *The Greater Trumps* (1932), and the gypsy Zeena reads the Tarot in William Lindsay Gresham's *Nightmare Alley* (1946). Froniga, a gentrified half-gypsy healer, confronts her premonitions through her grandfather's painted Tarot cards in Elizabeth Goudge's novel *The White Witch* (1958) set during the English Civil War, while the gypsy, Mouse, in Samuel R. Delany's *Nova* (1968) initially rejects the value of Tarot in a novel where it functions as a major theme.

In Charles Williams's *The Greater Trumps* (1932), Tarot meanings motivate action and offer paths to redemption.[7] This early novel anticipates the mixture of genres which characterizes post-modern writing, and for which the apparent randomness of Tarot readings becomes an apt metaphor. A subversively hybrid mix of Christian and pagan modalities is acted out through the interaction of the daughter of a middle-class family who possess a mysterious Tarot and her fiancé, a member of a Roma clan who own a corresponding set of animated

---

[7] My thanks to the late John Heath-Stubbs for pointing out that Williams's papers included one of Waite's pamphlets on Tarot.

chess figures. The aptly named Aunt Sybil helps the characters negotiate a series of epiphanic choices engendered by the ambiguous power of the Tarot deck (Groggin 2014: 427). On one level, *The Greater Trumps* is a conventional country-house thriller, but the Manichean interplay between the card game and the movement of chess-like figures may also reflect Williams's subtle use of Arthurian themes, specifically the way in which a board game between King Arthur and an opponent affects the outcome of a battle between human knights and supernatural ravens in *Breuddwyd Rhonabwy* ('Rhonabwy's dream') (Davies 2007: 214–28). Actions that have consequences in other dimensions are popular in more recent fantasies. In Piers Anthony's trilogy, *Tarot* (1979–80), set on a fictional planet of that name, characters experience both the threatening and didactic possibilities of a living Tarot deck, and in Laura Powells's urban fantasy with gothic overtones, *The Game of Triumphs*, the action moves between SoHo and the dream-like world of Arcanum.

The iconography of the 'The Hanged Man' – the unseen card in *The Waste Land's* Tarot reading – was influenced by medieval and Renaissance images with no esoteric overtones, but literary references to the card continue to associate it with the Dying God and with ritual interpretations of the grail story (Waite 1911: 'The Hanged Man'; Farley 2009: 170–3). In William Lindsay Gresham's noir thriller *Nightmare Alley* (1946), the Tarot is an ominous projection of the psychic scams of the carnival and the main character's arrogant self-deception. This hints at the use of Tarot in para-literary forms like urban gothic and noir fantasies which are a feature of post-1980s speculative fiction. On the original cover, a man with uplifted arms runs towards a mysterious figure hovering above an urban landscape. This figure recalls the Rider pack's Hanged Man card and reinforces the Tarot references in the chapter titles, and its use in the novel as a metaphor for moral and physical decay. Such motifs demonstrate the Tarot's continued influence on literature, and how the myth of the Fisher King, with its overtones of fragmentation and heroic quest journey, has provided some of the most compelling images for speculative fiction. The work of Eliot and Yeats created a dialogue between an esoteric Tarot and contemporary concerns of alienation and cultural dissociation (Johnson 2014), a dialogue which underpins two novels that bridge this early work and post-1980s speculative fiction.

Long seen as a classic of modern science fiction, Samuel R. Delany's *Nova* (1968) adapts the grail quest and Tarot motifs drawn from Eliot's poem, the Rider tarot, and Weston's *From Ritual to Romance* to post-modern political concerns about cultural syncretism and performative identity (Johnson 2014). In Delany's space opera novel, the romance quest expands into an open-ended myth in which Tarot provides a metaphor for the uncertainties of modern life, but also demands an understanding of the traditional esoteric Tarot quest. The central character, Lorq Von Ray, head of the culturally diverse Pleiades Federation, is simultaneously wounded like the Fisher King and the leader on a quest for a space-age talisman, a super metal with the power to transform society. In a reference to the card Madame Sosostris 'cannot find' in her reading, Lorq becomes identified with The Hanged Man, an indicator of the sacrifice he must make to achieve success. The metallic nature of this science fiction 'grail' and its location in a perilous environment has parallels with the traditional romance object. However, although the quest for the romance grail or the Celtic talisman from which it derives, can fail, there is no suggestion that its power can be subverted. In contrast, *Nova*'s quest object will destroy the world if it falls into the hands of the old-order Draco family. While Tarot in *Nova* underpins the perennial quest theme, the traditional imagery of castles and heroic journeys is replaced by shifting cultural identities played out in ambiguous spaces. Tarot cards in *Nova* foreshadow events, but more fundamentally, they simultaneously reinforce and challenge the mythic structure of the traditional quest in this heterotopian world of constant change. The characters belonging to the out-world Pleiades Federation – the wounded hero Lorq, the female alien Tarot reader Tyy, the scholarly Katin who is trying to write a Parsifal-themed novel and the gypsy Mouse who is reluctant to accept the power of the unseen – contrast sharply with the gothicized environs and inbred world of the Draco family. Initially the main characters seem to subvert their traditional roles. Lorq is both dying king and renewing seeker, Mouse the gypsy does not represent conventional Tarot wisdom but rather a lack of belief. Tyy is a doubly liminal wisdom figure, both female and alien, and Katin is seemingly writing the story that is already being acted out.

In 1973, the Ballantine Adult Fantasy series, an influential force behind a newly rekindled interest in the genre of fantasy literature, published a novel that incorporated Tarot and grail quest themes. The author, Sanders Anne Laubenthal, anchored her novel in an Arthurian world that included a quest for Excalibur and the grail, a wise Merlin-like figure, untried heroes, and two Tarot-reading sisters with connections to an ancient goddess religion (Laubenthal 1973).[8] Morgan facilitates the search for Excalibur, while Morgause covets the

---

[8] The novel has been reprinted (Ballantine 1977; Science Fiction Book Club, 2000) and is attracting a growing fan base – see: https://theshadowsanctuary.wordpress.com/2015/12/08/10-novels-that-informed-my-paganism/

grail's power for herself. In order to retrieve the talismans, Rhodri, a Welshman and Linette, Morgan's niece, must negotiate a sword bridge and other dangers in a frightening otherworld. Mixing Tarot with themes drawn from medieval Welsh tradition and an emphasis on female characters was a fresh approach to what has become an established trope in the modern fantasy genre. The setting is Mobile Alabama, supposed landfall of Prince Madog's mysterious voyage to the west (Clute 1999: 565; Pryce 2005), and the edges of Western Europe and eastern United States function as both geographic and metaphoric portals between real and supernatural worlds. The action moves between Wales, Alabama and a strange otherworld, as two women, Linette and the clairvoyant Christant, and two male characters, Rhodri and Anthony, search for Excalibur and the grail.

The novel appeared at the end of the Vietnam War, and its tone is surprisingly dark. The beautiful garden and mysterious Atlantic Tower at Silverthorne House, home of Linette's aunt, provide the interface to the location of the quest objects in the mythical city of Caer Mair (Mary's city). The real city of Mobile acquires a gothic quality through a vision of its destruction if evil harnesses the power of the grail. *Excalibur*'s Arthurian world, or more precisely post-Arthurian world, reflects the author's familiarity with a range of sources. The otherworld setting is reminiscent of C.S. Lewis's *Perelandra*, and T.H. White's Arthurian novel influenced the Morgan and Morgause characters. Narrative patterns from *Mabinogion* tales – the Welsh Owain romance *Owain neu Iarlles y Ffynnon* ('Owain or the Lady of the Fountain') and *Breuddwyd Macsen* ('The dream of Maxen') – inform a plot, which fuses medieval narrative and occult Tarot (see Davies 2007: 116–28, 103–10). Laubenthal's work also reflects the shift in attitudes to female figures that has come to characterize contemporary adaptations of Arthurian tradition in fantasy fiction and in significant areas of modern Tarot usage. Morgan contacts her sister by reading Tarot cards, which provides the mechanism to shift time and space in the novel, but also establishes a mystical link with the goddess religion to which the sisters belong. Laubenthal's novel created a dynamic between the masculine myth of discovery, Prince Madog's voyage and the idea of the feminine world of religion and mystery, accessed dangerously through Morgan's Tarot cards and more safely through the Merlin-like Julian's library. *Excalibur* looks back to the clear moral divisions in C.S. Lewis's fiction, rather than towards the conflict between a benevolent goddess religion and repressive Christianity that became fashionable in the work of later feminist writers. Nevertheless, the date of publication places this novel at the earlier end of a spectrum of the, then, new phenomenon of feminist

Arthurian literature, of which Marion Zimmer Bradley's *Mists of Avalon* (1983) is perhaps the most famous example.

Roger Zelasny set his ten-book series, *The Chronicles of Amber*, written between 1970 and 1991, in the contrasting worlds of Amber and Chaos and the numerous Shadow-worlds that lie between. The action centres on two characters, Corwin of Amber and his son, Merlin. Members of Amber's royal family receive personalized Tarot decks after they negotiate the mysterious labyrinthine Pattern, and Merlin, the protagonist of the second series, constructs a sentient computer based on Tarot Trumps. Titles such as *Knight of Shadows* (1989) and *Trumps of Doom* (1985) and the original cover art work of other novels, *The Guns of Avalon* (1970) and *Sign of the Unicorn* (1975), reference the cards. In addition, Tarot cards create a significant mechanism for plot development in which characters communicate psychically via Tarot or use them as transport between worlds. A striking feature of this series is that the changing characterization of the two protagonists mirrors the way in which the 'history' of the Celtic Tarot has been incorporated into speculative fiction as well as the changing nature of fantasy and science fiction writing over the period during which the books were written. Corwin typifies the questing immortal warrior and parallels both the grail seekers of medieval romance and the questing heroes of classical fantasy fiction, while Merlin in the second series is more an anti-hero like so many hacker protagonists of cyber punk fiction. Celtic and Arthurian references continue to characterize Zelasny's series. Alternate worlds are called 'Tir-na Nóg'th' and Avalon. Merlin is imprisoned for a time in a cave and retains his Arthurian aura as a magician/engineer, but his actions are directed at the creation of a Tarot-influenced computer. References to the grail myth are especially strong in the first five books. Initially, Corwin has no memory of his real identity. Like the medieval Perceval, he is unaware of his true nature, but as a 'seeker after knowledge', his character draws on the meaning of the Fool Tarot Trump as interpreted by Waite and other twentieth-century esotericists. Corwin's actions bring about a wasteland of black roads and sinister towers, causing him to undertake a quest to reclaim a talismanic object of immense power, the Jewel of Judgement.

Zelasny's Tarot references remain anchored by the Fisher King myth, but his novels reflect the author's interest in Jungian archetypes. Other modern fantasy novelists such as Stephen King and Tim Powers combine Tarot references and the Fisher King myth as refracted through Eliot's *The Waste Land* with Jungian archetypal metaphors. Robert Browning's poem 'Child Roland to the Dark Tower Came' provided the immediate inspiration for King's *Dark Tower* series

(1982–2004), but the Tarot reading at the end of the first book (*The Gunslinger* 1982) links the characters and the journey to the Dark Tower to specific Tarot cards. In the series' third book, *The Waste Lands* (1991), the main characters travel through a landscape, which is no longer that of medieval romance, but one populated by the mutant animals and mad cyborgs made familiar by modern science and fantasy fiction. Nevertheless, despite elements of the horror genre for which this author is so well-known, Roland, as the last survivor of King Arthur's line, must undertake a quest to save the Tower which holds the universe together. The Las Vegas setting of Tim Powers's *Last Call* frames a supernatural game of Tarot by which the villain, George Leon, takes over the bodies of his defeated opponents. This false Fisher King prolongs his existence by destroying the grail seekers rather than through the redemptive power of the grail. His wounded son, Scott, who is identified with the Page of Swords, returns to reclaim his place as Fisher King by defeating the father who wounded him with a set of Tarot cards. The journey back to Las Vegas is punctuated by 'quest' adventures such as defeating the henchmen 'knights' of his father's Tarot world. This is an ultimately positive novel in which Tarot cards become archetypal metaphors for the stages in an individual's journey of self-discovery. Once Scott returns to the Las Vegas casino, standing like a dangerous Tarot-derived Tower Trump at the centre of this wasteland, Scott symbolically overcomes the randomness of card gambling and uses the archetypal power of Tarot to control his own destiny and create order.

The mysterious grail-haunted countryside of Languedoc is the setting for Kate Mosse's second novel, *Sepulchre*, in which Tarot cards hold the key to a treasure and link the lives of two women from different historical periods. The time shift structure and motif of a secret unlocked by a talisman are popular tropes in the hybrid genres that characterize contemporary fantasy and speculative fiction. The re-drawn Tarot cards create a reciprocity between text and visual image through which the female protagonists, by deciphering a musical code, discover each other and by extension themselves. Mosse's novel focuses on a resurgence of feminine power rather than a Fisher King myth that dominated the mythic structure of *The Waste Land*. Although the Belladonna card in Eliot's poem hints at a female presence, the role of 'the feminine' was not as prominent in the work of Waite or Weston as it has become in the context of feminist and psychological Tarot use (Williams 2016: 312–30, 332–41). Nevertheless, by focusing on the Otherworld queen with her attendant crones in *Red Hanrahan*, Yeats re-created a primal Celtic sovereignty myth as it might have been, a myth in which the Tarot-themed objects offered to Hanrahan would reunite him with the queenly otherworld Sovereignty figure.

Although Grail motifs and Tarot references are not a major feature of J.K. Rowling's complex world, they are essential for the successful resolution of the overall plot and theme in the last two Harry Potter books. Rowling most directly evokes the Celtic world of the Tarot in the title of her final book, *Harry Potter and the Deathly Hallows*. Although it does not appear in mediaeval romance, the term 'grail hallows' was used by later critics and esoteric writers. Professor Sybill Trelawney, whose name combines the classical sibyl with the Cornish-sounding Trelawney, nods in the direction of both ancient and Celtic contexts for Tarot cards. On one level, she is a slightly dotty version of Madame Sosostris, but she correctly interprets the Tower arcana card as a prediction of Dumbledore's death-fall from an actual tower (Rowling 2005, see especially chapter twenty-five, 'The Seer Overheard', and chapter twenty-seven, 'The Lightning-Struck Tower'; see also Stratyner 2014). Harry and his friends travel through a wasted landscape searching for a mysterious trio of talismanic objects, which includes a literal descent from Dumbledore's tower, a journey through a dark forest, advice from a wise (deceased) mentor and a rebirth (Rowling 2007). The journey takes on characteristics of the classical *katabasis* of the mystery religions which so fascinated esoteric writers and which they applied to the grail quest.

Celtic-themed Tarot Cards as fantasy genre

Tarot reading has undergone a revival since the 1980s with the creation of new decks and an upsurge in books that 'explain or interpret Tarot by expanding its range of association into a modern or other cultural or symbolic context' (Auger 2002: 237). Professional certifications are available, and the cards have been adapted for teaching or as a psychological diagnostic tool. Celtic-themed Tarot decks and handbooks have made a particular contribution to this process. Speculation about Celtic origins has been supplemented by a search for new universals in the form of Jungian archetypes, but the Rider pack and Waite's exegesis of his 'rectified' Tarot continue to provide a popular template for interpretation (see Auger 2002; Aeclectic Tarot n.d.; Kenner 2009; Elmes 2013). Writers like Rachel Pollack (1980–83) and Caitlin Matthews (see Pollack and Matthews 1989) bridge the divide between novelists and practitioners who focus on Jungian or Celtic themes, but a review by folklorist Steve Winnick of a Celtic Tarot deck originally produced in 1990 illustrates the continued importance of an underlying 'Celtic' myth in this most recent revival of the occult (see Winnick n.d.).

Colman Smith's Rider deck illustrations remain a focus for reciprocity between image and text in contemporary Tarot decks and handbooks and provide inspiration for new images. The artwork in Celtic-themed decks typically evokes Celtic Twilight imagery with pale colours and mystic symbolism. A recent tarot produced by an American firm specializing in esoterica states: 'its watercolor imagery invites you into a mystic world of ancient forests, sensuous seascapes and wondrous waterfalls brimming with mystery, meaning and magic' (Ferguson 1995; Llewellyn n.d.). Celtic decks transmute Major arcana cards like the Wheel into the Winchester Round Table or Stonehenge, while The Tower becomes associated with Vortigern's dragons. Colman Smith's Emperor with his Holy Roman Emperor crown and Egyptian ankh is replaced by pensive figures in vaguely barbarian gear, or carrying a Scythian dragon banner in a nod to popular archaeology (Auger 2002: 234–6, 238–43, 246–7). The interpretations also reflect their Celtic heritage by invoking the supposed mythic world in medieval texts such as the Four Branches of the Mabinogi, 'a compelling Celtic story featuring Rhiannon as The Empress, Bran the Blessed as The Emperor, The Wild Herdsman as The Devil, Gwydion as The Magician, Llew (sic) Llaw Gyffes as the Bringer of Light and other figures from Welsh mythology' (Llewellyn n.d.). Guidebooks accompanying these decks interpret Arthurian and Celtic traditions through the prism of archetypal, neo-pagan and new age assumptions (Auger 2002: 234–6). For example, the *Hallowquest* Tarot Deck and Guidebook nods to the Grail Hallows of esoteric speculation as well as the Jungian archetypal world in its attempt to recreate Arthurian-nuanced archetypes as a living tradition that can be experienced through the tarot system (Matthews and Matthews 1990, 1997).

A secret tradition as a fragmented survival of an esoteric truth adapts easily to the multiple chance combinations possible in Tarot spreads. A number of decks employ Jungian psychology in reformulating Arthurian traditions in Tarot as portals to our inner being. Reinterpreted as a myth of regeneration, they reformulate the quest for a talisman into a narrative that is simultaneously Arthurian and esoteric and places the 'reader' in the role of questor (Nichols 1980; Paterson 1990). Unfortunately, this often obscures the actual history of Tarot, and there remains an implicit assumption among some practitioners that Tarot is somehow intrinsically meaningful, something more than a Renaissance game of chance which was given an esoteric spin and adapted as a literary conceit at the turn of twentieth century.

Conclusion

Images drawn from Tarot weave in and out of new fantasy forms and in divinatory meanings and symbolic correspondences that continue to read 'Celtic' myth, through the perspectives established by Waite, Weston and Yeats. The pattern of otherworld quest and testing, as expressed in Yeats's *Red Hanrahan* and in Eliot's *The Waste Land,* continues to influence speculative fiction, and modern Tarot decks continue to reflect the Golden Dawn hermeticism of the Rider pack. Earlier scholarship perceived similarities between objects in medieval romances, motifs in Irish and Welsh texts, and their potential survival in folk narrative and custom. In part, this reaction to nineteenth-century fears about industrial and moral decay brought about renewed interest in a medieval world as a time of wholeness and spiritual unity. This transforms the reader from a consumer to a producer of texts, which are infinitely adaptable to the mix of literary genres that characterize speculative fiction, Tarot guidebooks and visual meditation (Mountfort 2014: 187). The result is a participatory fantasy that encourages user-driven generation of personalized narratives rooted in a desire to accommodate both science and metaphysis and re-unite mind and body.

Writers readily discovered quasi-pagan Celtic origins beneath a subsequent Christian overlay, and the writings of W.B. Yeats and A.E. Waite together with Jessie Weston's quasi-esoteric book, *From Ritual to Romance*, connected these traditions to the Tarot and the idea of a spiritual journey. The belief that an esoteric quest characterized Celtic myth continues to underpin many contemporary uses of Tarot. The quest pattern is well-suited to postmodern genres, and Tarot symbolism has provided a model with which to allegorize the shifting realities expressed in this fiction. This chapter has attempted to draw attention to the pivotal importance of a 'Celtic' Tarot. This influential phenomenon has allowed its assumed ancient and esoteric meanings to be transmitted as a living tradition seeking to reclaim a spiritual wholeness which had seemingly been abandoned, but which continues to be recreated in hybrid fantasy forms that mix traditional heroic myth with gothic, detective and science fiction and steam-punk tropes. Despite the lack of historical or textual support for a myth about a Fisher King, the possibility of such a myth presents an attractive and imaginative vision of an alternate reality onto which it is possible to project multiple meanings. Current speculative literature, new Tarot books and the merchandising of innovative decks have created a new body of transmedia storytelling traditions that demand audience participation and continue to engage our imaginations.

References

Aeclectic Tarot, 'Celtic Tarot', http://www.aeclectic.net/tarot/cards/celtic/review.shtml, accessed 20 Jun. 2021.
American Tarot Association, 'Home Page', https://www.ata-tarot.com/, accessed 20 Jun. 2021.
Anthony, Piers (1979), *God of Tarot*, New York: HBJ.
Anthony, Piers (1980), *Vision of Tarot*, New York: Berkley.
Anthony, Piers (1980), *Faith of Tarot*, New York: Berkley.
Arnold, Matthew (1910), *On the Study of Celtic Literature, with introduction, notes, and appendix by Alfred Nutt*, London: David Nutt at the sign of the Phoenix Long Acre.
Auger, Emily (2002), 'Arthurian Legend in Tarot', in Donald Hoffman and Elizabeth Sklar (eds), *King Arthur in Popular Culture*, 233–48, Jefferson: McFarland.
Auger, Emily (2004), *Tarot and Other Meditation Decks: History, Theory, Aesthetics, Typology*, Jefferson, NC: London: McFarland.
Bayley, Harold (1909), *A New Light on the Renaissance Displayed in Contemporary Emblems*, London: J. M. Dent & Co.
Clute, John (1999), 'Laubenthal, Sanders Anne', in John Clute and John Grant (eds), *The Encyclopedia of Fantasy*, 565, London: Orbit.
Coldwell, Joan (1977), 'Pamela Colman Smith and the Yeats Family', *The Canadian Journal of Irish Studies*, 3 (2): 27–34.
Davies, Sioned, trans. (2007), *The Mabinogion*, Oxford: Oxford University Press.
Delany, Samuel R. (1968), *Nova*, Garden City, NY: Doubleday.
Dummett, Michael (1980), *Game of Tarot*, London: Duckworth.
Elmes, Melissa Ridley (2013), 'From Propaganda to Product: The Arthurian Legend in Modern Tarot Decks', *Relegere: Studies in Religion and Reception*, 2: 381–406.
Eliot, T.S. (1922), *The Waste Land*, with notes, New York: Boni & Liveright.
Farley, Helen (2009), *A Cultural History of Tarot: From Entertainment to Esotericism*, London: I.B.Tauris.
Ferguson, Anne-Marie (1995), *A Keeper of Words: 'Legend: The Arthurian Tarot'*, St Paul, MN: Llewelyn.
Frazer, James G. (1993), *The Golden Bough: A Study in Magic and Religion*, new abridgement of the classic work, Ware: Wordsworth.
Gibbons, Tom (1972), 'The Waste Land Tarot Identified', *Journal of Modern Literature*, 2: 560–5.
Gilbert, R.A. (1976), 'Arthur Machen and A.E. Waite: A Forgotten Collaboration', *Antiquarian Book Monthly Review*, 11 (4): 7–8.
Gilbert, R.A. (1983), *A.E. Waite: A Bibliography*, Wellingborough: Aquarian Press.
Goggin, Joyce (2014), '*The Greater Trumps*: Charles Williams and the Metaphysics of Otherness', in Emily E. Auger (ed.), *Tarot in Culture*, vol. 2, 411–38, Clifford, ON: Valleyhome Books.

Goudge, Elizabeth (1958), *The White Witch*, London: Hodder and Stoughton.
Grayson, Janet (1992), 'In Quest of Jessie Weston', in Richard Barber (ed.), *Arthurian Literature*, XI, 1–80, Cambridge: Boydell and Brewer.
Gresham, William Lindsay (1946), *Nightmare Alley*, New York: Rinehart and Co.
Guest, Lady Charlotte, trans. (1902), *The Mabinogion: Mediaeval Welsh Romances,* with notes by Alfred Nutt, London: David Nutt.
Hirsch, Edward (1981), '"And I Myself Created Hanrahan": Yeats, Folklore, and Fiction', *ELH*, 48 (4): 880–93.
Hyde, Douglas (1890), *Beside the Fire: A Collection of Irish Gaelic Folk Stories*, with additional notes by Alfred Nutt, London: David Nutt.
Johnson, Brian (2014), 'Tarot Infinite Grail-Quest of Samuel R. Delaney's *Nova*: Romance Science Fiction and the post-Modern Tarot', in Emily E. Auger (ed.), *Tarot in Culture*, vol. 2, 439–79, Clifford, ON: Valleyhome Books.
Kaplan, Stuart R. (2009), 'Artwork & Times of Pamela Colman Smith: Artist of the Rider-Waite Tarot Deck', in *Pamela Colman Smith Commemorative Set* [Book and Deck], U.S. Games Systems.
Kenner, Corrine (2009), *Tarot for Writers*, St Paul, MN: Llewellyn.
King, Stephen (1982–2004), *Dark Tower Series*, London: Sphere.
Laubenthal, Sanders Anne (1973), *Excalibur*, New York: Ballantine.
Llewellyn, 'The Llewellyn Tarot by Anne Marie Ferguson', https://www.llewellyn.com/product.php?ean=9780738702995, accessed 20 Jun. 2021.
Matthews, Caitlín and Matthews, John (1990), *The Arthurian Tarot: A Hallowquest Handbook*, illustrated by Miranda Gray, Wellingborough: Aquarian.
Matthews, Caitlín and Matthews, John (1997), *Hallowquest: The Arthurian Tarot Course*, London: Thorsons.
Mead, G.R.S. (1906), *Fragments of a Faith Forgotten: Some Short Sketches among the Gnostics, Mainly of the First Two Centuries: A Contribution to the Study of Christian Origins Based on the Most Recently Recovered Materials*, London: Theosophical Publishing Society.
Mosse, Kate (2007), *Sepulchre*, London: Orion.
Mountfort, Paul (2014), 'Tarot Guide Books as a Literary Genre: Narratives of Destiny', in Emily E. Auger (ed.), *Tarot in Culture*, vol. 1, 187–234, Clifford, ON: Valleyhome Books.
Nichols, Sallie (1980), *Jung and Tarot: An Archetypal Journey*, York Beach: Weiser.
Nutt, Alfred Trübner (1888), *Studies on the Legend of the Holy Grail: With Especial Reference to the Hypothesis of Its Celtic Origin*, Folk-lore Society Publication no. 23, London: D. Nutt.
Nutt, Alfred Trübner (1899), *The Influence of Celtic upon Medieval Romance*, Popular Studies in Mythology Romance and Folklore. no. 1, London: David Nutt.
Nutt, Alfred Trübner (1902), *The Legends of the Holy Grail*, Popular Studies in Mythology Romance and Folklore no. 14, London: David Nutt.

Paterson, Helena (1990), *The Celtic Tarot: Discover Celtic Myth and Legends in Your Tarot Deck*, book and card pack illustrated by Courtney Davis, Wellingborough: Aquarian.
Pollack, Rachel (1980–83), *Seventy Eight Degrees of Wisdom: A Book of Tarot*, Wellingborough: Aquarian.
Pollack, Rachel and Matthews, Caitlín, eds (1989), *Tarot Tales*, London: Legend.
Powell, Laura (2009), *The Game of Triumphs*, London: Orchard.
Powers, Tim (1992), *Last Call*, New York: William Morrow and Co.
Pryce, J. Malcolm (2005), *With Madog to the New World*, Talybont: Y Lolfa.
Raine, Kathleen (1972), *Yeats, the Tarot and the Golden Dawn*, Dublin: Dolmen Press.
Renan, Ernest (1859), *Essais de Morale et de Critique*, Paris: Calmann Levy.
Rowling, J.K. (2005), *Harry Potter and the Half-blood Prince*, London: Bloomsbury.
Rowling, J.K. (2007), *Harry Potter and the Deathly Hallows*, London: Bloomsbury.
Stratyner, Leslie (2014), 'Harry Potter and the Tarot: Divining the Half-blood Prince', in Emily E. Auger (ed.), *Tarot in Culture*, vol. 2, 481–502, Clifford, ON: Valleyhome Books.
Villemarqué, Théodore Hersart Vicomte de la (1842), *Contes Populaires des Anciens Bretons, Précédés d'un Essai sur l'Origine des Épopées Chevaleresques de la Table-Ronde*, Paris: W. Coquebert.
Waite, Arthur Edward (1896), *Devil-worship in France: or, the Question of Lucifer*, London: G. Redway.
Waite, Arthur Edward (1906), 'The Hidden Sacrament of the Holy Grail: A Mystery Play', in *Strange Houses of Sleep*, London: Philip Sinclair Wellby.
Waite, Arthur Edward (1909a), *The Hidden Church of the Holy Grail*, London: Rebman.
Waite, Arthur Edward (1909b), 'The Tarot: A Wheel of Fortune', *Occult Review*, 10 (6): 307–16.
Waite, Arthur Edward (1909c), 'Romance of the Holy Grail', *The Quest*, 1 (1): 90–107.
Waite, Arthur Edward (1910), *The Key to the Tarot: Being Fragments of a Secret Tradition under the Veil of Divination* [with a set of cards], London: William Rider & Son.
Waite, Arthur Edward (1911), *The Pictorial Key to the Tarot: Being Fragments of a Secret Tradition under the Veil of Divination*; with 78 Plates, Illustrating the Greater and Lesser Arcana, from Designs by Pamela Colman Smith, London: William Rider & Son.
Waite, Arthur Edward (1933), *The Holy Grail: Its Legends and Symbolism; an Explanatory Survey of Their Embodiment in Romance Literature and a Critical Study of the Interpretations Placed Thereon*, London: Rider and Co.
Waite, Arthur Edward (1961), *The Holy Grail: The Galahad Quest in Arthurian Literature*, New York: University Books.
Waitinas, Catherine (2014), 'Tarot as "Secret Tradition" in T.S. Eliot's The Waste Land: "These Fragments I Have Shored against My Ruins"', in Emily E. Auger (ed.), *Tarot in Culture*, vol. 2, 367–410, Clifford, ON: Valleyhome Books.
Weston, Jessie (1993), *From Ritual to Romance*, with a new foreword by Robert A. Segal, Princeton, NJ: Princeton University Press.

Williams, Charles (1989), *The Greater Trumps*, London: Paladin.
Williams, Mark (2016), *Ireland's Immortals: A History of the Gods of Irish Myth*, Princeton, NJ: Princeton University Press.
Winnick, Steve, 'Celtic Tarot Review by Steve Winick', http://www.aeclectic.net/tarot/cards/celtic/review.shtml, accessed 20 Jun. 2021.
Wood, Juliette (1998), 'The Celtic Tarot and the Secret Tradition: A Study in Modern Legend Making', *Folklore*, 109: 15–24.
Wood, Juliette (2000), 'The Holy Grail: From Romance Motif to Modern Genre', *Folklore*, 111 (2): 169–90.
Wood, Juliette (2002), 'The Search for the Holy Grail: Scholars, Critics and Occultists', in Kathryn Izzo and Katharine Olson (eds), *Proceedings of the Harvard Celtic Colloquium*, 22 (2002), 226–48, Cambridge, MA: Dept. of Celtic Languages and Literatures, Facuty of Arts and Sciences, Harvard University.
Wood, Juliette (2008), *Eternal Chalice: The Enduring Legend of the Holy Grail*, London: I.B. Tauris.
Wood, Juliette (2017), 'Jessie Weston and the Ancient Mystery of Arthurian Romance', *Journal of the International Arthurian Society*, 5 (1): 73–85.
Yeats, W.B. (1913), *Stories of Red Hanrahan*, London: A.H. Bullen.
Zelasny, Roger (1970–91), *Chronicles of Amber*, New York: Doubleday.

10

Celtic appropriation in twenty-first-century fantasy fan perceptions

Angela R. Cox

Other chapters in this book have addressed the use of Irish and Welsh source material, as well as classical texts and more recent folklore, as evidence of the ways in which contemporary fantasy has (re)imagined the Celtic past. This chapter, however, shifts focus for a moment to how fantasy fans as a collective group perceive the relationship between fantasy as a genre and the prevalent use of Celticism in that genre. As such, the research represented in this chapter employs Critical Discourse Analysis and a corpus of collected fan discussions from internet forums and blogs that represent a year of conversation to examine how fans perceive the role of 'Celtic' material in fantasy texts, rather than examining a specific authored text as an example. Considered through a postcolonial approach, some of the fantasy conventions, or 'tropes' as fan communities typically call them, indicate continued control or erasure of Celtic-speaking cultures' identities and cultural material in popular culture.

In the twenty-first century, the fantasy genre has become increasingly marked by the practice known as 'worldbuilding', and 'high' and 'epic' fantasies are largely distinguished not by their plot or themes as they might have been in other periods, but by their medievalized 'fantasy' setting. This setting often depends heavily on borrowing and appropriating cultural markers from cultures perceived as suitably exotic or mysterious and combining them together to create a novel 'original world'. Within this practice, cultures popularly lumped together as 'Celtic' (especially Irish and Welsh) are so commonly used in these appropriations, adaptations and borrowings that fans barely feel the need to mention their 'Celtic' origins; instead, they take the Celticity of fantasy for granted, attributing the Celtic-rooted conventions to notable seminal texts and legends (such as Tolkien or the medieval Arthurian tradition) without acknowledgement of the Celticity of these sources, resulting in a general erasure of Celticity, and its more specific Irishness and Welshness, even as the cultural materials continue to be used in fantasy as a matter of course.

It must first be acknowledged that the relationship between Western contemporary fantasy and Celticism is a long and complex one. No history of twentieth- or twenty-first-century fantasy would neglect to mention the influence of J.R.R. Tolkien's fiction, whether that history is generated by scholarship or fandom; and Tolkien's adaptation of medieval materials, including those from 'Celtic' cultures, is well-documented. Particularly relevant to the matter at hand is his use of Welsh and Irish language and cultural material in representing supernatural elements such as elves, as examined in detail by Fimi (2006). Likewise, although it is common to locate the origin of fantasy in the Gothic, many histories of fantasy, such as Cecire (2009) and de Camp (1976), point to the Arthurian tradition as a significant source for modern fantasy, or at the very least as 'early and medieval texts of great importance' to the earliest origins of fantasy, as Matthews (1997: 14) notes. Indicating Arthurian tradition as a major source for modern fantasy thus in turn traces fantasy to Welsh oral and literary tradition, as noted in the entry on Arthur in *The Encyclopedia of Fantasy* (Clute and Grant 1997: 57–63). As the other chapters in this book explore, these threads of medieval 'Celtic' material are strong and consistent throughout the modern fantasy canon. Indeed, I argue in this chapter that these threads are so strong, consistent and so enmeshed into the very definition of what the fantasy genre *is*, that they become indistinguishable from fantasy genre tropes, and thus functionally *invisible* to many fantasy readers and even fantasy writers or critics.

It may seem diminishingly academic and pedantic to be concerned about the Welsh and Irish influences on the fantasy genre – that is, its general 'Celticity' – as this state of affairs has existed more or less since Western fantasy's inception and generally does not seem to bother fantasy readers, writers or fandoms. Moreover, borrowing, appropriating and adapting cultural material in fantasy is a commonplace practice in the genre, and even something celebrated within the genre, so it may seem odd to single out 'Celtic' material in this way. However, there is some real damage being done of the colonial sort, albeit limited in many ways, through the normalization of fantasy's Celticity to the point of near invisibility behind 'fantasy tropes'. As I will discuss in this chapter, the transparent and ubiquitous Celticity of fantasy tropes perpetuates certain colonialist attitudes against Irish and Welsh cultures and treats the medieval cultural material used as something to which Western fantasy has an inherent right, rather than might consciously borrow with recognition as it does with other cultures.

Method

In contrast to most studies of a particular theme in a popular genre, the study described in this chapter looked not to the texts that are canonical, popular or influential in the fantasy genre, but rather to the fans themselves and how they discuss the genre amongst themselves. In that regard, the study is ethnographic in nature, collecting online discussions from two online self-identified fantasy fan communities over a span of a year, resulting in over 1,400 individual conversation threads. The larger community (Community A), which contributed 1,440 conversations and included 987 unique participants, was a forum for self-identified fantasy writers and fans; the smaller community (Community B), which contributed 214 conversations and included 112 participants, consisted of a central collaborative blog about fantasy and its regular commenters. Conversations were collected from public parts of the communities, although posting in the communities required membership registration. Both communities included a global presence, although the larger community was notably more global. All conversations were conducted in English, so that the sample tended to prefer participants in English-speaking countries, but did include participants conversing in English as their second language and discussions of non-English language texts. It is impossible to say, however, exactly the range of experience and geography represented in these communities; while member profiles in both communities allowed for personal information such as location, members often listed their location as fantasy locales or humorously vague locations, or else not at all. Significant for the purposes of this study, these communities are explicitly organized around interest in fantasy, although one stresses readership and the other stresses authorship more. The resulting corpus of archived, coded and databased anonymous conversations was not generated specifically for the present study, but rather for a larger project (Cox 2016) interested in defining the fantasy genre itself (and the very term *genre*) in descriptivist terms, with the understanding that the people best qualified to define a social space are the members of that social space. However, the corpus has proved useful for a number of other explorations of the fantasy genre.

The items in the corpus were stripped of identifying information and coded with five code families (and over 3,000 individual codes, as will become apparent) to examine different features of the fantasy genre being discussed. The families were 'actions for authority' (that is, instances of participants in the communities drawing attention to their own expertise in the fantasy genre); 'Attributions' (instances in which participants mention an authority, such as a fantasy text or author); 'Conventions' (instances where a participant names a particular textual feature as a fantasy convention); 'Definitions' (instances where a participant makes an explicit definition of a genre or sub-genre); and 'Values' (instances where a participant directly or indirectly expresses a value embedded in the fantasy genre or its surrounding communities).

Having thus converted the qualitative data into something more quantitative, the corpus can be analysed for any number of queries and combinations of these five families of codes or instances of specific codes within each of the families. Thus, we are able to explore how fantasy fandoms in the early twenty-first century are discussing the role of Celticism, Welsh and Irish cultures, authors known for their use of 'Celtic' material, and so forth.

For the question at hand, some of the most relevant codes were generally in the 'attributions of authority' family, specifically 'Attribution: Celtic Culture' (36 instances), used when participants specifically identify something as 'Celtic'; Attribution: Welsh Culture (sixteen instances), used when participants note Welsh origins of material specifically; Attribution: Arthurian Legend (forty-six entries), used when participants name the Arthurian tradition without specifying an author or origin; and Attribution: Irish Culture or Language (four instances, which largely co-occur with Attribution: Welsh Culture, indicating a strong inclination to pan-Celticism). Although these are minor codes in the corpus overall, they are nevertheless representative of the majority of codes in their frequency. While the most significant codes, such as attributions to J.R.R. Tolkien occurred over 300 times in the corpus, most codes occurred between twenty and forty times. Thus, references to Celtic culture and Arthurian legend are significant in their frequency, while we find that references to specific Celtic cultures (here, Irish and Welsh; other Celtic cultures, such as Scottish or Cornish, do not even occur in the corpus) are marginalized in favour of pan-Celtic references, but still present in discussions.

Results: Transparent Celticism

With this big-picture outline of the fantasy genre available, in which authors strongly value the incorporation of a range of cultural materials into fantasy texts, it becomes evident that the already documented enduring engagement of fantasy with the Celtic past remains strong, but not overtly so. Although many of the most attributed authorities in fantasy are known to have made use of 'Celtic' cultural materials and otherwise participated in Celticism, there is very little discussion of the use of Celtic-language materials, either by that name or, more properly, by more specific names such as Irish, or Welsh. Moreover, this stands in contrast to the common discussion of employing Norse, Japanese or other cultural material that is acknowledged as such.

Unsurprisingly, the most commonly attributed authority is J.R.R. Tolkien, with 361 distinct mentions, indicating that Tolkien is named on average in twenty-two per cent of discussions. Tolkien's dominance in the fantasy genre has undoubtedly been bolstered by recent adaptations, such as the films by Peter Jackson, as well as by other material that uses Tolkien's imagining of the medievalized fantasy setting such as the role-playing games *Dungeons & Dragons*. This bolstering is evident in the fact that discussions of *The Lord of the Rings* adaptations (whether individually named, or just generally referencing the series without specifying which film or version) are the third most common attribution, with 158 references, or occurring in approximately ten per cent of discussions. Attributions to *Dungeons & Dragons* are the eighth most common attributions, at 105 references, or approximately six per cent of conversations. Other authors occupying high-ranking positions in the attributions family of code tended to be more recent, such as George R.R. Martin (272 references, or sixteen per cent of conversations) or Brandon Sanderson (112 references, or seven per cent of conversations). This popularity and ubiquity is best explained in the cases of these other, more recent authors not by their staying power in fantasy (which remains to be seen), but rather by the period in which the data was collected, during which these authors were enjoying particular popularity (and, in Martin's case, popularity boosted by a multimedia presence through adaptation not unlike Tolkien's multimedia presence).

Tolkien's ubiquity and authority in the fantasy genre is reflected not only in direct attributions, but also in the conventions and values most frequently expressed by participants in the study. These conventions and values, however, also point to the importance of how Tolkien used cultural material from his medieval sources, and in turn how that use in fantasy has shaped popular perception of the medieval and Celticity. Although by far the most commonly named convention is the presence of magic in fantasy (197 instances), which cannot be ascribed to any particular culture, the ubiquity of *elves* (138 instances) in this case begins to paint a picture of the way that Celticism has been woven into the contemporary fantasy genre.

Although the term 'elves' is itself an English word in origin, the specific elves that are meant in the majority of these instances are Tolkienized elves, as one sees in Tolkien and derivative works such as *Dungeons & Dragons*, and *those* elves are associated with Celticity particularly through their associations with interlace or knotwork designs and other 'mystic' motifs in the most popular representations, such as the Peter Jackson films (see Fimi 2011), motifs that are commonly used to denote Celticity, especially popular notions of pre-Christian Irish material culture. When participants wish to be less conventional or more specific, they frequently turn to the less modern sounding term 'fae' (fifty-five instances), which has become in some ways interchangeable as a fantasy convention and seems to be perceived as more 'original' and in this situation more 'Irish'.

More than simply the conventions, though, the use of cultural source material to create coherent, believable worlds with magic *systems* is deeply embedded in the data concerning the 'values' family of codes, which is somewhat surprising considering that the fundamental aspect of the fantasy genre is the notion of the *fantastic*, which is to say that the genre is generally expected to be rooted in the unreal, impossible and imaginative. However, despite the fantastic being the most important *features* of fantasy, the most commonly expressed values in the fantasy communities studied were, in order of importance, *research* (173 instances), *worldbuilding* (144 instances), *scientific plausibility* (141 instances), *character building* (132 instances) and *realism* (127). Other commonly expressed values included originality, historical plausibility and believability. Indeed, the twenty-five longest threads (that is, those with the most replies, and thus the most discussion) collected from these communities were *all* designated as 'research' threads in the forums in which they appeared.

Thus, what appears to be valued most in twenty-first-century fantasy is not so much escapism or wonder, but rather the adaptation of historical and literary material into an original fantasy world. Significantly, this is what the communities appear to perceive Tolkien as having done with his Middle Earth books; thus, participants expressed aspirational desires to 'create a language' or to draw maps or otherwise emulate Tolkien, often neglecting to consider the medieval source material Tolkien used to do these things.

Additionally, it is significant that what qualifies as 'research' has a fairly low bar of admission within the fantasy genre, despite it being the single most commonly expressed value in the fantasy genre in this corpus. Thus, readers of fantasy most highly prize displays of research through the creative application of cultural material rather than the quality, accuracy or origins of that research. What matters, then, is that authors can demonstrate that there is some documented cultural parallel to the systems depicted in their fictional worlds, proving the believability of the element in question, even if the source of that parallel is dubious. Thus, parallels need not be vetted; sources supposedly closer to 'the originals' are prized for authenticity by merit of their age, but in many cases this means sources that emerged in the nationalistic push for folk origins in the eighteenth and nineteenth centuries, and the fantasy community is not especially picky in their choices of translations, either. The search for 'originals' also often ignores anything too old to be read without translation, or includes public domain translations that may not meet the standards of more recent research; these practices risk perpetuating mistranslations and nationalist attitudes.

Consider, for instance, in one conversation in which a participant writes 'I've started reading about King Arthur, Sir Lancelot and Guinevere. These are amazing tales. One shouldn't attempt a parody without reading the original stories'. However, 'original' here is ambiguous and, in the context of the conversation (which is a discussion of what medieval knights might carry on a journey), appears to refer more to English and French Arthurian tales such as *Sir Gawain and the Green Knight* or *Perceval*, rather than acknowledging Welsh origins of the Arthurian tales. Given the preference for modern, accessible texts overall, it might be assumed that the 'original stories' here would likely be those by T.H. White (who is attributed ten times in the corpus) or by Thomas Mallory (only one explicit attribution). Perhaps more significant, though, is that the participant here sees no need to clarify exactly which body of work is meant by 'the original stories' even while recommending that these be the foundation of any creative work using the Arthurian tradition.

Indeed, Arthurian tales are a particularly strong component of premodern erasures of Welsh culture in fantasy (and by extension, other Celtic erasures). Attributions to Arthurian legends appear with significant frequency relative to other attribution codes, at forty-six instances (which is statistically similar references to Shakespeare or to Greek Mythology, or to popular urban fantasy author Jim Butcher) and there are thirty instances of Arthurian legend treated as a convention of the genre rather than as a source; however, explicit attributions to Welsh culture occur only sixteen times, and to generalized 'Celtic' cultures thirty-six times. More significantly, attributions to Arthurian legends and to Welsh culture co-occur only four times, and three of those are in references to author Gillian Bradshaw's work. There is similarly little overlap between attributions to 'Celtic culture' and to Arthurianism; here, then, we see clear evidence of the invisibility of the Celtic influence on modern fantasy. While most participants see Arthurian legends as a pattern for high fantasy, Arthurianism seems to be either apart from history (lost to the mists of Avalon as it may be) or seen as a part of English history, and so the 'original legends' are accessed through later English versions of the legends such as Thomas Mallory's *Morte d'Arthur*. Such a conflation of English, Welsh, Irish and Scottish material into generally 'British' and then generally 'medieval' material is not unique or new to fantasy; it follows, for instance, Geoffrey of Monmouth's *History of the Kings of Britain*'s view of British history, as well as a number of other cultural materials that authors use as sources, and may even reflect the global nature of the fantasy genre in the twenty-first century. However, the effect of such conflation is part of a larger pattern of uncritical appropriation in fantasy, one that treats cultures as banks of discrete materials to be used at will and in combination with other elements, and in turn risks perpetuating colonial stereotypes that may date back to the middle ages.

Given the uncritical but voracious approach to research in fantasy communities, the erasure of Welshness in Arthurianism, and likewise the use of Irish source material to indicate otherworldliness in fantasy, is hardly surprising, as it follows from the general history of English use of marginalized 'Celtic' cultures. Fantasy communities' conflations of cultures in Britain and Ireland, as well as time periods, conform to the colonialist processes employed both in the modern era by the British Empire and also those employed by English rulers in the premodern eras. Such damage might be mitigated by a more nuanced approach to research or to what constitutes the so-called original stories in these cases as one more informed by typical folkloric transmission processes, and such voices *are* present in the fan communities, but they are a significant minority where outdated research that reflects antiquated attitudes towards authorship is generally more accessible to the fantasy fan community.

Yet another significant and simultaneous process evidenced by the erasure of Welshness in Arthurian legend and the plundering of source material in general in the fantasy genre is the othering of time; that is, the colonization by the modern era of the pre-modern era. This phenomenon is now well-documented, and fantasy functions as one of the main repositories of the invented medieval identity, one which conflates all of Europe together and approximately a millennium of human history into one period, largely for the purpose of having 'someplace exotic to fly to when modern life got too, well, modern. Or so that we could have a convenient Other against which to define ourselves' (Brown 2000: 550). It follows, then, that Celticity is a significant part of that Othered identity, both preserved as Other in English source materials as they are incorporated into fantasy fiction (where that presence becomes obscured in the adaptation) and as an active act of seeking out exotic, mystical cultures to use as research and inspiration for 'original' material in fantasy fiction (where the material may then be conflated with other cultures or overlaid on top of other cultural material subject to the same processes).

It must be noted, though, that the harm is minimal; in no way am I suggesting that the conflations common to fantasy are as damaging as other colonialization processes have been throughout history or in the present day. As Brown (2000) has noted, the harm of these practices is somewhat limited, in part because fantasy as a genre (as many other genres do) engages in continual self-examination, so that the genre's sources, history and expectations are constantly up for debate, remediation and re-interpretation. Indeed, the evidence in the corpus points directly to that debate. What is demonstrated in the corpus, then, is not the accepted status quo of fantasy, but rather the spaces of debate.

One of these spaces is the appropriate handling of research and source material. Although, as I have already said, research is a loose term with little rigor attached to it in fantasy spaces, it is nevertheless expected; moreover, consulting with other members of the community is common, as participants are seeking affirmation that what they have chosen to do with their source material is somehow acceptable in the boundaries of both the fantasy genre and modern sensibility about what is decent. This does not prevent the cultural appropriation, erasure or other colonial processes discussed above, but it does mean that these things are subject to discussion, even if that discussion may be less than precise in academic terms. Consider, for instance, in the context of a discussion of race and other real-world issues in fantasy, this participant's self-justification of a pastiche of human physiological and cultural markers:

> Fantasy is a nice genre to write in, because a fantasy world may not have the same issues as ours.
>
> For instance, my MC is what most people would consider Native American, but I chose to give his culture a Celtic base, and make them the dominant society in their little corner of the world. Therefore his brownish skin and black hair is normal. However, when he heads north on the obligatory quest, he's suddenly and acutely in the minority among the northern people, who have fair skin and black or red hair.
>
> (Community A, Participant 1)

Notice here that racial markers and cultural names are more or less interchangeable. There is a very complex process happening here, one that is both colonial and postcolonial at the same time. The participant is consciously trying to de-colonize this fictional space by presenting marginalized groups (Native Americans and the 'Celtic base') as 'the dominant society'; but at the same time, the participant has succeeded in further marginalizing these groups by conflating them, pushing them into a 'little corner of the world' (that is, a margin), and transplanting the protagonist from this space into a space where he becomes 'suddenly and acutely in the minority'.

More importantly for the present discussion, it is completely unclear what the participant meant by 'a Celtic base', nor does the further discussion take up this issue or call the participant to task on it. It is accepted as a reasonable move in fantasy, where such pastiche is common and even encouraged as a way to generate 'originality'. What *is* evident from the use of 'Celtic' here is that the participant fully means to conflate Irish, Welsh, etc. identities into one culture with either a unified mythos or singular racial identity, a notion of pan-Celticism that is reinforced by the relative prevalence of attributions to 'Celtic' culture in contrast to the lack of attributions to *specific* Celtic cultures. Again, as the thread demonstrates no objections to the use of the term in this way, it is evident that the other participants see this move as normal within the genre space, or at least beneath comment given the subject at hand (which was, nevertheless, a discussion of the role of race in fantasy). It may be that the author in this passage genuinely sees 'Celtic' as a unified identify, following the tendency from Romantic era literature towards pan-Celticism (Fimi 2017), or it may be that the author sees this as actually more correct than distinguishing or singling out an individual culture within the label 'Celtic'; the exact motivation here is a matter of speculation, but more significantly the acceptance of the term 'Celtic' is indicative of a general acceptance in the community of the term as an acceptable cultural marker.

What is also significant here is that Celticity is seen as a source generally for mysticism, another exoticizing approach. In general, the association of Celtic languages with mysticism is not new; Fimi (2017: 11) notes that English romanticism tended to mark the 'Celtic character as spiritual, natural, emotional, artistic, rural, and timeless' in a telling process of 'Othering'. Associating the 'Other' with nature, emotion and the mystical is a typical colonial move, and the characterization may be older still. In keeping with such characterization, when Celtic languages are referenced in this corpus of discussions of fantasy media, it is almost always in reference to some magical element in the story, be it to *fae*, *sidhe* or other material associated with magic or cult practice. In one discussion, participants debated the proper capitalization of *seelie* in English-language texts; the original post asks 'They're both faery, or faekind. Which do you think would be better?' and the first response is 'Seelie and Unseelie aren't races, they're Courts or kingdoms' to which the original poster answers 'In the original mythology, yes, they are courts of Faery. I've tweaked the legends however and in my novel they are used as races of faery'. Notice in this conversation the consistent use of *faery* over the more Anglicized *fairy* as an overt attempt to distinguish *these* supernatural creatures from other, more anglicized fairies and appear 'older' and more 'Celtic'; notice also that the centre of authority in the conversation rests on acknowledgement of 'original mythology' – something that, in discussing Celtic culture (Irish is not specifically named in this conversation, nor actually is it termed Celtic), is a specious notion at best, as such folkloric material lacks any 'original' in the modern sense of an authored text, nor are there available texts that pre-date Christian influence in Ireland to be considered 'original' in this sense.

In a similar conversation, another participant seems to want to demonstrate familiarity with Irish language as a way of displaying research, and asks:

> I am writing a contemporary/urban fantasy about the fae. The main character is ... well-read, especially in the medieval romances, because she knows enough to recognize that the word sidhe [...] means 'mound' with the sense of that being where the fae live. My question is this: when those who do not know Irish orthography see it, they would like pronounce is [*sic*] sid, or even sid.he [*sic*], when it should be shee [...] Would it be better to go with the traditional spelling ... or use a spelling that readers would be more likely to pronounce correctly?
>
> (Community A, Participant 2)

In this instance, the participant is deeply concerned with 'accuracy' and displaying research into the Irish language. It is notable, however, that there is no explicitly stated or intrinsic reason that being 'well read' in 'medieval romances' would confer upon someone a knowledge of 'Irish orthography', but nevertheless the participant treats this as a reasonable explanation; neither does any other participant object to the explanation. The lack of comment on this aspect of the discussed character here suggests an implicit assumption that what is medieval is also Celtic (and what is Irish is Celtic and vice versa). It is, however, worth noting a tension here: even while conflating the medieval, there remains a strong concern in discussions such as the one quoted above for preserving cultural material and attributing it accordingly. This is a generative tension in fantasy that helps produce worldbuilding and other significant fantasy genre activities, critical and uncritical, but the tension becomes problematic because even as participants debate the accuracy of research, they fail to criticize the epistemological assumptions under that research that risk perpetuating outdated and even harmful attitudes and assumptions about the nature of culture, language and race embedded in fantasy's inherited concepts such as pan-Celticism.

It is evident, then, that some of the most significant threads integrally woven into the modern Western fantasy genre have their origins in not only Celticism and Celticity, but in a complex history of relationships between cultures designated 'Celtic' and other Western European cultures that comprise the generally assumed source material for Western fantasy (German, English, French, Scandinavian, etc.). Fantasy readers, writers and fans *do* value historicity and research, but the method by which they value research and historicity tends to prize Celticity for its perceived exoticism and mysticism, but at the same time to assume and even overlook its inclusion in fantasy because of its familiarity as a fantasy trope dating back to medieval Arthurian romances.

Perhaps nowhere is this invisible ubiquity as obvious as it is with the discussions of music in the corpus. Music in fantasy, much like Celticity, is highly influential but so ubiquitous that it garners very little discussion in the corpus. Although this method of study is advantageous in privileging the real-world discussions and concerns of participants in fantasy communities of practice, it must be assumed that the things that are largely taken for granted in the community will not stand out in the codings, because there is little point in discussing that which is known and accepted. Music is such a thing; while these communities discuss source material, research resources and genre-specific books, films and games extensively, there is relatively little reference to music. However, upon closer examination, participants in the communities who self-identify as fantasy authors discuss music in ways that make it evident that it is a fundamental part of their process. Moreover, whenever music is mentioned, it frequently includes 'Celtic' music. In the most telling thread in the corpus, the original post asks if participants 'listen to music for ideas' or 'to unlock your imagination'. In the ensuing discussion, most participants discuss using music in some way in their composition process. More importantly for the present discussion, much of that music is 'Celtic'.

Participants argued that they selected music to match the writing they were engaged in – that is, to match the fantasy genre. As a result, the most common choices of music were metal, Celtic/New Age, soundtracks and electronica. The soundtracks selected tend to already occupy a fantasy genre space, as with the commonly cited Howard Shore soundtrack from Peter Jackson's *Lord of the Rings* films, which notably includes contributions from Irish musician Enya (Fimi 2011).

Indeed, it seems that Celtic music, which is often lumped with New Age music in part because of the association of Celticity with Neopaganism and mysticism, is a common choice among participants in fantasy communities, in part *because* it is perceived as Other and mysterious, somehow tapping into a raw mystical past. Several participants claimed to listen to 'exotic' music, and proceeded to name Celtic music as one of the genres included in that label.

Thus, Celticity holds an ever-present position in fantasy media, but in so doing it becomes effectively invisible because it becomes associated with the fantasy genre rather than with any particular source culture. The effect is a strange overlapping of Celticity in modern fantasy; when participants look for a more mystical source material, they often seek out overtly 'Celtic' material (such as Celtic music) to consciously weave into an already Arthurian and Tolkienized milieu that serves as the default 'fantasy' mode. This creates a sort of Celtic 'double exposure' in many fantasy texts, not unlike the strange incorporation of Welshness in the medieval *Perceval* by Chrétien de Troyes, in which then-contemporary stereotypes of Welsh people complete with a movement from the Welsh margin to the English centre were overlaid on top of the already Welsh Arthurian tradition, all as read through a French romance tradition.

The modern Western fantasy genre has done precisely this double exposure several times over. By forgetting the already Celtic milieu of modern fantasy's origins, as traced through Arthurian legends, popularly translated texts such as the *Mabinogion*, and Tolkien himself, modern fantasy continues to look to Irish and Welsh cultures for mysticism, exoticism and otherness, overlaying on top of that tradition another layer of perceptions of Celticity. And, because the fantasy genre's values encourage research but little criticism of that research beyond seeking 'originals', medieval, early modern and romantic interpretations of Irish, Welsh and other Celtic cultures become folded into the mix and further entrenched in popular imagination.

The end result of these layers of adaptation and appropriation is that when most people casually see material coded as 'Celtic', they often label it as 'fantasy', and in reverse when people seek to enact the 'fantasy' genre they often encode it by using 'Celtic' material, so that the two in many ways become more or less synonymous, and in so doing, the Celtic gets enmeshed transparently into the fabric of the fantastic.

References

Brown, C. (2000), 'In the Middle', *Journal of Medieval and Early Modern Studies*, 30 (3): 547–74.

Calvo-Sotelo, J. C. (2016), 'I Celti, la prima Europa: The Role of Celtic Myth and Celtic Music in the Construction of European Identity', *Popular Music and Society*, 40 (4): 369–89.

Cecire, M. S. (2009), 'Medievalism, Popular Culture and National Identity in Children's Fantasy Literature', *Studies in Ethnicity and Nationalism*, 9 (3): 396–409.

Clute, J., and Grant, J. (1997), *The Encyclopedia of Fantasy*, New York: St Martin's.

Cox, A. R. (2016), 'The Power Fantastic: How Genre Expectations Mediate Authority', PhD diss., Fayetteville: University of Arkansas.

Dagenais, J., and Greer, M. R. (2000), 'Decolonizing the Middle Ages: Introduction', *Journal of Medieval and Early Modern Studies*, 30 (3): 431–48.

Davies, R. R. (2000), *The First English Empire*, New York: Oxford University Press.

Davis, K. (1998), 'National Writing in the Ninth Century: A Reminder for Postcolonial Thinking about the Nation', *Journal of Medieval and Early Modern Studies*, 28 (3): 611–37.

de Camp, L. S. (1976), *Literary Swordsmen and Sorcerers: The Makers of Heroic Fantasy*, Sauk City: Arkham House.

Duggan, J. J. (1999), 'Afterword', in C. de Troyes, *Perceval by Chrétien de Troyes*, trans B. Raffel, New Haven: Yale University Press.

Fimi, D. (2006), '"Mad" Elves and "Elusive Beauty": Some Celtic Strands of Tolkien's Mythology', *Folklore*, 117 (2): 156–70.

Fimi, D. (2011), 'Filming Folklore: Adapting Fantasy for the Big Screen through Peter Jackson's Lord of the Rings', in J. M. Bogstad and P. E. Kaveny (eds), *Picturing Tolkien: Essays on Peter Jackson's The Lord of the Rings Film Trilogy*, 84–101, Jefferson: McFarland.

Fimi, D. (2017), *Celtic Myth in Contemporary Children's Fantasy*, London: Palgrave Macmillan.

Holsinger, B. (2002), 'Medieval Studies, Postcolonial Studies, and the Genealogies of Critique', *Speculum*, 77 (4): 1195–227.

Jauss, H. R. (1979), 'The Alterity and Modernity of Medieval Literature', *New Literary History*, 10 (2): 181–229.

Matthews, R. (1997), *Fantasy: The Liberation of Imagination*, New York: Twayne.

Pike, S. M. (2001), *Earthly Bodies, Magical Selves*, Berkeley: University of California Press.

Shippey, T. (2003), *The Road to Middle-earth*, New York: Houghton Mifflin.

Tolkien, J.R.R. (1984), 'On Fairy-Stories', in J. R. R. Tolkien, *The Monsters and the Critics and Other Essays*, ed. C. Tolkien, 109–61, Boston: Houghton Mifflin.

Index

Acallam na Senórach ('Dialogue of [or with] the Old Men') 58, 63
Aengus Óg/Oengus Mac ind Óc
    in the Irish material 45, 57
    in McIsaac's work 63
Aífe/Aoife
    in the Irish material 163, 165, 166, 167
    in MacLeòid's work 163
Ailill 60
Aislinge Oengusa ('The Dream of Oengus') 33, 45
Alderley Edge 29–30, 31, 41, 42, 43, 47–50
Allingham, William
    'The Fairies' 56
Altromh Tige Dá Medar ('The Nurturing of the House of Two Milk Vessels') 57
The Annals of the Four Masters 60
Annwn
    in Kennealy-Morrison's work 129
    in Silhol's work 141, 148
    in the Welsh material 124, 125, 148
Anthony, Piers
    Tarot trilogy 183
Arawn
    in Silhol's work 141
    in the Welsh material 32, 141
archaeology 1–3, 7, 30, 87, 106, 107, 118, 122, 189
Arminius 110–11
Arthur, King 41, 45, 63
    in Kennealy-Morrison's work 121, 124–5, 127, 128
Arthurian legend 6, 39, 41, 45, 117, 121, 128, 195, 196, 206
    in the evolution of the Tarot 179, 183, 189
    in fandom 198, 201, 202, 207
    in Garner's work 41, 45
    in Kennealy-Morrison's work 117
    in King's work 187
    in Laubenthal's work 184, 185
    in Silhol's work 138–9, 140, 141, 148
    in Zelasny's work 186
Atlantis 117, 119–20, 123
Avalon
    in Arthurian legend 41
    in Kennealy-Morrison's work 126
    in Zelasny's work 186

Baring-Gould, Sabine 177
Benedeit
    Le Voyage de Saint Brendan 145
Beowulf 80, 169
Bertilak/Bert
    in Arthurian legend 45
    in Garner's work 45
Book of Fermoy 55, 57, 58
Book of Taliesin 124, 125
Boudica/Boudicca 102–3, 109, 123
Branwen 47
Bres 119
Breuddwyd Macsen ('The dream of Maxen') 185
Breuddwyd Rhonabwy ('Rhonabwy's dream') 33, 183
Brexit 14, 16
Brigit/Bríg/Saint Brigit
    in the Irish material 7, 54, 59–60, 63–6, 67
    in McIsaac's work 53, 59–60, 61, 62–6
Bull, Emma
    War for the Oaks 138
Butcher, Jim 201

Cad Goddau ('The Battle of the Trees') 125, 128, 129
Cadellin
    in Garner's work 35, 38–42, 45, 46, 48
    in the Welsh material 41
Caesar 92, 97–107, 109, 110, 112
    De Bello Gallico/Gallic Wars 73, 86, 97
    De Re Militari 73, 110

Index

Calgacus 92, 103, 109–10
Carmina Gadelica 60
Cath Maige Tuired ('The [Second] Battle of Mag Tuired') 125
Cathbad 82, 83
Celtiberi 101
Celtic/Anglo-Irish/Irish (Literary) Revival 2, 125, 140, 177
Celtic character, *See under* 'Celts', the
Celtic languages
    Breton 1
    Irish 1, 2, 12, 18, 22, 23, 59, 196, 198, 205
    Scots Gaelic 1, 2, 5, 12, 22, 23, 155–8, 160, 161, 164, 166–9
    Welsh 1, 2, 30, 121, 196
Celtic music 206–7
Celticism 4, 195, 196, 198–9, 206
Celticity 4–7, 11, 47–50, 73, 86, 87, 127, 130, 131, 141, 152, 169, 195–6, 199–200, 202, 204, 206–7
'Celts', the
    and 'Celtic' character 17, 204
    and classical perceptions 73, 86, 93–4, 101–5
    conventional history of 2–3
    and Hallstatt culture 2
    and interlace design 2, 122, 200
    and Iron Age archaeology 74, 86–7
    and La Tène culture 2
    and Romanticism 1–3, 7, 12, 18, 105, 108, 138, 140–3, 152, 156, 177, 179, 204, 207
changeling 57, 142
Cheshire 31, 37–8
Chrétien de Troyes 37, 207
Clarke, Susanna
    Jonathan Strange & Mr Norrell 5, 7, 11–28, 138
    The Ladies of Grace Adieu and Other Stories 12, 23
Coimín, Micheál
    The Lay of Oisín in the Land of Youth 57
Colman Smith, Pamela 175–6, 178, 189
Conchobar 81, 82, 163
Coranians 117, 119, 121, 124
Cormac's Glossary 65
Crowley, Aleister
    'Book of Thoth' Tarot 182

Cú Chulainn
    in Gemmell's work 73, 75–87, 91, 92, 108–9, 111
    in the Irish material 6, 44, 75–87, 91, 92, 108–9, 111, 161, 162, 163, 164
Culhwch ac Olwen ('Culhwch and Olwen') 30, 41, 128

Dagda, the/Thagda, the
    in Gemmell's work 74, 87, 91
    in the Irish material 7, 74, 87, 91, 125, 147, 148
    in Silhol's work 147, 148
Daoine Sidhe, *See under* fairies/fairy folk/faerie folk/Fays/fae
Delany, Samuel R.
    Nova 182, 183
Dream of Rhonabwy, *See under Breuddwyd Rhonabwy* ('Rhonabwy's dream')
Druids
    in classical accounts 104, 106–7
    in Gemmell's work 81, 82, 106–7, 108
    in Kennealy-Morrison's work 127, 129, 131
    in McIsaac's work 57, 61
    in the Irish material 82, 83
Dungeons & Dragons 199

Eliot, T.S.
    The Waste Land 175, 181, 183, 186, 187, 190
Emain Macha 108, 163
Emer/Eimhir
    in the Irish material 84, 161, 163
    in MacLeòid's work 157, 161, 163, 166
Englishness 7, 14, 16–17
Erikson, Steven
    Malazan Book of the Fallen 160
Étaín
    in the Irish tradition 46, 47, 48
    in Kennealy-Morrison's work 129
Evans-Wentz, Walter
    Fairy Faith in Celtic Countries 55

Faerie/Faërie/Faery
    in Clarke's work (Faerie) 13, 15, 17, 18, 20–5, 27
    in fandom (Faery) 205
    in Silhol's work (Faërie) 137, 140, 141, 144–50

see also Tír na nÓg/Tir-na Nóg'th and Otherworld
fairies/fairy folk/faerie folk/Fays/fae/faekind
  in Clarke's work (Daoine Sidhe/fairies) 11, 12, 17–21, 23, 24–5, 138
  Daoine Sidhe 11, 12, 19, 20, 21, 137, 138–9, 141
  in fandom 200, 204–5
  in Gemmell's work (Seidh) 74–5, 78–80, 82–3, 91
  in Kennealy-Morrison's work (faerie people/Sidhe) 127–9
  in McIsaac's work (fairies) 53, 56–7
  in Silhol's work (Sidhe/fairies) 137–47, 149–52
fandom 5, 6, 195–207
Fenrir 166
Fer Diad 82, 163
Fhriseal, Anna
  'An Dùdach' ('The Horn') 157
Fionn mac Cumhaill/Finn mac Cool
  in the Irish material 57, 63
  in McIsaac's work 63, 65, 66
Fisher King 37, 176, 180–1, 183–4, 186–7, 190
Fitzpatrick, Jim
  The Book of Conquests 119
folklore
  British 140
  'Celtic', 124, 138, 139, 140, 143, 147, 148, 151, 152
  Eastern Asian 145
  Gaelic 60, 137, 138, 146, 148, 159, 161, 164, 166, 169
  Irish 6, 11, 55–7, 139
  Japanese 145
  Scottish 6, 141, 146
  Welsh 137, 140, 141, 146, 148
Fomorians 119, 125, 126
Frazer, James G. 180
Frost, Gregory
  Remscela 75
  Táin 75

Gabaldon, Diana
  Outlander 62
Gae-bolg 163
Gàidhealach 156, 161, 163, 166, 168–9
Galatai 101

Galli 101
Garner, Alan
  Boneland 29–50
  The Moon of Gomrath 29–32, 35–6, 38–9, 41, 43–6, 48–50
  The Owl Service 49
  Strandloper 49
  The Voice that Thunders 29, 49
  The Weirdstone of Brisingamen 29–33, 35–6, 38, 41, 43–50
  Weirdstone trilogy 29, 47
Gauls 2, 98, 101–4, 109
geis (pl. *gessi*)/geasa
  in Gemmell's work 77–8, 87, 109
  in the Irish material 76–7, 87, 109, 127
  in Kennealy-Morrison's work 127
Gemmell, David
  Lord of the Silver Bow 87
  Midnight Falcon 73–87, 105–12
  Rigante series 73–87, 105–12
  Sword in the Storm 73–87, 105–12
Geoffrey of Monmouth
  Historia Regum Britanniae/History of the Kings of Britain 39, 120, 202
  Vita Merlini 38, 39, 40
Giraldus Cambrensis (Gerald of Wales) 59
Golden Dawn, The Hermetic Order of the 175, 176, 178–9, 190
Goudge, Elizabeth
  The White Witch 182
grail romances 176–80, 182, 184
Graves, Robert
  The White Goddess 31–2, 37, 44–6, 118, 121, 124–5, 129–31
Gregory, Lady Augusta 57, 118
Gresham, William Lynsey
  Nightmare Alley 182–3

Hand, Elizabeth
  Waking the Moon 120
Hellenism 94
Herne the Hunter 150
Herodotus 86, 92, 95–6, 100
Holdstock, Robert 4
Holy Grail 36–7, 148, 175, 176–80, 183–9
Homer 96
  Iliad 94, 100
  Odyssey 80, 93
Horslips
  The Book of Invasions 119

Imramma 146

Jackson, Peter 161, 199–200, 206
Jungian psychology/archetypes 31, 49, 176, 186, 188–9

Keightley, Thomas
   Fairy Mythology 140, 142
Keltoi
   in classical texts 1, 2, 6, 101
   in Gemmell's work 73, 75–7, 79, 83, 85–6, 105–10
   in Kennealy-Morrison's work (Kelts) 117–131
Kennealy-Morrison, Patricia
   Blackmantle 117
   The Copper Crown 117–19, 122, 124, 127, 129–30
   The Deer's Cry 117
   The Hawk's Grey Feather 117
   The Hedge of Mist, 117
   Keltiad series 117–31
   The Oak Above the Kings 117
   The Silver Branch 117–19
   Tales of the Spiral Castle: Stories of the Keltiad 117
The Throne of Scone 117, 120, 124, 126
King, Stephen
   Dark Tower series 186–7
   The Gunslinger 187
   The Waste Lands 187

Laubenthal, Sanders Anne
   Excalibur 194–5
Laxdæla Saga 167–8
Le Guin, Ursula K. 158, 160
   The Farthest Shore 160
Lebar Gabála Érenn ('The Book of Invasions/Takings of Ireland') 3, 55, 58, 119–20, 125, 147
Lewis, C.S.
   Perelandra 185
Lichtenberger, André
   Les Centaures 139
Lindsay, Coinneach
   A' Choille Fhiadhaich ('The Wild Wood') 157
Livy 101
Llywelyn, Morgan
   The Red Branch 75

Lug/Lugh
   in the Irish material 81, 82, 85, 125
   in Silhol's work 147, 148, 149–50

Mabinogi
   First Branch of the 32
   Four Branches of the 189
   Second Branch of the 47
Mabinogion 2, 3, 32, 105, 119, 177, 185, 207
Mac an t-Saoir, Màrtainn
   'Oisein ann an Tìr nan Òg' ('Oisein in the Land of Youth') 157
Macha 54, 60, 61, 67
Machen, Arthur 179
MacLean, Sorley
   Dàin do Eimhir ('Poems to Eimhir') 161
MacLeòid, Fionnlagh
   Gormshuil an Rìgh 162
MacLeòid, Iain F.
   Am Bounty 158
   Ìmpireachd 165, 168
   An Sgoil Dhubh ('The Black School') 155–69
   An Taistealach 158
Mallory, Thomas 201, 202
   Morte D'Arthur 202
Marie de France
   Lais 141
Martin, George R.R. 199
Matthews, Caitlin 189
McGinley, Patrick
   The Trick of the Ga Bolga 75
McGuire, Seanan
   October Daye series 138
McIsaac, Jodi
   Among the Unseen 53, 61
   Beyond the Pale 53, 57
   Bury the Living 53, 62, 65
   Into the Fire 53, 58, 61
   Revolutionary series 5, 53, 62–6, 67
   Summon the Queen 53, 65
   The Thin Veil series 5, 53, 54–62, 63, 66, 67
   Through the Door 53, 54, 57, 58, 61
Mead, G.R.S. 176, 179
Medb/Maedhbh
   in the Irish material 54, 60–1, 67
   in MacLeòid's work 161–2, 166
   in Silhol's work 148
Merlin 38–43, 48

Morgan le Fay 45, 48
Morganwg, Iolo 128, 131
  Coelbren y Beirdd 128
Morrígan/Morrigan/Morrigu, the
  in Garner's work 30, 31, 42, 43–7, 48, 49
  in Gemmell's work 74, 78–81, 83, 87, 91, 108, 111
  in the Irish material 7, 31, 43–7, 48, 49, 74, 78–81, 87, 91, 108
Morrison, Jim 117
Mosse, Kate
  Sepulchre 187
Myrddin Wyllt 31, 38–43, 47, 48, 49
Mythology
  Celtic/'Celtic', 6, 7, 11, 29, 30, 31, 32, 38, 46, 48, 50, 54, 61, 74, 91, 92, 105, 106, 130, 138–9, 143, 144, 175, 176–7, 178, 179, 180, 187, 188, 190
  Egyptian 7, 99, 119–20, 179, 182
  Greek 95, 96, 119, 143, 145, 201
  Irish 6, 7, 31, 32, 33, 34, 35, 43–5, 47, 49, 53, 57, 60, 66, 91, 145, 147, 148, 182
  Norse 139
  Welsh 6, 31, 32, 33, 43, 49, 130, 146, 189

Navigatio Sancti Brendani Abbatis 146
Neopaganism 189, 206
New Age 189, 206
Nutt, Alfred Trübner 80–1, 177

Oidheadh Chon Culainn ('The violent death of Cú Chulainn') 44
Otherworld 20, 23, 30, 31, 32–8, 40, 42, 45–9, 53, 54, 57–8, 124, 125, 139, 141, 148, 182, 185, 187, 190
  see also Faerie/Faërie/Faery and Tír na nÓg/Tir-na Nóg'th
Owain neu Iarlles y Ffynnon ('Owain or the Lady of the Fountain') 185

pan-Celticism 6, 31, 32, 37, 38, 45, 46, 48, 118, 124, 130, 198, 204, 205
Paolini, Christopher
  Brisingr 167
Perceval 37, 186, 201, 207
Peredur 37
Peter Pan 141
Pollack, Rachel 188
Powells, Laura
  The Game of Triumphs 183

Powers, Tim 186, 187
  Last Call 187
Pratchett, Terry 159–60
  Guards! Guards! 159
  Mort 160
Preideu Annwfyn ('Spoils of the Otherworld') 124, 125
Púca 130
Pwyll 32

Renan, Ernest 177
Ríastrad 76, 78, 84, 108
Rider and Co. 177
Rider pack (Tarot) 175, 178, 180, 181–3, 188–90
Roman Empire/Roman Britain/Rome 1, 2, 37, 73, 87, 97–104, 110–11
Rowling, J.K.
  Harry Potter and the Deathly Hallows 188
  Harry Potter and the Half-blood Prince 188
  Harry Potter series 188

Saint Brigit, *See under* Brigit/Bríg
Sallust
  The Jugurthine War 100
Scáthach 83, 84, 163
Scél Tuáin meic Cairill ('The Tale of Tuáin son of Cairell') 55
Seelie Court 145–6, 149, 204
Seidh, *See under* fairies/fairy folk/faerie folk/Fays/fae
Shakespeare, William 128, 146, 149, 150, 201
  A Midsummer Night's Dream 146
síd (pl. síde)/sidh (pl. sidhe) (mound)
  in fandom 205
  in the Irish material 20, 23, 34–5, 91
  in McIsaac's work 54–8, 61
Sidhe, *See under* fairies/fairy folk/faerie folk/Fays/fae
Silhol, Léa
  Avant l'Hiver: Architectonique des Clartés 137, 144, 148, 149
  Emblèmes hors-série 2: Les Fées 140
  Frontier series 5, 137–9, 142–8, 150, 151
  Il Était Une Fée 140
  La Glace et la Nuit: Opus un. Nigredo 137, 139, 141–2, 144–5, 147–50
  Musiques de la Frontière 137, 150
  Possession Point 137, 139, 144, 150

Sacra, Parfums d'Isenne et d'ailleurs: Opus deux: Nulle âme invincible 137, 144, 145, 147
Seppenko Monogatari sequence 137, 145, 150
La Sève et le Givre 137, 141–2, 145–6, 149
Sous le lierre 150
la Trame 137, 143–4
Vertigen series 5, 137–9, 141–2, 144–51
Sir Gawain and the Green Knight 45, 201
Society for Creative Anachronism (SCA) 118
Suetonius 97, 110

Tacitus 86, 92–3, 97, 99–100, 102–3, 105–12
  Agricola 93, 100, 102–3, 106, 108, 110
  Germania 97, 99–100, 102, 106, 111
Táin Bó Cuailnge ('The Cattle Raid of Cooley') 2, 44, 60, 75, 76, 78, 91, 105, 163–4
Taliesin 30, 45, 124, 130
Tara 58, 120, 125, 126, 129, 148, 149
Tarot 175–90
Thagda, *See under* Dagda, the/Thagda, the
Thucydides 92, 95–7
  The Peloponnesian War 95–6
Tír na nÓg/Tir-na Nóg'th
  in the Irish material 53
  in McIsaac's work 54–61, 66
  in Silhol's work 148
  in Zelazny's work 186
  see also Faerie/Faërie/Faery and Otherworld
Tochmarc Étaíne ('The Wooing of Étaín') 46
Tolkien, J.R.R., 4, 87, 110, 129, 131, 139, 141, 148, 158, 159, 161, 195, 196, 198, 199, 200, 207
  The Hobbit 165
  The Lord of the Rings 129, 133, 159, 161, 165, 193, 206
Tuatha Dé Danann
  four treasures/Grail Hallows of the 58, 124–5, 128, 130, 147–8, 179

  in the Irish material 11, 20, 23, 35, 53, 55, 57, 58, 74, 91, 119, 141, 145
  in McIsaac's work 53, 54–8, 60–1, 63, 66
  in Silhol's work 141, 145, 148, 149

Ulster cycle 44, 73
Unseelie Court 145–6, 149, 204

Vercingetorix 73, 86–7, 98, 109–10
Villemarqué, Theodore de la 177
Virgil
  Aeneid 107, 120

Waite, Arthur Edward 175–6, 178–80, 182, 183, 186, 187, 188, 190
Weston, Jessie 175–6, 179–80, 183, 187, 190
  From Ritual to Romance 180, 183, 190
White, T.H. 185, 201
Williams, Charles
  The Greater Trumps 182
Wolfe, Gene 158–60
  The Book of the New Sun 160
  Sword of the Lictor 160
Worldbuilding 3, 5, 74, 92, 119, 163, 195, 200, 205

Yeats, W.B., 56, 57, 118, 140, 147, 175, 176, 178, 181–2, 183, 187, 190
  The Book of Fairy and Folk Tales of Ireland 140
  'The Stolen Child', 56
  Stories of Red Hanrahan 181–2, 187, 190

Zelazny, Roger
  The Chronicles of Amber series 186
  The Guns of Avalon 186
  Knight of Shadows 186
  Sign of the Unicorn 186
  Trumps of Doom 186
Zimmer Bradley, Marion
  The Mists of Avalon 186

www.ingramcontent.com/pod-product-compliance
Lightning Source LLC
Chambersburg PA
CBHW062221300426
44115CB00012BA/2171